# PRAISE FOR *THE TRUFF[LE]*

"Jacobs is an unstoppable and captiva[...] underbelly of the world's most glamorous rungus. This is the ultimate truffle true-crime tale."

**—BIANCA BOSKER**, *New York Times* bestselling author of *Cork Dork*

"It is totally unlikely that I will ever be a truffle hunter, but thanks to Ryan Jacobs's thrilling book, I have experienced truffle sales no less shady than a parking lot drug deal, escaped bandits with my haul intact, witnessed truffle heists, and mastered the scientific mysteries of their growth. And best of all, as a reward for having (not at all) lived through such mayhem, I feel entitled to say to the waiter, 'Why, yes, I will add truffles to my pasta for [exorbitant amount of money].'"

**—ALEXIS COE**, author of *Alice + Freda Forever: A Murder in Memphis*

"Holy hell, this is a good book. With prose that is often as seductive as the elusive fungus itself, *The Truffle Underground* transports the reader to an intoxicating world of aromatic forests and international intrigue. It's full of passion, promise, and danger, and as gripping as any HBO prestige drama. This impressively researched and beautifully written debut is a must-read for anyone interested in how our food makes its way to our plate from its origin in the wild world. I found myself reading it far into the night, thinking again and again just a few pages more."

**—SUMMER BRENNAN**, author of *The Oyster War*

"[A] fascinating work....This deeply researched and eye-opening account of the lengths people will go for wealth, gratification, and a taste of the prized fungus will captivate readers."

**—PUBLISHERS WEEKLY**

"Investigative journalist and first-time author Jacobs does a remarkable job reporting from the frontlines of the truffle industry, bringing to vivid life French black-truffle farmers, Italian white-truffle foragers, and their marvelously well-trained dogs."

**—BOOKLIST**

"Fans of weird true crime will eat it up."

**—BUZZFEED**

# THE TRUFFLE UNDERGROUND

*A Tale of Mystery, Mayhem, and Manipulation
in the Shadowy Market of the World's
Most Expensive Fungus*

RYAN JACOBS

CLARKSON POTTER/PUBLISHERS
NEW YORK

*For Emily and Olive,*
*who was born during revisions*

Published in the United States by Clarkson Potter/
Publishers, an imprint of the Crown Publishing
Group, a division of Penguin Random House LLC,
New York.
crownpublishing.com
clarksonpotter.com

CLARKSON POTTER is a trademark and POTTER
with colophon is a registered trademark of Penguin
Random House LLC.

Library of Congress Cataloging-in-Publication Data
Names: Jacobs, Ryan McMahon, 1989– author.
Title: The truffle underground : a tale of mystery,
mayhem, and manipulation in the shadowy market of
the world's most expensive fungus / Ryan Jacobs.
Description: First edition. | New York : Clarkson
Potter, [2019] | Includes bibliographical references.
Identifiers: LCCN 2018053998 (print) | LCCN
2018055700 (ebook) | ISBN 9780451495709 (Ebook)
| ISBN 9780451495693 (paperback)
Subjects: LCSH: Truffle industry—France—
History—19th century. | Truffle industry—
Italy—History—19th century. | Truffle culture. |
Smuggling. | Black market.
Classification: LCC HD9235.T782 (ebook) |
LCC HD9235.T782 F833 2019 (print) | DDC
381/.4158—dc23
LC record available at https://lccn.loc
.gov/2018053998

ISBN 978-0-451-49569-3
Ebook ISBN 978-0-451-49570-9

Printed in the United States of America

Cover design by Ian Dingman
Book design by Jen Wang

10 9 8 7 6 5 4 3 2 1

First Edition

# CONTENTS

# AUTHOR'S NOTE

ALL EVENTS, CHARACTERS, AND LOCATIONS PORTRAYED IN THIS AC-count are real. No names have been changed, but some sources have been kept anonymous. Crime and vice are difficult to observe firsthand, so all scenes at which I was not present are based upon extensive interviews with victims, law enforcement officials, or other sources with credible knowledge about how they occurred. Other relevant source material is listed in the Notes section.

In a few instances, minor details—lost to history, sources' memories, or industry secrecy—have been supposed in a way that is consistent with other available facts. This is especially applicable to sections that focus on the early- and mid-nineteenth century, which are supported by contemporaneous but sparse accounts. These suppositions were considered carefully and always aim to get the reader closer to the reality of what happened.

Much of my reporting was conducted through French and Italian translators. In favor of avoiding distraction, distinctions between interviews conducted in English and those conducted in a foreign language were not made unless they were directly relevant to the story.

Where does it ever say, anywhere, that only bad
can come from bad actions? Maybe sometimes—
the wrong way is the right way? You can take the
wrong path and it still comes out where you want to
be? Or, spin it another way, sometimes you can do
everything wrong and it still turns out to be right?

—Boris, in Donna Tartt's *The Goldfinch* (2013)


Good food, good eating, is all about blood and
organs, cruelty and decay.

—Anthony Bourdain, in *The New Yorker* (1999)

PROLOGUE:

# UNDERGROUND

THREADS OF FUNGUS SWIRL THROUGH THE HEAT AND DARK OF THE rocky soil. They spend years twisting, extending, contorting, in perpetual search of nutrients to bring back to their host tree. It took thirty years and a series of improbable incidents for the fungus to connect with the roots to begin with, and now it will take even more luck for the colony burrowing through the dirt to find a fungal mate.

But if it happens, an invisible knot will bubble up from this fateful connection sometime in the spring: a primordium, a jumble of tissue that, under a microscope, resembles a ball of haphazardly assembled yarn. Over a few weeks, the microscopic cells bulk into something more complex. Structures materialize: Bits of skin come into focus; a maze of white veins unfurls, marbling a black interior. Eventually, a miniature, immature truffle has formed. When the heat of the sun washes over the soil in the first days of summer, its cells fall into a warm slumber. At summer's end, it rests, waiting for the hulking clouds of a thunderstorm to swing in its direction.

One day in early autumn, lightning shoots into the forest canopies, and a smack of thunder rumbles over the forest floor. Rain falls. Droplets trickle from the leaves and seep into the soil, past the surface layer and into the root zone. The cells of the fungus are jolted out of dormancy by the flood. Growth begins anew.

One night in early winter, some signal of moisture, temperature, or magic presses into the depth, and spores bloom in the truffle's interior. The developed cells begin sucking water out of the soil like a vacuum, bloating the fruit to full maturity.

Then, and only then, is an edible, aromatic truffle born into its dark soil.

But somewhere above, another underground awaits.

# PART I

# THE FIELD · THEFT

The essence of pearl mixed with essence of men and a curious dark residue was precipitated. Every man suddenly became related to Kino's pearl, and Kino's pearl went into the dreams, the speculations, the schemes, the plans, the futures, the wishes, the needs, the lusts, the hungers, of everyone, and only one person stood in the way and that was Kino, so that he became curiously every man's enemy. The news stirred up something infinitely black and evil in the town; the black distillate was like the scorpion, or like hunger in the smell of food, or like loneliness when love is withheld. The poison sacs of the town began to manufacture venom, and the town swelled and puffed with the pressure of it.

—John Steinbeck, *The Pearl* (1947)

# CHAPTER ONE

# Black Diamond Bandits

AT NIGHTFALL, THE THIEVES DROPPED ROPE LADDERS THROUGH CEIL-
ing ducts and drove trucks through warehouse walls. They scaled
roofs, broke locks, ripped refrigerator doors off their hinges. They
wore night-vision goggles and slinked into private oak groves,
their guards holding rifles and standing watch. Their hounds wove
quietly through columns of stalky trees, snouts working chalky
soils for a scent of the quarry. When the hounds' paws scratched,
the men darted toward patches of burnt earth and shoveled shal-
low holes with precision and speed. When their bags bulged, they
screeched past moonlit vineyards onto country roads, into darkness. And they did all this not for cash, or for jewelry, or for art. It
was for *les truffes,* the truffles.

By the time the winter sun rose each morning over the dusty peak
of Mont Ventoux in 2005, large quantities of Provence's finest black

winter truffle—worth €500, €600, or even €1,000 per kilo on the commercial market—had vanished from company storage rooms, middlemen's refrigerators, and, most frequently, the soils where hopeful farmers in the region of Vaucluse had once planted oak saplings inoculated with fungal spores. Victims reported the losses to the local gendarmerie, France's military police, but the heists— occurring randomly across large stretches of agricultural land— proved difficult to solve and to marshal serious resources for. The village authorities occasionally recovered abandoned trucks and stolen rope but rarely located the product or witnesses with useful leads. Though American eaters typically think of truffles as for- aged foods, found in misty stands of wild forest, the majority of the French supply of black winter truffles comes from the small and in- consistent yields of cultivated oak groves on the outskirts of several rural villages in the southeastern section of the country; farmers still have to search for the truffles, but at least they have some sense of where to look, as do the thieves.

On the narrow streets of Carpentras and Richerenches, the vil- lages where the region's two main truffle markets are held, farmers swapped intelligence on the latest trespasses and nervously won- dered if they would be targeted next. The thousands or even tens of thousands in lost sales would slow and harden the passage of winter, when there were few other things to nurture or sell. And the poachers' careless digging would disrupt the delicate symbio- sis the truffle spores had found with their host tree's roots, cutting into a lifetime of potential earnings and violating the sanctity of a years- and sometimes generations-long relationship between a man and his capricious grove. Only farmers who had planted, irrigated, pruned, and worried over their trees had the right to dig for their buried fruit; only they understood the improbability of their enter-prise and the importance of scraping damp soil back over the holes.

Eventually, rumors devolved into paranoia and fear. Farmers suspected jealous neighbors and business rivals, and began patrol-ling their groves late on cold winter nights, clutching their hunting rifles.

Out of caution, some took out insurance policies on their prod-uct. The victims who already had them filed claims. One targeted trader was reimbursed with €76,000, on the condition that he im-prove his security system. The way the insurance brokers spoke about the necessity of the improvements, it was as if the country-men had suddenly developed a weakness for exhibiting rare pieces of Chagall or wearing custom designs from Cartier.

But these missing black winter truffles were not unlike stolen jew-els. The species *Tuber melanosporum*, known by the French as the black diamond or black pearl, is revered as one of the finest, scarc-est, and most valuable ingredients in fine dining.

Even without criminal interference, a truffle's journey from spore to plate is so fraught with biological uncertainty, economic competition, and logistical headaches that a single shaving could be understood as a testament to the wonder of human civilization. After farmers plant inoculated saplings in suitable soil, the fruiting bodies of the fungi can take a decade before materializing below host trees, and even then, a hot summer, a pruning mishap, or an unexplained stroke of fate can rip them away. After decades of study, scientists still don't fully understand the mechanics of their growth. Yields in France have fallen dramatically for more than a century, first because of disruptions to and closures of truffle orchards during the world wars and later from rural development, declining precipitation, and higher temperatures. Or at least that's what most truffle scientists theorize. No one seems to truly understand why farmers have had such trouble returning to the gilded yields of the twentieth century's turn.

And when truffles do form, a farmer doesn't harvest as much as he hunts. Unlike most crops, they don't all come in at once. Over a few months, they appear in fits and spurts, in different places throughout the grove, and with little to no external clues about where they are. A farmer dawdles through his rows with an expensive and expertly trained dog, until the pet locates the scent of a black bulb buried in mud. Mark by mark, the farmer digs upon his canine's indication, often with no results. The farmer must pry his prizes from the hound's mouth, drive them to market, and approach a middleman, who has the audacity to haggle him down from his asking price, if he's intrigued enough by the shape and quality of the specimens to make an offer at all. It's a medieval undertaking in a smartphone world.

Once sold, the truffle makes its way, occasionally through secretive back channels, from a middleman's hand to a restaurant's kitchen, usually in less than thirty-six hours. The truffle is as fleeting as a cloud: With each passing minute, the fungus shrinks in size, dissipates in aroma and flavor, and edges closer to rot. No serious restaurant will buy a truffle that is more than ten days old.

Each winter, the world's fine-dining chefs compete—sometimes hysterically—over a limited global supply, personally inspect them for flaws the instant they arrive in the kitchen, and prepare the dishes they're featured on with the precision and concern a master gemologist takes to the polish of a final setting. The gnarled and pebbled black lumps are finally shaved—often at the table—over buttered tagliatelle noodles, farm-raised eggs, or foie gras, at a cost of more than a hundred dollars per serving. The thin slivers reveal brilliant white veins that snake through the dark center of the fungus. But by themselves, whole truffles look a bit like the strange, mangled droppings of a forest troll.

Truffles can make the people who eat them behave in strange ways. Puff Daddy once indelicately requested that the French celebrity chef Daniel Boulud (of Daniel in Manhattan) "shave that bitch" over his plate. Oprah refuses to travel without ensuring that she, her assistant, and her security detail have packed surplus truffle salt. In 2010, at an international auction benefitting charity, the Macau casino tycoon Stanley Ho placed a winning bid of $330,000 for two large pieces of white truffle, or *Tuber magnatum pico*—a rarer, smoother-surfaced, and more expensive species (a kilo routinely wholesales for more than $7,000) with a pale yellow-brown complexion that cannot be cultivated and can only be found in a few places on earth. The anonymously wealthy ask their pilots to fly their helicopters directly from Monte Carlo to northern Italy for the express purpose of eating large, fresh white truffles at lunch, complete with €1,500 tips for the waitstaff. Others jet from Florida mansions to New York warehouses just to inspect their truffles before they purchase them.

But the task of cogently explicating the allure of truffles can transform even the fiercest food critics into hopeless, salivating romantics. The late *Time* magazine columnist Josh Ozersky once mused that the white truffle's scent recalled "the pungent memory of lost youth and old love affairs." Truffles, he wrote, gave him "something to aspire to, to talk about, to dream of and to save up for. In a world where essentially everything is available to everybody at all times, give or take a few seasonal vegetables, [their] rarity is luminous and riveting."

Asking even seasoned chefs and truffle industry insiders to describe what the fungus tastes or smells like is a bit like asking a priest why he believes in God. There are words and descriptors, sure, but they are only symbols of an experience. The truffle smells of cold mountain air, of forest and leaf litter, of wet earth. Its taste corresponds to these wild smells, but it also transcends them: It is one of the few foods that can take a mind to its source, even if the person that mind belongs to has never traveled there before. You are eating years of nature's labor, many mornings of a truffle dog's sniffing search, and a moment of exhilarating discovery. You are eating secrets, mystery, and danger too.

If you do not believe in magic or religion, eating a truffle may inspire reconsideration. In southeastern France, the veneration of the ingredient does border on religious fervor. Farmers and traders there proudly proclaim that they were "born in truffles," as if to intimate a baptism by dirt rather than water. At the beginning of each year's truffle season, on the first Saturday after November 15, the Confrérie du Diamant Noir, a self-appointed fraternity of local truffle farmers, dresses in black robes and marches through the streets of Richerenches, a place where roughly €300,000 are exchanged for truffles each week. A "grand master" announces that the harvest and markets are officially open for the season, which lasts until March. On the third Sunday in January, the townspeople gather for the formal truffle Mass in honor of Saint Antoine, the patron saint of truffle farmers; congregants ask God to bless the year's harvest, and according to the lead curator at the town's truffle museum the "happiest priest in France" presides. "When the collection basket is passed," one of the museum's placards reads, "truffle growers traditionally place their best truffle from that week's harvest in the basket as their offering."

It is here, in this sleepy rural milieu—among gangly oaks, fields of fresh lavender, and sprawling vineyards, among campy traditions and romantic ideals—where criminals saw an opportunity to strike. Soon, everyone—farmers, middlemen, and even large distributors—had their own tales about the thieves.

Truffle farmers in the department of Vaucluse had dealt with poaching neighbors since at least the nineteenth century—the ones who'd wander over the property line, dig for a few truffles, and then claim they'd been confused about where they were when caught—but sometime in the early aughts, the thefts evolved into more than just simple crimes of opportunity. In their search for kilos rather than handfuls, bandits turned entire groves into archaeological excavation sites. In their selection of a wide range of rotating targets, they seemed to employ both reconnaissance and human intel and moved—always at night—with the lightness and imperceptibility of country foxes. On rare encounters with interlopers, they flashed weapons. Increasingly, farmers came to regard these nighttime incidents as the handiwork of a well-connected network of professional thieves.

"It's a mafia, you know?"

With his yellowish hoodie, mussed brown hair, thick sideburns, and plump face, truffle grower Nicolas Valayer comported himself with the air of a friendly stoner, but when it came to the prospect of organized thievery, he spoke with grave solemnity. To him, the existence of such a group wasn't a question; it was a conviction, bred by scars of the past.

On a Christmas morning in the mid-1980s, at the modest house on the estate where we now stood, robbers placed a cold pistol on his uncle André's temple. They grabbed his cash and all of his recently harvested truffles and fled in his car. But in the years since, brute, isolated efforts had matured into a more sophisticated paramilitary ballet. "They're organized," Valayer said. "There are twenty people. At night, with a big flashlight, good dogs. So, the only solution is to go very often in your truffle groves. And as long as there's a problem, you can go with a gun."

His three-year-old black cocker spaniel and springer mix, Melano, after *melanosporum*, bounded forth on a yellow leash, cutting a trail between the property's large vineyards—Syrah, Grenache, Mourvèdre, and Carignan—and the spindly green and white oaks at the edge of one of the family's six truffle plantations. It requires almost two days to cover every corner of each, making protective, preemptive harvests a chore. Melano's tail wagged furiously, but he hadn't caught a promising scent all afternoon. The moon was in the wrong phase, and young Melano wasn't exactly a "broom," what Valayer called dogs that were capable of digging up truffles and returning them without direct commands. Perhaps Melano also knew that expectations on a brief security sweep wouldn't be as high as on a mid-season hunt.

As the setting sun blew a spectacular dusky glow into the sky and farm machinery ground in the distance, Valayer told me that vigilante justice had taken hold. Years earlier, when members of the gendarmerie were first overwhelmed with reports and complaints, they had made the mistake of endorsing nighttime patrols. For the most part, the region's farmers found real law enforcers feckless. The last time the gendarmes nabbed someone near Richerenches, the thief—a local wine producer—had been spared jail time. He paid a fine, and his dog—used during the course of the crime—was seized. The targeted farmer was less than pleased with the severity of the punishment. Two months after the arrest, the thief walked into his winery one morning to find the farmer's revenge: In the night, he had drained every tank in the building.

◆

I would probably never have found myself wandering around tiny truffle villages in southeastern France, attempting to grasp the subtleties of rural thievery, if I hadn't developed a habit of cataloging every strange headline I spotted in a foreign publication, especially if it contained a hint of mystery. But back in 2013, as a reporter on the global desk of *The Atlantic*, I discovered a particularly titillating offering from *Der Spiegel*: "Mushroom Thieves at Large in German Forests." Somewhere outside the town of Bad Münstereifel, on the western side of the country, four porcini foragers had evaded a forestry worker's questioning by running him over with their vehicle. In a statement cited by the magazine, police said, "While the forestry official struggled to his feet, the car reversed back toward him, rolled onto his foot, and stopped." The report seemed to intimate that the men, one of whom brandished a knife and was referred to by his acolytes as "the boss," belonged to some kind of shadowy poaching group. Soon after reading, I placed an international call to an expert porcini forager based in the U.K., hoping he'd have a juicy lead. In his view, what had transpired in Germany was an outlier in the trade. But he didn't get off the phone before giving me a tip. If what I was really after was a crime story, he said, I ought to investigate the truffle business.

With that small morsel, I was off. At the time, I didn't know much about truffles beyond the fact that I couldn't afford to eat them. But it wasn't long before people were revealing slivers of an underworld, driven by a combination of extreme scarcity and exorbitant value. Demand from chefs and private clients had long outpaced supply, and smaller harvests—thought to be associated with climatic shifts in truffle-growing regions—inspired corresponding surges in crime. Basic secrecy and deception were standard traditions of the market, but economic desperation had amplified a casual culture of illegality and scandal, and it went far beyond theft: tax evasion, mislabeling, wholesale fraud, sabotage, poison, and, occasionally, violence. There were manipulative backroom deals, gut-wrenching betrayals, vicious rivalries, and lots of lies. This hidden reality seemed almost outlandishly improbable, which made investigating it all the more intoxicating.

I had covered international carbon market scams and diamond heists, but the truffle crimes were perpetrated with more personality and spite and usually demanded a fuller understanding of the target industry's eccentricities. They didn't occur just at the top or only at the bottom. They seemed to haunt the whole supply chain, until the moment a plate passed from the kitchen into the dining room. Their variance was as striking as their ubiquity. And what united them all was a general lack of law enforcement scrutiny. Because the risks were relatively low and the rewards were at times comically high, the ingredient became an easy accessory to crimes of greed and cruelty.

At certain times, trying to square a particular fact or story about the business, I felt as if I were standing in a house of mirrors, each one reflecting a more alluring tangle of light. Sources contradicted each other on seemingly straightforward details; they ignored my requests for interviews; and even friendly sources asked me to turn my tape recorder off the moment I began digging in the wrong direction. I was often cautioned about powerful forces and about the difficulty of overcoming the trade's culture of silence. At one point near the beginning of my reporting, a criminal intelligence analyst at Interpol, who had come across mislabeled truffles during a larger European sweep for counterfeit foods, told me the organization was investigating the potential involvement of organized crime in truffle and caviar fraud. My imagination ran.

In the imagination of American eaters, though, the truffle represents something else entirely: a luxury born of tradition, ritual, and romance. As a twee fascination and object of delight among aristocrats, shavings of whole truffles became an aspiration for a food-obsessed upper-middle class. Diners pay for the legendary flavor, of course, but they also pay for a momentary escape into a universe the menu or their server draws for them: a man, his dog, the mountains outside some tiny outpost in France or Italy—usually Alba (whites) or Périgord (blacks)—the find just a day ago, delivered fresh. Perhaps the purchase is also for the story they could later tell themselves and their friends, about a transformative plate of food that demonstrates their refined sensibilities and class. The story adds to the dish's flavor. For those who can't afford to order it, the ingredient can be consumed as an aspirational idea or as a derivative. The truffle has become so pleasantly mainstream that it was a focal point for a date on *The Bachelor* and appears—courtesy of cheap, dressed-down truffle oil—on the menus of more quotidian restaurants: truffle fries, truffle mac and cheese, truffle anything. In choice international markets, McDonald's has experimented with truffle mayonnaise. A taste of luxury without the cost.

But what if the story the industry sold to diners, and diners sold to themselves, was all wrong? What if the truffle they were all dreaming of and saving for, as Ozersky did, was not a genteel product of graceful provenance and, in fact, was party to secrets that were darker than we ever imagined? And what if our blind willingness, as an eating public, to shell out top dollar for fresh truffle shavings and the fantasy they afford us—or even just a couple extra bucks for some truffle-oil-drizzled fries at a chain restaurant—was actually part of the problem? Maybe a single shaving of a truffle was not just a testament to the wonder of civilization but also a keyhole to its failures, rogue operators, and even evil. And perhaps the modern truffle bon vivant just happened to be a perfect mark in an epic con.

Then again, the majority of the people in this industry had no direct hand in treachery. They simply dealt with scarcity, honestly. They were victims and innocents who persisted, in pursuit of adventure or love or tradition or the ineffable flavor, despite ruthless competition and economic hardship. By documenting the industry's crimes, I thought I might gain a richer and fuller understanding of its beauty, and of the good and grit of people who chose not to yield to its worst tendencies, even when bending in those directions seemed fair or, at the very least, more profitable.

I knew the truffle underground couldn't be understood from afar. To see the crimes the fungus encountered, I had to shadow it on a bumpy journey from ground to plate, through embattled orchards, peculiar history, secretive science, wild forests and foothills, deceptive markets, byzantine law enforcement investigations, cutthroat companies, and fancy dining rooms. Along this route, the truth about its handlers would be difficult to obscure. And so, in the autumn of 2015, in the overlapping period between white and black truffle seasons, I boarded a plane for Europe, bent on shaving off the industry's artifice.

In the fragrant department of Vaucluse, the supply beneath the farmers' truffle groves didn't always satiate the thieves' appetites.

Sometimes, despite higher risks, middlemen, and distributors—the people who regularly purchased from hundreds of the region's farmers—made more appealing targets. Back in 2005, Valayer's older cousin Pierre-Andre—a quiet, discerning middleman found every Saturday at the Richerenches market during the season, peering at various truffles from under a newsboy cap with a skepticism approximating that of a rare-jewel appraiser at Christie's—lost 150 kilos to the thieves. They broke through the roof of his storeroom, slipped down a rope ladder, and pried open a locked refrigerator. A stolen truck was later found abandoned, along with the rope. In a separate incident, bandits stopped one of his Carpentras colleagues out on the road and demanded he hand over their loot. "Like a Western," Pierre-Andre said, as he waited pensively one morning for another truffle farmer to walk tautly up to his open Golf hatchback. It was impossible for Pierre-Andre and his fellow middlemen to know how many of the truffles they were buying were previously stolen. In a fast, hyper-competitive market, most traders only have the time to scrutinize the product, not the sellers.

The thieves also preyed upon one of Pierre-Andre's best clients, a renowned truffle company called Plantin, based in the countryside between Carpentras and Richerenches, near the village of Puyméras. One winter night, the same year that Pierre-Andre's 150 kilos went missing, a whole crew—three cars and one truck—drove down the long dirt driveway to the company's squat warehouse. They employed the truck as a battering ram, smashing through the sidewall, straight into the main truffle-sorting area. The loud bang of metal and crunch of concrete roused nearby neighbors from their sleep. Once inside, the team carried out as much product as they could find near the mess of their entry and loaded it into their vehicles. Most of it was canned—preserved for use during the off-season—but they managed to grab some fresh truffles too. Roughly five minutes after they drove in, they careened out onto a country road, €400,000 richer.

Originally founded by Marcel Plantin in 1930, Plantin had come to dominate the country's fresh truffle trade. Unlike its competitors, the company—which had been purchased by a Frenchman named Hervé Poron in 1986—focuses most heavily on whole black winter truffles and their preserved versions in cans, selling to luxury restaurants and hotels in France, Macau, Japan, the United States, and across the world. Plantin mostly left the wild white truffle and the derivative product market—truffle oils, creams, butter, and a hundred other variations on the same idea, including truffle wasabi—to the two largest Italian firms, Urbani Tartufi and Sabatino Tartufi.

The truck-blast heist was not the company's first bout with thieves. Christoph Poron, Hervé's son and one of Plantin's two current co-owners, recalled at least two other break-ins at the facility, both around Christmas or New Year's Day, when demand for black winter truffles is highest. "There are times—I'm not even sure how they entered here," Poron said, after showing me around the warehouse floor, a jumble of metal tabletops, scales, cardboard, and truffles below hanging fluorescents and a vaulted ceiling.

In his black Plantin apron, jeans, and white hygiene cap, Poron looked a bit like a cross between a business wunderkind and a school cafeteria worker. He was short, lean, and springy, as if his body were built too small to contain all his energy and unflinching affability. He smiled often and frequently trailed into a chuckle, even when discussing the most troubling of matters. The singsong in his French accent was so pronounced that it almost seemed vaudevillian. When he wasn't negotiating directly with middlemen like

Pierre-Andre on the market or buying from farmers on the production floor, he was traveling all over the world, convincing gourmet chefs that his company's truffles were the best.

After the heist in 2005, an insurance company notified Plantin that it could no longer offer the company coverage. Poron and Hervé decided to lock the most expensive product into a dim, underground bunker, protected with the installation of a heavy, unmarked metal door that resembled the entrance to a vault. "It's not like a bank, but everything here is done—if we get robbed—to slow them as much as possible," Poron said. "You cannot avoid people from coming, but you can slow them." They also installed surveillance cameras and hired a professional guard to sit on the property every night of the year. "We are well guarded now."

The company never recovered the €400,000 worth of product it lost during the 2005 incident, and the thieves were never caught. Poron suspected they had already secured a willing buyer and that the goods were fenced immediately. I asked whether he had any suspicions about the identities of the thieves.

"I have no idea," he said. "Absolutely no idea. I don't think it was someone from our profession, but at the end you never know. The good thing is with our main competitors in France we have a very good relationship. When we see each other on the market, we talk to each other. Each of us has a different way of working. Then we fight on the market to get our customers. We have a very good relationship among each other, I think. Mostly."

By 2008, when Poron bought the company from his father, the new security system seemed to be working. The break-ins had stopped. But thievery in the region's truffle groves only seemed to worsen. Every other night, it seemed, another one of Poron's farmers was hit.

"I heard stories," Poron said. "I wasn't there. There are well-organized—I'm going to say gangs. You have a guy with a dog, people posted here and there with guns. I don't know if it's real life or not. I wouldn't run in there if I was one of the farmers. It's not worth getting killed for."

He began to see conducting truffle hunts as frequently as possible as the only effective strategy for protecting the product from the region's pilferers. "The farmers try to go every day, every two days, in their fields to harvest the truffles because, if the guy tries to come during the night, he doesn't find anything," Poron said. "He's not going to come back. That, for me, is the best way to protect yourself. Protect your harvest."

# CHAPTER TWO

# Death in the Grove

THE GRAINY BLACK-AND-WHITE IMAGE FROM THE INFRARED CAMERA flashed onto the truffle farmer's mobile phone sometime before six in the evening. Perched about seven feet up the trunk of a tree, the camera was positioned high enough above the thieves' sight lines that the red blink of light didn't attract notice. The farmer quickly dialed André Faugier, one of the gendarmerie's chief commanders, at a special phone line dedicated to the truffle-surveillance detail he ran. "Okay, come here," the farmer said. "The camera just worked. There is a robber."

It was New Year's Eve 2013, and Faugier was behind the wheel of his patrol car, driving along a country road, not far from the village of Montségur-sur-Lauzon in the Vaucluse department's northern neighbor, Drôme. He sped toward the scene of the unfolding crime. A few minutes later, Faugier's phone rang again: The thief had already driven off the farmer's property. The car, an old, beat-up white sedan, appeared to be heading in the direction of Richer-enches.

Faugier texted the information to his entire list of truffle farm-ers, who exchanged information with him constantly. They peeked through their windows and doors into their fields to check if the thief had yet landed at their properties.

A few truffle farmers who happened to be near the traffic circle outside Richerenches reported the car's direction back to the gen-darmerie. By this point, officers from the nearby villages of Saint-Paul-Trois-Châteaux to the west, and Valréas to the east, had been scrambled for the pursuit.

Eventually, the gendarmerie cars caught up, and the thief ac-celerated far beyond the speed limit of the country road. Heaving into a sharp curve, the car skidded off the pavement and lurched to a halt in a truffle orchard.

The officers pulled over, exited their vehicles, and marched out into the field to inspect the wreck. Instead of one thief, they found two. And instead of hardened convicts, they found boys. One was nineteen; the other was just seventeen. They discovered eight hun-dred grams of fresh black winter truffles in the car, an €800 stop in what was likely to have been a most eventful evening for the teenagers.

By this point, the young men had crossed from Faugier's ju-risdiction in the Drôme department into Vaucluse, so one of the officers from that department handcuffed the suspects and drove them to jail. Vaucluse's laws were far more lenient on truffle theft than Drôme's, so the thieves were released not long after the arrest with nothing more than a petty fine.

Faugier was not surprised. He had come to expect nabbing

young suspects and seeing meager punishments. In much the same fashion as America, French law demands leniency for minors. Faugier suspected that gang leaders deliberately recruited young, impressionable minions to insulate the organization from potential consequences. Though there were some instances of rival farmers sneaking onto each other's properties at night, the majority of the people Faugier and his colleagues had arrested with stolen truffles were members of a larger gang of thieves who associated on the basis of their shared Roma ethnic ancestry and lived an itinerant lifestyle in the countryside. The Roma people trace their roots back to northern India, but their members live in various places throughout Europe, where they are frequently marginalized and scapegoated as the drivers of high urban crime rates.

Some farmers reported having spotted suspects under the age of fifteen, even primary-school-age children. The on-the-ground crews were constantly shifting. The few adults Faugier did manage to apprehend were likely selected because they had no formal criminal records and were therefore also subject to legal leniency. Without ever catching the criminal minds that plotted and ordered the heists, he had difficulty stanching them.

❦

Faugier has all the attributes of a handsome man: dark hair, olive skin, brown eyes, cleanly shaven, medium build. But despite the added flair of heading up a secretive surveillance operation, something about him is decidedly unsexy. He reads more bookish than daring, looks more like a librarian than a detective. But it was his personality that had cultivated trust among the truffle farmers: He is soft-spoken, calm, gentle, and passionate about investigating crimes other gendarmerie officers would yawn at. He avoids the frenetic impulse of the French language and pauses every so often to chuckle at himself, mostly in deprecation. His expressive bushy eyebrows give him a whimsical lightness. He specializes in the investigation of truffle theft, which means he also specializes in soothing nerves.

The region Faugier oversees is home to approximately twenty-five hundred truffle growers, who together produce a substantial portion of the country's national supply. And those are only official numbers; many of the farmers do not formally declare their production and revenues to the French government. To report theft, a farmer must first prove to Faugier that he officially owns the goods. When we met, Faugier wore a light blue polo shirt and an unzipped blue gendarmerie jacket with a horizontal white stripe over the breast. Soon after I arrived, he walked into the kitchen to fix me an espresso, a spoon clanked in the distance, and he came back with a small red cup. He wasn't nearly as intimidating as I supposed he would be after the battle with the gendarmerie to get a meeting with him. The day before, a local truffle farmer named Joel Barthélémy had told me that Faugier never discussed his top secret operations, not even with his closest friends. But suddenly here he was, ready to talk. I was delighted to listen.

His office lies on a quiet, narrow street on the edge of the small fifteen-hundred-person village of Grignan, which is surrounded by lavender fields, vineyards, and truffle plantations. The modern beige building with a slanted tiled roof and a French tricolor "Gendarmerie" sign stands in stark contrast to the eleventh-century stone, Roman tile, and pastel shutters nearby. The room he works in is the size of a rich man's closet, and when I visited, it was crowded with chairs and a desk for another officer. There were yellow walls and darker yellow window frames. A map of the region, with the Drôme department outlined in pink highlighter, was posted near his desk. A Cibox 4 GB thumb drive was plugged into his computer; the key chain label read, "Truffes."

The ever-humble Faugier couldn't remember when he became chief commander in Grignan; he took his glasses off and pursed his lips. We settled on a few years ago.

⸺

Faugier grew up about twenty minutes away from his office, in a commune close to where he and his colleagues chased the teenage thieves, Saint-Paul-Trois-Châteaux. Before he arrived in Grignan, he served in his hometown and in another small Drôme village named Suze-la-Rousse, but his work always seemed to take him out of the agency's provincial boundaries. He began working as a gendarmerie officer around 2001, and not too long after he started, the farmers, individually, began visiting him to tell him there was a major problem with theft. One farmer's fields were dug one night, and then the next week another farmer's long-awaited fungi had been stolen as well.

Back then, the gendarmerie in Drôme was not keeping a close eye on truffle thefts, so the men decided to organize among themselves as a band of crop-guarding vigilantes. They went out into their fields with sticks and waited for the thieves to trespass.

Concerned about potential violence and spurred by the farmers' tips, Faugier finally told them he would lobby for an official surveillance program. He filed a formal request with France's Ministry of the Interior, and eventually it was granted. His superiors even gave him a small budget for some basic surveillance equipment. The farmers were ecstatic. They told him they were prepared to help Faugier in whatever way they could to combat the thieves. He was born in the same rural landscape they were, and they trusted him.

He accompanied the farmers into their fields and had them show him which groves had been hit. During the summer, he sent his men on foot and bike patrols through the orchards to identify the most productive sections in the most secluded areas, the ones that were sure to catch the eyes of thieves. The patches were marked by bright leaves produced from well-irrigated soils, careful pruning, and the right type of rocky soil. The thieves, they suspected, were walking the same paths, casing the groves to see which trees would be worth returning to when winter fell. Had the thieves had the property or the means to buy truffle saplings, they were so observant that they would have made excellent truffle cultivators. They always seemed to know where the best truffle trees stood.

Faugier had become a member of the union of truffle farmers and requested that they consider purchasing an infrared camera so he could see what time and which days the thieves preferred for their pilferage. They complied. Each year, he helped place it in a tree of a grove he was certain would be targeted based on previous years' reports and told the farmer to bury a collection of fresh truffles in a few places around it so the thieves' dogs would linger long enough that he could ensure a clear shot of their faces.

Before each truffle season began, Faugier held meetings with the farmers to lecture them about how they could contribute to the investigations, to collect intelligence, and to instruct them about what their rights were when they encountered a trespasser. He toured southeastern France and even held a meeting on the other side of the country, in Périgord, an area now poor in truffle production but rich in reputation. (Long ago, the southwestern side of the country had many more truffles, and when companies first attempted to build an international market in the late-nineteenth century, they called all the truffles Périgord—no matter where they came from—because they hoped to ride the coattails of its international reputation for canned foie gras. The name never faded.) He advised them to put up "Private Property" signs so the thieves could have no excuses about wandering off in the wrong direction.

When the season formally began, the gendarmes organized night patrols near the spots with the highest likelihood of heists. Still the thieves came. "They always have one step in advance," Faugier said. The farmers, as well as Faugier and his officers, feared the dark chases through the cold woods as much as they relished them. Amid the crisscrossing of flashlights and the chaos of the pursuits, the men easily lost track of the thieves in the nooks of the forest. They openly wondered how many suspects they were looking for and whether they were armed. The robbers learned to look around for red lights from the infrared cameras, and they came prepared with night-vision goggles that were nicer than the models Faugier and his men had access to.

Faugier suspected they purchased the goggles on the cheap at the border of France and Spain, where products are sold without the in-country 20 percent tax. Meanwhile, Faugier's office remained strapped. The camera they used was bulky and five years behind the current technology. They patrolled mainly on foot, bicycles, and in smaller patrol cars. They were able to use a helicopter and motorbikes for a few months but then had to return them. They couldn't possibly be everywhere at once.

During the course of the patrols, thieves threw their digging tools at approaching farmers. They hurled stones. When farmers fired warning shots into the sky, the thieves returned fire, so they could escape while farmers weighed the risks of pursuit. Sometimes, the thieves fired preemptively. Farmers, especially those who patrolled alone, walked the edges of their oak groves, increasingly petrified about what lurked in the darkness. They feared that their livelihood and years of work would be erased in a night under the moonlight, that a bullet shot in warning might end up lodged in their chest.

Faugier and his men considered the thieves armed and dangerous. Faugier took great precautions to ensure security; at a minimum, he required three officers per suspect. On a more recent pursuit involving four suspects near the village of Saint-Restitut, thirty-two officers participated, seventeen of them working out in the field.

Early on, Faugier ruled out sending his truffle surveillance team undercover. The robbers knew each other too well; they'd smell a gendarme from the other end of the oak grove. Occasionally, the thieves claimed they were farmers, but, as Faugier suggested, his men aren't idiots either.

Not wanting to pursue a formal covert op and knowing he wouldn't receive contact or full transparency from every farmer, Faugier found a digital avenue for his investigation as well. He created a handle on a French truffle-farming web forum—where producers troubleshoot growing techniques and exchange information about yields and recent trespasses—and began lurking. Using information gleaned there, as well as intelligence from farmers, he began plotting trends. He and his colleagues posted patrols in areas that were repeatedly hit, and soon, in and around the villages of Saint-Paul and Suze-la-Rousse, where Faugier focused most of his energies, the thefts began to drop.

⁂

But Faugier also had a secret, someone who allowed him to see things his foot patrols and his single infrared camera and even his truffle forum handle couldn't. His name was Ernest Pardo, a giant man with hulking logs for arms, a barrel of a chest, short-cropped gray hair, and soft, tired brown eyes. At six feet seven and 240 pounds, he looked not unlike a retired NFL linebacker. His hands were comically large, the size of a child's head. And the size of his feet compelled some who encountered him to call him Bigfoot. He was of Roma descent and had loose associations with some of the suspected truffle thieves. He lived with his spouse and two children in a nondescript modern apartment building in Saint-Paul. By day, he worked part-time on an ambulance. By night, he was a car and jewel thief of some renown. He did most of his criminal work in the much larger city of Avignon. He had an intimate understanding of crimes in the region, of who worked with whom, and of where they would be next.

Faugier had grown up with Pardo in Saint-Paul. They attended the same middle school, shared friends and classmates. One became a thief, the other a detective. Pardo eventually became Faugier's truffle crime informant. The pair began meeting around town, never at the gendarmerie station, and Pardo told him where the thieves planned to strike. It was as if they were playing cops and robbers again, except this time it was real.

Pardo always came to him. Faugier never shared anything about the details of the investigation or the theories he was operating upon. Pardo always had a new lead, and usually it led to something. He had established himself as something of a professional informant. In one instance, he told the gendarmerie in one of the local villages about an upcoming jewel heist so large that an important judge from the city of Valence to the north drove all the way down to get the details.

But Pardo wasn't only an informant; over the course of their collaboration, he became a real friend to Faugier. He was warm.

Faugier used a French expression to describe him: "The hand on the heart." A salt-of-the-earth, pat-your-back kind of guy. He also just happened to steal.

---

Some time before 2010, Faugier began to develop a reference map for truffle thievery. With assistance from farmers across Drôme, he marked the paper with more than a dozen little red circles, which represented the most vulnerable areas in his slice of the department. These were places where farmers had lost sizable quantities during the night, usually on more than one occasion. He soon noticed that the sleepy village of Grignan seemed to occupy a relatively blank space on the map. Though there were plenty of truffle groves there and he had made himself accessible, he hadn't received a single report of theft from farmers in the area.

For some reason, the people there seemed to labor under the illusion that there were no crimes in their quiet, cloistered little village. It was as if they rather their idyllic existence not be marred by the facts of the thieves. The silence hung over the landscape like a fog, curling them into its wispy grasp. But one day, the mistral would blow in, and there would no longer be a comfortable cloak with which to conceal the truth.

It wasn't just the truffles that colored the town's secrecy. People in Grignan simply liked to keep to themselves. Though Faugier had been working there for the better part of two years when I met him and continually reached out to farmers there as he had elsewhere, he felt no real connection to its community. In fact, there was an eerie absence of community. People remained in their country homes and subscribed to their own views. Certain little villages in Provence have the propensity to close themselves to outsiders, and to isolate their insiders as well, and Grignan happened to be one of them.

The village's abundance of truffles made the private community more hermetic, even paranoid about what might walk out of the shadows. Without reports about thefts or even knowledge about who grew truffles on their properties, Faugier was operating in both literal and figurative darkness. It wasn't clear who had chosen to patrol, what their plan of action was, or how angry they were. The silence seemed destined to morph into fury.

Laurent Rambaud was quiet, just like the rest of Grignan. He worked as an administrator at a bank and managed his truffle orchard during the season to earn his family some extra cash. He served as the president of the department's young farmers' union and was a member of the volunteer fire department. Rambaud had dark brown hair, cut short at the sides with longer curls at top, and a big nose. When he was stressed, he pressed his lips tightly together, curling one or the other into his mouth. His wife managed the family's lavender fields, which produced the raw material for a line of products. And Rambaud's father, Albert, oversaw their property's vineyard operations. They all kept to themselves. The family was not so much an exception to Grignan's milieu as its silent touchstone.

The family lived directly across the road from the gendarmerie station. The officers could see the property from their windows. The Rambauds didn't have problems with anyone in the village, and no one had any issues with them.

On Saturday mornings, like many of the other truffle growers in the region, Rambaud showed up at the Richerenches market to sell his recent harvests. He also drove out to Puyméras to sell directly to Plantin's Christoph Poron on the warehouse floor.

In the truffle season of 2010, farmers in the Grignan area were waking up to truffle groves pockmarked with holes, footprints, and tiny mounds of dirt. A small group of farmers began gossiping about the problem among themselves, but no one reported anything to the gendarmerie. Each day, a new property was hit. Rambaud and Albert grew concerned that their oak groves would be next. A few farmers installed surveillance cameras in their groves and pooled information about where the thieves had been and where they suspected they were likely to go next. Rambaud and Albert took turns patrolling their grove at night with guns.

One evening, out in the grove, Rambaud encountered trespassers who didn't leave without muttering threats. On another occasion, a car edged into the grove and drove dangerously close to Rambaud, before speeding off. At some point, the family discovered that someone had broken into his mother's car.

After work on December 20, 2010, Rambaud was anxious, as many other farmers were that season, and enraged by the prospect of losing his valuable product during the night. The sun began to dip beyond the lavender fields and the hills in the distance, and twilight set in. Rambaud's father asked him whether he planned to go out into the truffle groves to patrol. He retrieved his 12-gauge shotgun and walked down the dirt pathway, past the lavender fields and vineyard, and out to the grove. He loaded the shells into the gun as he approached.

When he came upon the edge of the grove, he spotted a lumbering silhouette and a dainty shadow lingering near its rear. A man and his dog. Startled, Rambaud bent down and steadied his weapon. Fearing that the small object the man held in his hands was a pistol, and not comforted by his sudden movements, Rambaud fired. The shot pierced the front of the man's thigh, and he fell to the ground. But moments later, the man staggered to his feet and turned to run, out from the grove and toward a low stone wall at the edge of the property. He had parked his Citroën C15 van just on the other side. All he had to do was hop over before Rambaud was able to get a closer look at his face. Its location seemed planned for easy escape.

But Rambaud pulled the trigger again.

The second round of pellets tore through the back of the man's scalp. He stumbled and collapsed. His body slumped over the wall. Blood poured over the cold stone.

With the assistance of his brother, Dominique, who met him at the scene, Rambaud phoned the authorities in a panic. His father, Albert, felt a desperate rush of paternal responsibility. Before the gendarmes arrived, he hid the unregistered weapon and put his own legally declared rifle in its place.

When the gendarmerie officers arrived on the scene, they recognized the bleeding giant. It was Faugier's informant, Ernest Pardo. He was unarmed and dead.

Soon after pulling in, the officers placed Laurent Rambaud under arrest.

⁂

Back at the gendarmerie station in Saint-Paul-Trois-Châteaux, Faugier was heartbroken, especially for Pardo's widow and his two young children. But he was also stunned. He couldn't quite believe that his old informant chum was stealing black diamonds along with real ones and, in the process, betraying their alliance. He knew that Pardo had dabbled in wild truffle hunting, as the old Provençal men used to favor, but had no idea that he was among the very truffle thieves he was trying to catch. Faugier had thought that Pardo's illicit activity was centered on Avignon and rarely, if ever, extended into his home department. He had believed that Pardo abided by some kind of unwritten criminal code: stealing from outside the neighborhood rather than within it.

The killing also left Faugier somewhat lost professionally. Most of his compelling inside leads evaporated with Rambaud's two pulls. He knew most growers and thieves had guns and understood that ceaseless fear could precipitate further tragedy.

I couldn't tell whether the personal or professional loss saddened him more. When he spoke of losing his informant's tips, he wiped a faux tear from his eye.

Meanwhile, the prosecutor Gilbert Emery charged Rambaud with murder.

Faugier raised his eyebrows when I asked about Rambaud. He looked hesitant, even embarrassed to tell me how he truly felt. Though he had been working in Grignan since 2013, he hadn't spoken with the family, even though they lived directly across the street from his office. He suggested that people around the village wouldn't necessarily stop to tout the family's special qualities. He couldn't say much about Rambaud other than that he was "a secret man, like Grignan," but I sensed he had little sympathy for Rambaud's ordeal. I sensed he liked Rambaud about as much as someone could like a person who had killed his friend.

What sympathy Faugier lacked, though, the eighth-generation truffle farmer Joel Barthélémy more than compensated for. As the president of the region's truffle-farming union, he'd known Rambaud for years through the Richerenches market and by function of the smallness of the industry. A few days after the shooting, he and about two hundred other farmers protested with comrades in the streets of Grignan. They opposed the charges against Rambaud and what they perceived as the police's failure in managing the thieves' unrelenting trespass. Lately, farmers in and around Grignan had been complaining among themselves of a thief they called Bigfoot, because of the size of the footprints he left in their groves.

*

"The truth is really complicated," Barthélémy said, in his low, flat, and measured tone, his customary method of delivery. Dark had fallen over his thirty acres of stately truffle oaks near Suze-la-Rousse, and his two Rottweilers, friendly during the day but ferocious at night, had begun to roam the estate. "And everyone is talking about that. But the end is someone has been killed. The real question is, why is it like that now? Why someone innocent killed another?" For Barthélémy, the answers to that question are a lack of proper protection by the police, and the desperation of farmers organizing themselves against freely prowling thieves. He doubts the thieves grasp that growers cannot simply venture into their groves and pluck truffles at will. He believes that when they sneak onto a property, they imagine a farmer of luxury and ease rather than one carrying the constant pain of uncertainty. Cold, fear, darkness, rage, and guns tend not to produce tidy results. There was a fatalism to his vision, but it made sense: If Rambaud hadn't pulled the trigger, another farmer would have.

Around the same time as the protest in Grignan, about three hundred people flooded the streets of Saint-Paul, Pardo's hometown, to rally against Rambaud's deadly decision. Pardo "did not deserve to be killed like a dog," the gathered grievers told reporters.

Though he'd purchased truffles from Rambaud before, Poron's thinking was closer to Faugier's. "Some people live off selling truffles, so of course it's like taking away the bread from their table," he said. "But I cannot approve of somebody killing somebody. Whatever they do. You know, a lot of people—not going to say they approved—but supported the guy, in the fact that every-body's pissed off. The farmers want to be protected. The police do a lot of surveillance to try to figure out what's happening. At some point, there's only so much you can do."

A couple years after Rambaud was arrested, another band of thieves began preying upon Saint-Restitut, a commune southwest of Grignan. Faugier was having trouble making any breaks in the case, until the gendarmerie in Carpentras, the Vaucluse town to the south where one of the largest truffle markets is held, arrested two Roma thieves, who were willing to provide intelligence on what was happening up north. The information led Faugier to four arrests.

The Rambaud family was not pleased that the gendarmerie continued to develop informant relationships with the Roma gangs. They did not want to see the criminals responsible for sending Rambaud to prison getting off easy or forming another relationship they would betray. Of course, Faugier said, informants were one of the only avenues the gendarmerie had to pursue and prevent the truffle crimes.

Despite his informant's death and the fact that thieves were still sneaking into local groves days before we spoke, Faugier seemed to think he was making a kind of progress. When he began his truffle investigations, the French penal code treated truffles in the same way as mushrooms; offenders had to steal at least ten kilos to generate any kind of notice, even though truffles were far more valuable. In credit to Faugier's lobbying, that rule shifted to include judicial punishments for the theft of even a single truffle. If the criminal had no previous criminal record, a stolen truffle might lead to a hefty fine. If it were the thief's second or third offense, the punishment could lead to jail time. "That's why all the robbers are always young or changing teams," Faugier said. The punishment is more severe if the thieves are wearing masks, carrying weapons, or working in more than a pair.

In the end, though, neither Pardo's death nor the new laws really discouraged the thieves.

A few years later, in 2015, Rambaud was brought to trial. On the day of his sentencing, May 29, a Pardo family friend and attorney, Naceur Derbel, spoke to the court on behalf of Pardo's widow and children. "We talked about the atmosphere of fear that hung in the world of truffle growers," he said. "There was a parade of witnesses to come and talk about it. A parade of witnesses who have not had a look or a word to the family of the victims. . . . The death of Mr. Pardo became an accessory to worries of truffle related thefts."

Of Rambaud's decision to pull the trigger twice, he added, "I see no fear in it. I see only the methodical and the rational." He stressed that Rambaud was out in his grove plotting to kill anyone he saw. "Your decision will not be trivial," he said, addressing the jury. "It will be a sacred message. It will open the door to anarchy, or be a reminder of what is a society of law."

Another man, speaking on behalf of Pardo's parents, told the court that he "had two good reasons" for being in the grove. He was "picking up the materials" from a local business and dropping off "a lawn mower to a friend." "The pickax"—the truffle digging tool recovered near the body—"was not in the hand of the victim when he was shot," he said.

Another attorney representing Pardo's spouse revealed that she had been pregnant with their third child when he was killed. He relayed her thoughts in the days after the murder: "Am I going to be able to give birth to this child who will remind me every day of the father he does not have, the father who was taken away from him?"

Then the prosecutor, Gilbert Emery, gave his parting thoughts to the jury: "We must understand why Laurent Rambaud killed a man. . . . He executed without trial Ernest Pardo, who probably would have given anything to be entitled to a trial. . . . Is Ernest Pardo a truffle thief? Was he stealing? For him, there was no presumption of innocence."

Emery criticized Rambaud's legal team for introducing the victim's criminal record in witness testimony. "When someone dies," he said, "his criminal record is blocked. It is forbidden to consult. I condemn the method of interrogating a police officer to know the record of a victim. But, Monsieur Rambaud! You shot a criminal record or a man!?

"I remain firmly convinced that [it] was Rambaud's obsession to flush out the thief," he said. The prosecutor recommended a twelve-year sentence to the jury.

Alain Fort, Rambaud's defense lawyer, stood up next. "I do not like hate," he said. "I do not understand the violence of words you have just heard. Why so much hatred toward Laurent Rambaud?

"How do you ask for twelve years' imprisonment for a man who never in his life violated the law and who has dedicated his life to others? . . . This case is that of a man who, alone in the night, was panicked.

"These are two shots fired by a man in full panic. He thought he was in danger. For four years, every moment, he thinks of the Pardo family and his."

After his other defense lawyer finished, Rambaud—who had remained mute and stone-faced throughout the proceedings unless directly questioned—rose to address the court.

"I never wanted to kill Monsieur Pardo," he said. "I ask the family to forgive me."

Fort's vigorous defense of his client—which hinged on painting a poignant picture of just how fearful and desperate farmers in the region were becoming because of the nightly heists by armed thieves—convinced the jury. For killing Pardo, Rambaud was sentenced to less than the prosecutor's recommendation: eight years.

After one of their own was sentenced to prison, some farmers wavered on the necessity of patrols. "After this man was killed, some people, finally they were back in reality," Nicolas Valayer, the farmer in Richerenches, told me. "They said, 'That is the life of someone against a few grams of truffles'—perhaps it's not exactly the same value." Others had a difficult time resisting the compulsion to defend their groves. A farmer in Saint-Restitut told *The Telegraph* that he "often had to fight a primal instinct to take justice into my own hands, despite the tragedy of Grignan."

Even after the trial had concluded and Rambaud began serving his sentence in prison, the exact events on the night of December 20, 2010, remained shrouded in mystery. Besides Rambaud, no one knew for certain what happened in that grove. And especially what pushed Rambaud to fire. Given the opportunity to tell the full story without his future in jeopardy, could Rambaud make his decision seem less senseless? Would Pardo seem more threatening than the testimony let on?

Through his attorney, I tried to arrange a visit with Rambaud in prison during the truffle season following his sentencing. Caught up in another high-profile murder case at the time I was visiting France, the attorney and his secretary brushed off the requests.

Both Faugier's and Rambaud's old acquaintance Barthélémy

agreed there was more to the story than what was discussed in court.

For instance, less than two hours after the shooting, Pardo's dog was found at home in his apartment back in Saint-Paul-Trois-Châteaux, more than six miles away. "Of course, he wasn't alone," Barthélémy said. Dogs don't fly, Barthélémy reminded me. "Why did he shoot two times?" Barthélémy said. Isn't a shell full of pellets enough for one man?

Faugier, too, was convinced that someone besides Pardo had been in the grove. He pointed to the dog's presence back at Pardo's home as evidence of an accomplice.

When I pressed for more about that night, Barthélémy reminded me that he could only tell me what he knew. Tensions and anxiety had died down since Rambaud had been sentenced, and he didn't want to stir the pot. Rambaud is expected to be released before he has served his full term, and many in the truffle community agreed that opening old wounds would serve no one. The silence was designed to allow Rambaud and his family to reclaim their old lives of privacy. Barthélémy subscribed to the old French proverb "A closed mouth catches no flies."

I walked along the low stone wall at the edge of the Rambauds' estate. The air smelled of burning firewood and dead lavender. The old stone house, with its lavender doors and shutters, stood at the end of the dirt driveway. A child's swing set sat on the grass in front of the home. Purple signs advertised some kind of lavender product.

Feeling somewhat hesitant, I crossed the property line and paced toward the home. To the left, a wide, open lavender field stood between the dwelling and the small truffle orchard at the other end of the property. A set of ganglier truffle oaks rose out from the back end of the property, past the haystacks and farm employees milling near the working shed.

Two black curly-haired truffle dogs barked from inside their gated cage as I edged closer to the front door. The entranceway was at the crux of the L-shaped structure.

I rapped the wood portion of the pane-glass door. Nothing but a yappy white house dog answered the call.

I paced past the garage toward the chicken pen, where red- and orange-feathered birds milled and balked. I was staring into the pen at about the moment a car, headlights on, rolled up the end of the driveway. I froze for a moment, considering that I was now trespassing on the Rambauds' property.

The car came closer, and I walked farther toward the entrance, where my translator had headed after being spooked by my skulking. She doubled back to help me speak to Ms. Rambaud.

After parking near the front door, Ms. Rambaud exited the vehicle and walked toward us, leaving her young son wriggling in the front seat. The translator told Rambaud that I was working on a book, had spoken to others in the region about truffle production, and hoped she would answer some of my questions. She understood what was going on. It had the distinct flavor of an ambush.

She said the truffle plantation was her husband's domain and that she wouldn't talk about anything, including the incident, without his express permission. "It's my husband's life, not mine," she said. "Just talk to the lawyer."

But, I stammered, I had already contacted the lawyer, with multiple requests. "That's strange because my husband didn't mention that," she said. Either the lawyer hadn't shared the request with the family, or Rambaud had chosen not to tell his wife.

As anyone surprised at home by a foreign journalist might be, she was stiff. I could sense the tension as the translator explained the situation. It obviously wasn't the best time or circumstance for a conversation, but I was due to meet an Interpol detective in Lyon the next morning. The conversation quickly fizzled; it didn't make sense to stay around to talk about everything but her husband, and she had to attend to her young son.

The translator and I turned and walked past the dogs, along the low wall, to the front of the gendarmerie station, where we had parked. The sun had begun to set.

After the translator drove off, I got back in my car, resolving to do some further reconnaissance. I made a left onto the road I had just walked along and drove away from the house toward the young truffle orchard. I drove until it forked right, where the pavement turned to dirt and a private track led down a steep hill toward a large set of fields. Down below in the distance, a tractor drove in my direction. I reversed up the hill and turned back out onto the paved road. I drove slowly, hoping to snap some photographs of the property. The tractor caught up and passed me on the road toward the house. It turned in to the dirt driveway, pulled toward the stone, and came to a halt. An older gentleman was driving. I suspected it was Rambaud's father, Albert.

Not wanting to draw any further attention, I drove off in the other direction, making the first left, tracking the other side of the property. There was a stunning orange and pink glow in the sky. The grove at the back of the property extended for quite a distance, at least for a full minute down the road. I kept driving, until I spotted another low stone wall at the grove's edge. It was either here or at the other end of the property where Pardo had been shot. No one would have noticed if I pulled over and wandered into the grove.

But I turned around and drove out of town. I pulled over on the side of the road and looked out onto a field of dry lavender and out at the hill in the distance upon which the village of Grignan stood. The sky had drained of its late afternoon light and twilight had crept in. It was roughly the same time of day and the same time of year that Rambaud had killed Pardo.

When I returned to the United States, Rambaud's lawyer continued to ignore my emails and calls. I could no longer talk to the man who died stealing truffles, so I wanted to talk to the man who killed to protect them. I wanted badly to understand what the killing revealed about the truffle's power. But I still felt as if I were sitting in silence on the outskirts of Grignan, staring into a sky losing its light.

# PART II

# THE LABORATORY · SECRECY

There is not a crime, there is not a dodge, there is not a trick, there is not a swindle, there is not a vice which does not live by secrecy.

—Joseph Pulitzer

# CHAPTER THREE

# The Peasant's Golden Secret

THE MORE I CONSIDERED RAMBAUD'S FEAR—AND HIS DEADLY DETER-
mination to protect what he had grown—the more I realized that
its true cause could be found not in Pardo's silhouette but, as his
lawyer Alain Fort suggested, in the intense culture of suspicion
and paranoia among the region's truffle farmers. The men believed
they were being tailed on the way home from market and watched
as they moved about their groves. They speculated that the thieves
drove up to their farms from their hideouts in Marseille, famous for
its armed Mafia. At night, as they wandered their rows, mulled over
the latest rumors, and imagined armed men lurking in the shadows,
the resulting phantasms were perhaps more frightening than the
actual thieves. Fort described the collective dread leading up to the
incident as a "climate of psychosis."

But this fear was not a new affliction. Truffle farmers' compulsion to conceal and protect their buried treasure from shadows in

the forest began with the very origins of truffle cultivation more than two centuries ago, on a hill seventy miles south of the grove where Rambaud fired his shots.

Sometime around 1818, fate appointed a peasant named Joseph Talon the sole guardian of a secret that had been sought since ancient Amorite servants dug hopelessly into the sands of Mesopotamia, searching for the mysterious desert truffles, or *terfez*, that kings demanded as a centerpiece in lavish royal meals, next to fried locusts and chickpea salad. Based on contemporaneous accounts, it's easy to imagine the way it happened. Talon approached the limestone outcropping at the crest of the hill near his modest house in the hamlet of Croagnes, when his pig squealed and bolted down the slope. By the time he was able to sprint back to her, his satchel swinging at his side, she was digging furiously at the soil beneath one of the holm oaks he had planted. He had never seen the languid creature so kinetic. Before he was able to command her to cease the nonsense, a black blur came tumbling across the dead grass. The sow scooped it up and tore uphill, and Talon chased after her.

Once up on the scrubby plateau, Talon managed to use what strength he had to pin the pig against a boulder and take her down to the ground. He squeezed her snout and yanked open her stubborn jaws. She squirmed so wildly that she knocked off his beret and emptied his satchel full of acorns onto the ground. Finally, with a panting grunt, she relented and spat the object out. She eyed him in anticipation of a morsel of bread, as if what had just transpired were worthy of reward.

He held the object in the air, rubbing its pebbly surface between his thumb and his forefinger underneath the heat of the morning sun. It was a black winter truffle.

It was the same kind that chefs had been stuffing into turkeys and serving to aristocrats in the well-appointed dining rooms of the Hôtel des Américains, the Hôtel de Provence, and in all the most fashionable smoky restaurants across Paris. "The meal is almost unknown in which no truffled dish occurs," the French writer Jean Anthelme Brillat-Savarin would soon observe. "However good in itself an entrée may be, it makes but a poor appearance if it be not garnished with truffles. Who has not felt his mouth water at the very mention of truffles a *la Provençale?*" European royalty had long relished the ingredient—the Dukes of Savoy, the Medicis, King Louis XIV, and Napoleon ate them—but ordinary nobles and men of means had come to lust after them too.

Lately, Parisian dealers, noticing how truffles enhanced diners' enjoyment at the table, had dispatched their deputies south to Carpentras and Apt, two villages not far from Croagnes, offering peasants numbers of francs they had never held before. They arranged mail couriers and express coaches to race the truffles back north, where demand had exploded. Soon, it seemed, every farmer in the southeast had also become a truffle hunter, or *rabassière,* in the Provençal dialect.

I imagine Talon returned to the hole and stuck his fingers into the soil, scraping away where the pig had shoved her snout. Soon, he plucked out a few more truffles. They were large and aromatic—of far superior quality to the ones he'd seen dealers fussing over at the market in Apt.

These truffles could make a peasant like Talon rich.

The rest of the parched landscape on the acres he owned was fitful or completely barren, a place where he could hardly will thyme to grow. It was sloping, ragged, rocky, and exposed to the elements, and several years before he had become seized with desperation. Before he departed to fight in one of Napoleon's wars, he resorted to collecting acorns from underneath the wild white and holm oaks growing here and there on the hill and planting them in rows surrounding his fallow farmland. He hoped to shelter his meager crops from the roiling winds of the Luberon valley, and in absence of any success on this measure, he figured he could trim the trees for bundles of firewood and let his pigs feed on the resulting acorns.

But desperation was not the only driver; there was curiosity too. On wild truffle hunts through the scrubby foothills, he had noticed that whenever his pig came upon a truffle, there was always an oak tree not too far away. Part of him might have hoped that his grove might do more than improve crop yields; perhaps his grove would serve as an experiment for a theory he had developed in the woods: The truffle, he suspected, wasn't possible without the oak. The land was already useless; if the experiment didn't work, at least he'd have useless land covered in oaks and showered in acorns.

The great Greek and Roman scholars had not been as practical as the insolvent farmer in their hypotheses about the fragrant, underground lumps, which grew with no apparent seeds or connections to other plants. They yearned for a grandiose, numinous origin: Some thought thunder ushered them into existence; others speculated about sorcery. The naturalists and scientists of the eighteenth century had convinced themselves of the notion that simply burying a wild truffle—sometimes with elaborate, alchemical mixtures of leaves, bark, and sawdust—could lead to its reproduction. For thirty-five hundred years, the greatest agricultural minds wondered how truffles could be tamed.

But now, roughly eight years after planting the oaks, the twenty-five-year-old peasant had finally cracked the code. Peering down at the result—the first truffles to ever be successfully cultivated—he must have realized the sheer absurdity of his discovery.

Oaks. Trees. Plant them, and you may have truffles. He'd stumbled onto a fertile El Dorado. It was the kind of discovery usually reserved for learned men, not diminutive sons of soil.

But the revelation also meant vulnerability. Fellow farmers would be intrigued. If Talon disclosed his methodology, he would create his own competitors and reduce his fortune.

Talon gathered every acorn he could find from the trees he'd planted, loaded them into a basket, and emptied them near his house. He believed the acorns themselves carried some special capacity for germinating into truffle trees, and he couldn't let anyone else come across them. Perhaps he retrieved a pickax and crushed them into dust. Or perhaps he threw them into a fire—started with his wood bundles—or fed them to his pigs. But he spent the afternoon destroying all of the extras he could find, ensuring no neighbors would divine their importance and lay claim to his innovation.

As the sun crept behind his hill, he began planting the remainders in rows throughout his property. He would visit his neighbors soon to see about buying more parcels of land; they would be more than willing to sell their infertile plots.

In the scrubland on the edge of the property, though, Talon's cousin, also named Joseph, was carefully studying Talon's harried movements. As he approached, perhaps he had noticed how furiously his relative was swinging his pickax and decided to step back into the bushes to spy for a moment. There was limited logic to what he witnessed. First, there was the wholesale destruction of hundreds of acorns, but then Talon delicately planted the hillside with them, with the elation of someone who'd just been visited by a deity.

⬧

Soon Talon's cousin learned that Talon had begun buying up rocky, valueless parcels from neighbors near his home. He'd never shown any interest in the land next to his own fallow patch. The cousin was beginning to think there was a kind of magic to that landscape and to those trees no one had considered.

Over time, he began to understand what Talon was doing as he planted the acorns incessantly, in every open parcel he could find. He noticed that Talon tended to the saplings as he might tend to a garden. He plowed the space between the rows, ripping up the grass and weeds. And he kept his pigs out of the plot.

When Talon came to market in Apt with a full basket of truffles, the other peasants swooned over the man's good fortune. But the cousin knew that luck hadn't been the only factor. As he arranged his own meager crops, he decided to gather and plant some acorns himself.

⬧

Each season, more truffles materialized, and Talon became less and less a peasant. By 1820, he had sown almost five acres of oaks.

He bought more land from his neighbors, who, by then, probably wondered what Talon knew about the land that they didn't. Talon might have been a peasant, but he wasn't dim-witted. Once he discovered the secret behind cultivation, he didn't talk about it with anyone.

But his cousin did. He began telling others of his expected fortune, about how oak acorns could produce treasure. Monsieur Étienne Carbonnel, who lived in the same hamlet as the cousin, a place called Clavaillant to the west, soon followed with a plantation of his own. Word spread to Monsieur Vaison in Fontaube, Monsieur Vendran in Bédoin, and Dr. Bernard in Valsorgues. The secret crept through the Luberon valley and beyond. "A veritable school of trufficulture" arose, the French botanist Jules-Émile Planchon wrote, but the secret remained, for a time, in the narrow thread of hamlets surrounding Apt.

At some point, Talon settled on a refinement of his method—planting only acorns that he'd recovered at the base of truffle-producing trees. In his fieldwork, he possessed a rare mixture of patience and wisdom. At one point, he discovered that the shade of some of the oaks seemed to be reducing the harvests, so he sacrificed one out of every two of his rows.

Soon, he'd planted almost twenty-five acres, and after the eight or ten years they took to mature, each produced roughly forty kilos of truffles. He was the first, and most successful, truffle farmer in the world.

◆

Eventually, word of Talon's success reached Auguste Rousseau, a powerful and sly trader in Carpentras, across the hills and through the gorges to the west.

Rousseau rode over the hills to Croagnes to see Talon's property and gathered acorns from the most productive oaks in the batch, with Talon's assistance. At this point, in 1847, Talon had realized his methods had become somewhat public and had forfeited his attempts at secrecy.

When Rousseau looked upon Puits-du-Plant, a six-acre parcel he owned near Carpentras's gates, all he could see was the potential of the Talon method. The dirt managed to spit out only 180 francs of rye and straw per hectare (or around two and a half acres). Just like Talon's soil, the topsoil teemed with pebbles and limestone, and the subsoil had the quality of "an impenetrable pudding," as if the only thing it wanted, the only thing it could bear, were oak saplings. One November day, Rousseau walked from north to south, planting small holm oak seedlings, hunching every six feet or so to bury a new one. He spaced the rows roughly seventeen feet apart, enough space to nurture grape vines between the trees.

In 1853, he recovered just three truffles. By 1854, there were four kilograms. In 1855, Rousseau was able to harvest fifteen kilos of shapely truffles from his oldest trees.

Rousseau canned the best truffles from the harvest with the newly minted Appert method and brought them to the Exposition Universelle, held at the Palais de l'Industrie at Marigny Square in Paris. The judges honored his product with a first-class medal, alongside Algerian oranges, "admirable for size, finesse and flavor," and "very fine Corinthian grapes." Parisian journalists swarmed, announcing the successful cultivation of the truffle, which was then still thought to be damned to the wild.

"Here are the products I have gathered at the bottom of *truffière* oaks," Rousseau told those who would listen. "They are perfectly my work, and have nothing in common with those which are harvested in abandoned woods given to nature. If you will take the trouble to come to Puits-du-Plant, you will see that the question of artificial truffles, so often debated, has definitely entered the domain of practice." The scientists in attendance were not convinced; they couldn't believe that where the men of science had failed, a rustic merchant had excelled.

Struck by the development, the Count of Gasparin, a French politician and scientist, arranged an introduction through the head of the Vaucluse department's farm school and proposed a visit to investigate. Rousseau agreed, and the count planned a stop on his next return to France from his home in Switzerland. On February 3, 1856, he arrived at the truffle farm on the outskirts of the village, with his brother and a group of agricultural enthusiasts in tow.

Rousseau's pig ran wildly through the rows of miniature holm and common oaks, which rose only a few feet from the ground. Her snout detected a scent, and she darted twenty paces forward, to the base of one of the oaks. She would have swallowed her discovery if Rousseau hadn't rapped her snout with his stick. He bent down and offered her a dry chestnut as a reward. The pig seemed to pay the most attention to the trees that Rousseau had already marked as productive with a splotch of white paint at their base. And she avoided the common oaks, which sat in the shade of a nearby house. After an hour of walking the grove, Rousseau and his sow had unearthed one kilogram of cultivated truffles in front of Gasparin.

When Gasparin returned home, he issued his report to the jurors back in Paris. "There is not the slightest doubt that truffle plots can be formed at will in the south of France by seedlings of oaks," he wrote. The count made no mention of Talon in his report, presumably because Rousseau never bothered to tell the count where he'd learned the techniques that produced his "prodigious results."

The count reported his observations to the prefect of Vaucluse. In November 1856, the prefect circulated a pamphlet instructing local officials and citizens to plant as many acorns as they could in the vacant spaces surrounding their towns. Farmers paid notice. They colored the dry foothills of Mont Ventoux in green. The truffle saplings grew with abandon.

The adoption was so widespread that by 1866 Rousseau's truffle-canning business had grown from fewer than ten tons to fifty-four.

Meanwhile, Talon's truffle harvests continued to grow. In a

report, filed in 1869, Henri Bonnet, an agricultural official in Apt, called them "excellent." "This is where I came into the world," Talon told his children, gesturing to the field where his oldest oaks grew.

Around the same period that wide adoption of Talon's method took off, France's grapevines began to yellow and rot from a then-unknown disease. The tiny insect phylloxera was destroying vineyards all over France, and desperate vineyard owners pivoted to the new business. Between 1862 and 1886, farmers planted thousands of acres of oaks. Talon's discovery had provided them with a savior from financial demise, but Rousseau was the one who was publicly honored and remembered.

—

Thieves recognized the development of truffle cultivation before the courts did. Knowing that a forest code, rather than the penal code, governed conduct in the woods—even woods lying on private property—they trespassed in the new truffle groves without concern. A judge in northern France ruled that the penal code could not be applied to any product of the forest, including truffles. The laws failed to recognize that truffles were no longer exclusively a foraged food, especially in the south.

Aware of the law's failure, farmers in the southeast erected watchtowers on their land and trekked out together at night with lanterns. A book from the late nineteenth century reads as if it were penned by the truffle farmers who protested Rambaud's indictment in 2010. "This monitoring, often inefficient, [was] very dangerous. Truffle poachers, like game poachers, were not always of good composition."

A judge in the Court of Apt, not far from Talon's land, made the first favorable ruling for truffle farmers on December 14, 1865, applying the penal code to the crime. It sentenced a repeat truffle thief, who worked with a sow, to ten days in prison and a fine of 16 francs. He had already been caught and sentenced for four previous infractions. In 1878, another man in Carpentras received a one-year sentence after he was discovered digging with his dog and a pickax in someone's grove, but he appealed the ruling, and the sentence was chopped to a month. The judge stipulated that though the sentence would be changed, the crime would still be recognized as a violation of the penal code. He recognized that throughout Vaucluse truffles had become a product of a farmer's labor, time, and effort. In a later ruling the same year, the court in Loudun, in the Vienne department, empathized with the truffle farmers battling against " 'armed and feared' marauders" who ravaged the roots of truffle oaks that had been nurtured for many years.

⚬

Meanwhile, in Paris, at a remove from the rural thievery, wealthy diners came to expect restaurants to serve truffles as they served olives. A meal without them was regarded as foul. In the southwestern corner of the country, in Périgueux and Périgord, food manufacturers rose along the Isle River to meet the demand. They bottled them, tinned them, added them to jellies, and mixed them into pâtés of partridge, hare, and foie gras. In 1885, France consumed one thousand tons of its supply, and the companies exported tens of thousands of kilos to England, Germany, and Belgium. Truffle farmers could not produce enough to satisfy their brokers. Twenty thousand kilos' worth had to be imported, predominantly from Italy, to feed the manic obsession.

By 1895, Talon's method of cultivation had spread throughout southern France. In what became known as the golden age of truffle production, the country produced roughly fifteen hundred tons of the black fungus each year.

And then the truffles began to disappear. The world wars had a major impact, because properties were destroyed and many farmers left their land, perishing in wars or later joining the movement to live in cities. The groves fell into disorder, and without the generations-honed skills and constant upkeep of the land, the practice of truffle cultivation was almost lost.

But in the 1970s, a group of French scientists began using some of what Talon had learned to reintroduce the practice by inoculating saplings with truffle spores and distributing them through France's national agricultural laboratory, INRA. Every scientist and farmer longed for a return to the golden age, but it was a guessing game, and reliable commercial cultivation still remained a mystery. Despite a more technologically advanced method, the annual French harvest hovered only around thirty tons, and occasionally fell far lower. The scientists believed a combination of poor orchard management, competing fungal organisms, rising temperatures, and reduced summer rainfall accounted for low yields, but no one seemed certain. The people who thrived tended to approach their land with the same intensity and care as Talon, but scarcity made them even more desperate to protect their secrets.

I drove over the hills from the town of Carpentras, where Rousseau canned his truffles, through a rocky gorge—where some sections narrowed for the passage of only one vehicle—and down hills of evergreen into a vast valley. I passed collections of vineyards and farms, and finally drove up a hill into Saint-Saturnin-les-Apt, the pastel-and-shutters village that had become synonymous with Talon's legacy. The community had placed a stone statue of Talon in the center of the village, to commemorate their native son's connection to the craft of truffle cultivation. He knelt on one leg, a large brownish truffle in his left hand and a satchel slung over his shoulder. His beret and mustachioed face were bent toward the earth, as if in prayer. The town overlooked a flatter section of the rolling Luberon valley, where truffle orchards and vineyards stretched among beige villas with French tile, toward a hill sloping out of the flats. The light of the sun glinted, barely, through a tapestry of dark, low-lying clouds.

When the statue was first installed in the 1980s, the sculpture artist had placed a black volcanic rock, in the shape of a truffle, in Talon's outstretched hand. A month later, the fake truffle vanished. Someone stole it.

Two old local historians I met with in town didn't know much more about Talon than I did. Most of the original documents about his life had not survived. They handed me a slim historical journal they assured me contained all that was known about Talon. The section about him was just fourteen pages long, including charts, a bibliography, and a genealogy of the Talon family.

Truffle farms still flourished in the area; one of the historians had a plot. When I asked how many truffles he was able to harvest, he declined to answer. Chuckling, he asked whether I was an FBI agent interested in tax investigations. A long, hot summer, with only light rainfall, had driven down production and driven up prices at market; average winter truffles were going for as much as €700 a kilo.

As the earliest generation did, the farmers in the area still feared thieves. The historians mentioned one notorious thief in Saint-Saturnin-les-Apt who had been caught and allegedly beaten so brutally that he was hospitalized for months. Some farmers appointed special guards to patrol their groves.

Realizing that Talon was a mysterious figure even to the experts, I asked if they knew where exactly in the area I could find his land. I thought walking the hallowed soil might provide me with a glimmer of the past.

Apparently, the little hamlet of Croagnes was still there. The men told me to follow the signs to it a few kilometers outside Saint-Saturnin-les-Apt. Some of his descendants, they said, might even live there. "It's such a mysterious thing, how it grows," one of them said. "It does make people have fantasies."

The hamlet of Croagnes was not more than several stone buildings at a bend in a country road. There were no cafés or businesses of any kind, and no one busied themselves outside their homes. I drove onto the gravel, past a few dwellings, and made a turn. Up ahead, a Frenchman smoking a hand-rolled cigarette pushed a wheelbarrow near what looked to be a one-man construction project. The quiet hillside that stood below us was planted with oaks by the man who invented truffle farming, but when I asked the man about Talon, he looked at me with complete bewilderment. He remarked that there was an American nearby, then led me toward his door.

The American turned out to be a middle-aged Englishman, visiting from his home in Texas to tend to his sick mother.

After I asked him where I might find Talon's property, he pointed at a stately château down the road and added that Talon had constructed it himself. He'd call someone over there and see if they knew anything, but he was uncertain about whether anyone over there spoke English. In the meantime, I told him that I wanted to see where Talon had been buried. He told me there was a cemetery at the bottom of the hill. "He's probably there," the Brit said in a hurry, before heading back inside his mother's home.

I got back into the car and turned down the narrow track. Halfway down the slope, I stopped. At the other end of a large dirt expanse, I saw the faintest sign of headstones. Trudging through the soil, I realized that the graves were actually agricultural nets, protecting dozens of truffle oak seedlings. The land Talon had used to develop the earliest method for growing truffles was being used, more than two hundred years later, for the very same purpose.

A little bit farther down the road, I spotted the entrance to a small, ornate cemetery, surrounded by marble walls and a vineyard.

Among chirping birds and dead flowers, I scanned the graves. The distinct sound of clothes flapping in the wind slid down the hill. The only sign of modernity was the rattling of a tractor in the distance. It wasn't long before I found a "Talon" on a large beige stone with a star. But it was the burial site of the Famille of Louis Paul Talon, and Joseph wasn't there.

I returned to the car and drove back up the hill, to the estate. A strong wind rustled the leaves of the tall trees that lined the driveway.

Without warning, two dogs appeared. The darker of the two barked ferociously, but as he came closer, I noticed he was limping. My heart thumped as I bent down and held out my open palm. I felt a rush of relief as they both calmly lay down in the dirt just off the driveway.

A lanky man, with a reddish complexion and short-cropped hair, appeared as suddenly as the dogs and wheeled toward me. He didn't seem perturbed by my presence, but spoke very little English. When I asked where Talon lived, he pointed back down the driveway at an old stone building with a wooden door. It looked like an excellent place for storing grain but unlike a home.

We walked over to his front garden, where a statue of Saint Antoine—the patron saint of truffles—stood, a truffle-hunting sow at his feet. I realized with some wonderment that I was in the right place. He lit a cigarette and took a deep pull.

"And here," he said, "this house is built with the *argent* of the *truffe*."

"The money of the truffle?"

"The money of the *truffe*."

When he couldn't find the word he was looking for, he snapped his fingers repeatedly.

He walked me over to a low wall at the property's edge, which overlooked the hill and the saplings I had seen in the dirt below.

"All there, there's no wine," he said, gesturing into the distance. "And there are *chênes, chênes, des chênes, des chênes, des chênes, des chênes, des chênes*." Oaks.

He rustled closer to the wall. Another gust blew through the trees. He explained that he had determined that his green oaks were better at producing truffles than the whites—something the Count of Gasparin had noted as well. That was what he had recently planted in the field.

But, unlike Talon, he suggested he'd be lucky if even twenty out of a hundred green oaks produced truffles.

"The *truffe* is *mystère*. I don't know the *mystère*."

The wind blew fiercely again.

"You're not related to him?" I asked.

"No, no."

"Are they still living in the area, the descendants?"

He had an uncertain look on his face. "I don't know. I think no."

I thanked him, waved good-bye, and walked back down the dirt driveway.

＊

I rang the doorbell of the house connected to what was supposedly Talon's stone home. An old woman answered but did not speak any English. She didn't seem to know anything about Joseph Talon but knew that her house had been built in 1789, a few years before Talon was born. Confused, she led me back to the British Texan's door. I was now officially going in circles.

The Brit and I walked back toward my car, parked near the driveway of the château. Even though the man living inside the château had pointed, with seeming certainty, at the stone structure we were now standing in front of, the Brit seemed convinced that sometime in the nineteenth century Talon had built or invested in the lanky man's house. The château, I had corroborated, was built with truffle money, but just whose truffle money was it?

The Brit ventured that Talon had helped build the château and many of the other buildings in the hamlet, which, by now, I had thoroughly traversed. Perhaps he lived in one for a time and built another after his truffle business took off.

And then, as we stood between what were both allegedly Talon properties, things grew stranger than I'd expected.

Talon or someone else in the family, according to hamlet folklore, had supposedly put all of the truffle cash into physical gold. There were rumors in the hamlet, the Brit said, that at some point the treasure had been buried somewhere near Talon's property. A lot of it was hearsay, he said, but he supposed that was why the man in the château hadn't been forthcoming about Talon's role in building his property. Perhaps the truffle farmer was searching for Talon's fortune and was fending off someone who he speculated was an interested party.

Because I knew the Talon story, the whole thing didn't seem that implausible. I later found mention of Joseph's son, Hilarion Talon, buried within an old manuscript from 1875. After his father's death in 1873, he expanded his father's wealth. He bought up parcels of rotting vines in the valley plains and planted even more truffle trees. His father's methods were so effective that he regularly brought fifteen to twenty kilos to the Apt market each week. It seemed he realized the threat of publicizing his fortune, because the historical record doesn't reveal what he did with it. Among jealous marauders, he might have realized that he needed to hide his fortune and techniques better than his father concealed his acorns.

I began to realize that Joseph Talon's legacy was not just his discovery but also the speed with which he lost his grip on the industry's first trade secret, even after an immediate, cunning effort to conceal it. His failure to thwart his spy and, later, to claim proper credit for his methodology may have inspired paranoia in his son and in generations of truffle farmers who followed. The truffle and the techniques used to will it into existence became objects increasingly worthy of protection, anxiety, and misdirection. Sharing knowledge would likely have made the orchardists' lives easier, but each seemed to think he possessed the shrewdness required to solve the mystery of commercial cultivation himself.

As yields continued to dwindle over the latter half of the twentieth century and demand for the ingredient continued to rise, the allure of untangling the enigma became an entrancing fantasy, propelling the same flickers of grandeur and terror that accompany the end of good dreams. Just as the achievement seemed within grasp, a farmer had to remind himself that his labor, time, thoughtful adjustments—quirks of irrigation, pruning, and tree spacing—and even his legacy were subject to erasure. The prospect of success—or, more likely, the illusion of it—bred conspiratorial thinking.

# CHAPTER FOUR

# A Scientific Mystery

TALON HAD PROVEN THAT THE TRUFFLE WAS NOT SIMPLY A SPONTANE-
ous wart of the earth. His method—and its somewhat successful
replication throughout France—confirmed that a truffle could not
exist in absence of a tree. But the farmers and scientists who followed him had other mysteries to solve: the mechanics of what was
actually happening beneath the ground, and how to manage the
trees in a way that would lead to commercial harvests. It became
clear, however, that such a task would be impossible without first
understanding how the truffles matured naturally in the wild.

Jim Trappe, referred to by some as the grandfather of truffle
science, was born in 1931. In photographs, he looks a bit like Santa
Claus—a full white beard on a roundish face, a pair of wide spec-
tacles magnifying gentle eyes, a bald head—but his age hasn't de-
pleted his intellectual vigor. In fact, he remains livelier and more
articulate than most early-career scientists I've spoken to. The force

of his wry humor reveals itself almost immediately. I reached him on the phone at home, not far from his old laboratory at Oregon State University, and asked him to start from the beginning. "You mean like when God created heaven and earth and so forth?" he asked.

We didn't start quite that far back. But in the 1950s, in a University of Washington classroom, listening to Professor Daniel Stuntz wax poetic about the forest floor and its dizzying array of pathogens, Trappe knew fungal science would be his calling. It was Stuntz's brilliance, his elegant way of unspooling a complicated concept, that drew Trappe in. But it was also Stuntz's unconventional character: He was calm, generous, and unpretentious, unlike so many other members of the tenured academic elite in that era. His white hair, thick-lens glasses, perpetually donned lab coat, and extravagant taste for fine dining, expensive bottles of wine, and classical music helped cement him among students as something of a legend: He was the professor every student dreamed of. Trappe yearned to learn from this man, to join his ranks, to live in his small academic fiefdom of fungi.

After graduating, Trappe settled on pursuing a Ph.D. in mycology, or fungal science, under Stuntz, focusing on mycorrhizae, the types of fungi that form in symbiosis with the roots of trees or other plants. By no error, his choice would allow him to spend time collecting data in the forest, a place he first fell in love with on family trips as a child to the wilds of Idaho and later, in college, as a trail hand for the U.S. Forest Service in a remote part of the Chelan National Forest.

Not long after he began the Ph.D. program, he ventured out into one of the university's research forests to excavate some Douglas fir roots. Once he started extracting them, though, he came across strange-looking fungus bodies that he didn't recognize. When he brought them back to the laboratory, Stuntz explained that what he had discovered was some kind of truffle. "There is not much known about this particular group," Stuntz said, "but Alexander Smith at the University of Michigan is working on them, so take some notes on them, we'll dry them, and send them to Dr. Smith." Trappe prepared the package, sent it, and waited for a response. A week or so after mailing the specimens, Trappe received a reply from the professor in Michigan. "This is a wonderful find. It's the first report of this species from Washington State," Smith wrote. "Get more."

And so Trappe went back out to the woods and searched, shipping new pieces of truffle halfway across the country to Smith. Letters flowed. "This is a new species. Get more," the professor wrote. The excitement of new discoveries, of uncharted territory, drove Trappe to focus his fungal expertise on truffles. "Not a heck of a lot was known about native North American truffles," Trappe said, the melody of his voice revealing richness of use, of someone who has given a thousand lectures, who knows just where to pause, which words to elongate, and which tones to hit for dramatic or explanatory effect. "So I said, 'Well, that looks like a place that could use my interest.' And so it was."

Stuntz taught Trappe how to search the literature, which, back then, meant combing manually through print journals at the university library. When the rain and cold swept over Seattle in the winter, Trappe retreated there to gather all that was scientifically known about truffles. There wasn't very much.

———

There are hundreds of truffle species, but only a handful of them generate any kind of culinary fervor. White truffles (*Tuber magnatum pico*)—the rarest, palest, and smoothest fungal mounds—and black winter truffles (*Tuber melanosporum*) are the crown jewels, of course, followed—at a long distance and price differential—by the summer truffle (*Tuber aestivum*); its fall equivalent, the hooked truffle (*Tuber uncinatum*); the small white, or *bianchetto* (*Tuber borchii*); and *Tuber oregonense*, which blooms in Oregon. The rest—*Tuber brumale*; *Tuber mesentericum*; several truffles from the large genus of *Terfeẓia*, known as desert truffles; and *Tuber indicum* and *Tuber himalayensis*, which grow in China—are essentially regarded as third tier: edible but not worth much—or sometimes anything—on the market . . . unless passed off as their more precious relatives. The ones Trappe was initially identifying belonged to a group below even this, a group that was valuable to the forest and to the soil but not necessarily to culture. However, studying North American truffles would help Trappe quickly make his mark as one of the world's preeminent experts, and soon he found himself yearning to explore the more valuable realm of the black winter truffle and the great mystery of cultivating it.

In 1967, Trappe took a year of sabbatical from the U.S. Forest Service's Pacific Northwest Research Station—where he'd found work as a researcher after finishing his Ph.D. coursework—to study Italy's growing conditions. One of his many stops on a journey through truffle country was near the village of Scheggino in the region of Umbria, at the world's leading exporter of truffles, Urbani Tartufi. The company did not yet have much business in the United States. Trappe was its first American guest.

Carlo Urbani, then the leader of the company and Trappe's primary guide, did not speak any English. Trappe could only manage basic Italian. For two or three days, they communicated through a younger man who translated fluently. Carlo showed Trappe around the warehouse, took him out into the forests, and treated him to "the best truffle dinner I've ever eaten."

Urbani had bushy eyebrows and a short, stocky build. "The old Carlo, he dressed like a peasant," Trappe said. "He had worn black pants and a tattered black sport coat with a gray shirt buttoned up to the neck—no tie. He looked like a real Italian country boy. A farmer type. Son of the soil."

Notwithstanding his countrified manner, he was paid the deference of a nobleman. And not unlike royalty, he employed the services of sentries. At the edge of the wild oak forests the company tended to for black truffle production, guards—donning formal uniforms and badges—stood watch with large guns at their hips. They were stationed there to prevent poachers from trespassing.

"Well, how many times have they shot people for trespassing?" Trappe asked.

"Oh, I issue only guns, not bullets," Carlo said.

Carlo had an answer for all of Trappe's many questions, even the proprietary ones. Even in those early days, company employees were maintaining detailed records about production on hundreds of acres of forest, learning the tendencies and tells of a productive patch. They soon learned that the soil responded the best to trees hosting roughly 40 percent of their full canopies, leaving enough space in the leaves for the sun to filter through and down to the ground. They began pruning the rest of the trees in the forest to match that optimal spatial proportion.

Over years of observation, the company's forest managers also noted that new trees began hosting the first decent truffle growth after about four or five years, and then levels of production declined precipitously after the tree turned thirty. At that juncture, mushrooms and other fungi began appearing at a much higher rate at the base of the trunk, outcompeting the truffles buried below. As a productive tree neared the turning point, officials—taking a page from Talon's notebook—dug holes and planted new seedlings in a circle in its shadow. They allowed five years to pass and then felled the older and diminishingly productive tree in the center. The fungi underneath the younger trees, meanwhile, began producing their biggest, most consistent fruit. Leaves were pruned to optimal levels, and a new cycle began. Trappe took notes.

Two decades later, Trappe mentored a smart young graduate student named Tom Michaels who had settled on focusing his thesis on growing *Tuber melanosporum* mycelium, the filaments that eventually germinate into the fungus that produces the truffle, in pure culture. He needed some raw product from which he could gather spores, and no one else in American academia was yet working on the species. So Trappe called Urbani Tartufi's U.S. office in New Jersey, which was then run by Carlo's nephew Paul Urbani, to see whether the company could help.

Over the phone, Trappe explained the situation: He was strapped for funding and needed several samples of the very expensive product for his driven graduate student.

"How many do you need?" Urbani asked.

"Maybe half a dozen good-sized ones," Trappe said.

Urbani liked the idea that the truffle was getting attention from American scientists and agreed to ship them, free of charge, to Oregon.

Trappe was enthused but also surprised at how little convincing Urbani needed. "Are you not worried about the potential of truffle industry starting here and competing with your import company?"

"No," Urbani said. "Look, we can only supply about a fourth of the demand that we have from importing European truffles. The more people that are producing truffles, the better the market is going to become, because you need that for people to learn about truffles and try them."

Urbani explained that if the Americans were ever to pose a competitive challenge, the Europeans would be forced to develop a coherent marketing strategy, which, at the time, was modest at best.

As a scientist, Trappe agreed with Paul's open-source philosophy: The more people sharing knowledge and resources, the better the chances were that truffle cultivation and the truffle industry at large would thrive.

But not long after his pleasant exchange with Urbani, Trappe heard about the experience of an Oregon entrepreneur who had less friendly dealings with the company that had treated him and his student well.

The man sought out the services of an amateur mycologist who could use spores to inoculate tree seedlings that would be planted on a large property in Texas. They'd selected the location carefully: ideal limestone soil, good growing climate. They invested in the construction of greenhouses and labs and were hopeful about making a profit. The mycologist called Urbani and told the company that he needed a huge supply of black truffles for the inoculation of the seedlings. He was interested in minimizing cost and decided that he didn't need the biggest or most beautifully shaped specimens: He said he'd take the rejects for a fourth of the cost. "You know, the penny-wise, pound-foolish approach," Trappe said.

A few years later, when the orchard began to fruit, the only kind of truffle that was growing underneath the soil was *Tuber brumale,* an inferior and hypercompetitive form of fungi with little market value. "In fact, at that time, it wasn't even being sold," Trappe said. "They were just rejected.

"Urbani must have known that they wanted these truffles for inoculum, and they didn't object to them buying the rejects," Trappe said. "So that was a little bit of a different attitude than Paul Urbani who gave us the Périgords a few years before." After the initial disaster, the company went out of business, the trees were ripped from the ground, and the land was sold.

Trappe continued to study truffles at the U.S. Forest Service for thirty years, until he retired from the agency in 1986. He then received an appointment as a research professor at Oregon State University, where he led experiments and mentored graduate students for another ten years, until 1996. Despite a lifelong study of the fungus, he still can't say he has a complete understanding of the specific mechanics behind the truffle's growth.

But now, after a long career, he does understand just how preposterously complicated a journey a fungal spore must take before it is transformed into the edible and redolent thing harvested by hunters. The truffle's existence and scarcity depend on a long and circuitous collision of natural events that the spore and later fungus must encounter before it even has the chance to fruit. Against chance, many hundreds of conditions and variables must align. And even when they do, the truffle presents only a narrow window of opportunity for foragers to harvest, before it rots in the ground.

Truffles' spores, which act as a sort of seed for the fungus, cannot be dispersed by wind, which is the customary method of distribution for most other forms of forest fungi. Fittingly, then, the story of a wild truffle's development begins in darkness, a blackness that is abruptly disrupted by an animal's search for a meal. But for all the challenge in finding them, the truffle wants to be eaten. The strength of its musk increases as its spore count rises, and the aroma attracts squirrels, chipmunks, shrews, rabbits, wild boar, and other digging forest animals, which then gnaw at its tough, pebbled skin, ingesting the spores buried beneath the surface of the fruiting body.

Once the truffle has been consumed, the animal carries the spores away, and the spores move through the digestive tract, waiting for their release back into the outside world in the form of defecation, hopefully on the forest floor. The package of spores in the fecal pellet must then find its way back beneath ground. Usually, a heavy rainfall or an industrious dung beetle or worm can push the spores back down into the root zone underground, where they need to be positioned to have any chance at growing into fungus.

If the spores manage to get down to the necessary depth, then the real probability game begins. The spore cluster can only germinate when it has found tree roots that have not already been targeted by the many other fungi already living in that same layer of soil. This is usually not a casual kind of search. "The spores can reside in the soil—we have some evidence up to maybe thirty or forty years, just waiting," Trappe said.

Part of the problem is location; the spore cluster must, by chance, end up relatively close to an available root for the germination process to begin, or possibly stay in place long enough for a root to grow into its vicinity. "The root is probably sending out some chemical signal," Trappe said. "It can either be a gas or an enzyme or maybe a hormone—nobody knows for sure—that stimulates spores to germinate." Once the spores receive that signal, they bubble into filaments, long strands of fungal matter that snake through the soil in order to attach to the rootlet. That's what we think, anyway. "Since the damn things insist on being below-ground, they are a little bit hard to observe in nature without disrupting the whole system," Trappe said.

The fungal filament eventually burrows into the space between cells on the outer surface of the root and begins receiving transfers of sugar—and therefore energy—from the tree. This energy allows the fungus to grow, gradually forming "a mantle" around the entire circumference of the root. Once this process has finished, the formal symbiosis has begun: As the root's energy powers the extension of the fungal filament into the soil, the fungus, in turn, returns critical soil nutrients and water back to the root. The root system has root hairs and rootlets for collection of nutrients, but fungal systems—of which the truffle is one of many—can increase those root systems' surface area by up to two thousand times. "It's sort of a difference between a fishhook and a fishnet," Trappe said. Without the different fungal systems, the roots alone would not be able to soak up enough water and soil nutrients to keep the tree functioning. And without the roots, the fungus would have no efficient process for transforming water and nutrients into sugars for further growth. It would be like a person with hands and a mouth but no stomach. Without these symbiotic relationships, the world might not have had forests—or the life supported by them, for that matter. Without truffles and other fungi, the earth might have instead stagnated with blooms of algae and lichen and the more simple organisms that could subsist off such a desolate environment.

As the fungal structure grows, it expands even farther out into the soil, with even more filaments. On this journey, the structure must make contact with another fungal colony of the same species but of compatible mating type. If this happens, and the colonies fuse together and exchange genetic material, they will be one step closer to forming a truffle.

Sometime in the spring, a tiny knot of fungus emerges from the crossing of those colonies. Over a couple of weeks or a month, the cells grow and organize into a baby truffle without spores—that is, immature, incapable of reproduction, and therefore nonaromatic. Then, as summer arrives, the warmth puts the cells to rest, and they await the next signal.

In early autumn, rain from thunderstorms makes its way down into the root zone. The cells of the fungus come back alive, growing again through the season. As the season changes again, the truffle receives another signal; it's unknown whether it's temperature, moisture, or an undiscovered microbial reaction. As a result, the truffle produces spores, and the knob bulks to maturity. This is the fruiting body that we eat, steal, and hunt for at nearly any cost.

But how or what finally edges the process to completion, what pushes the larger fungal system to form the mature truffle that we eat, remains an utter mystery. And at any step along the way, something can—or will likely—derail the entire process. The theories as to why it works never tend to pan out. "Nobody knows," Trappe said. "However, for the fifty or sixty years I have been working with truffles, half a dozen times at least, I think I got it figured out. Okay, you need this kind of weather pattern and so forth. And then there comes along a year that totally destroys what I have thought I had understood the process to be." He laughed.

"So that makes it kind of interesting," he said, still giggling. "This year, for example, it was a very poor crop of native truffles in western Oregon, hardly any were found by anyone until almost

January, and yet it was wet. We had no idea why they did not start. I don't know if anybody can figure it out."

⁓

Even in the modern age, because these many variables and elements of the growth process still defy our understanding, reliable, commercial cultivation remains not much more than the hope of foolhardy obsessives. The ones who believe they've somehow cracked the code are a strange mixture of technical experts and alchemists. "The process is so much more complicated than we are even close to understanding," Trappe said. "I talk about the signals, you know, the truffle 'gets the signals,' but we have no idea what that signal is and how it is transmitted to the fungus from the tree."

Since leaving his position at Oregon State, Trappe hasn't really stopped trying to improve his understanding of the truffle mystery. As a scientist emeritus at the Pacific Northwest Research Station in Corvallis, he's continued to produce academic papers at a prolific rate—the total number now sits at 488, with 7 in press, 12 in stages of preparation when we spoke—coauthored two reference books, and travels the world in search of new truffle and trufflelike species, even though he's already discovered 184, with 15 more in preparation. ("The world is full of yet undiscovered new truffle species," he said.) "Could do more but not enough time in the day," he wrote to me. "I'm old and wise enough, however, to not obsess on numbers. I'm doing it because I love doing it."

He's now been truffle hunting on all but two continents, Antarctica and Africa. Most recently, though, he's developed an obsession with the wealth of truffle diversity and the promise of cultivation in Australia. "I was in truffle heaven," Trappe said, remembering some government fieldwork he'd done with an Australian colleague who first contacted him as a graduate student and asked him to serve as an adviser, even though he was more than seven thousand miles away. "We estimated two thousand or more species of truffles in Australia, of which maybe three hundred had been collected and described, so that leaves only seventeen hundred for me to work on there," he added, laughing. In a few months, Trappe would leave Oregon for another excursion in the eucalyptus forests there. "And we are still finding a lot of new stuff in North America as well," he said. "It has been great fun, I tell you, Ryan. I could not have asked for a more satisfying and pleasurable career."

Bruce Hatch and Billy Griner had an acorn problem. The bachelors lived at a beautiful little bend in the redwood forest about twenty miles north of the nearest town, at 9000 Spyrock Road in the northern section of fog-drenched Mendocino County, in California. And they were "eyeball deep" in acorns. They fell from tan oaks and valley oaks, which rose gangly and wild like weeds across the property.

It was 1982. Hatch and Griner had met in San Francisco the decade before and decided to decamp north. Hatch bought a forty-acre property in the middle of nowhere, to live off the land and invited his friend Griner to live with him. Hatch was burned out, having spent years building out recording studios and film postproduction facilities in the city. Griner, a laconic guy who loved rocks and had dirt in his bones, was eager to return to the country, to reconnect with his childhood memories of working the land on his father's New England farm, where he wasn't permitted to return home until the tractor ran out of gas.

As soon as they arrived, Griner, who wore his long blond hair in a ponytail, rooted around the property, disappearing into the forest to prospect the creek and ravines for gold. He liked to fashion jewelry, and when he wasn't in the forest, he spent time working on his pieces. Hatch, an uncomplicated man of simple pleasures, soon settled into living cheaply and watching his friend bask in the isolation and calm of their backwoods estate. Together, they passed the time flirting with local women, sitting around and drinking beer, exploring the lush landscape, and slipping on acorns.

One day, one or the other picked up a regional newspaper, the Santa Rosa *Press Democrat*, and, thumbing through the classifieds, noticed an advertisement. A Frenchman named François Picart who ran a tree nursery in Santa Rosa, in Sonoma County to the south, wanted to buy acorns, especially those falling from oaks. The men looked out to their acorn mounds with new purpose.

They stuffed as many bags as they could with their bounty. They threw them in the back of the car, and Griner drove out to the highway for the two-and-a-half-hour trip south to meet Picart for the sale.

In the years before Griner visited him, François Picart had attempted to corner the California market for escargot. By the time Griner arrived, Picart, a fast-talking huckster with curly hair, a dark goatee, and a long face, was tending to several hundred thousand writhing snails. He shipped frozen ones to restaurants and specialty food stores and live ones to aspiring snail farmers. In 1978, he wrote a seventy-four-page illustrated guidebook about how to raise them in a garden. Some of his snails were escaping, and locals were finding them in curious places across their properties in Santa Rosa. But lately, Picart had realized that there was no way he could outcompete the Taiwanese, who had recently started sending cheap Chinese snails to California by the boatload, and so he decided to pivot to an even more improbable enterprise.

In 1980, Picart—who grew up watching pigs devour wild truffles in Périgord, France—had licensed a black truffle inoculation technology that scientists at the French enterprise Agri-Truffe had developed several years before. Saplings inoculated with the method produced their first successful harvest in France in 1978. Picart creatively called his American spin-off Agri-Truffle. He was selling truffle-inoculated saplings to anyone he could interest in his effort. He was experimenting with different kinds of host trees, both indigenous and not. He hoped sapling sales and, more urgently, starting his own commercial truffle farm could save him from the terrors of the snail business. "I'm snailed out," he told a reporter from the *Detroit Free Press*.

After some investigation, he had already settled on planting his own trees in the limestone-rich soils of Dripping Springs, Texas. He was plotting to turn Texas hill country into the truffle capital of the world. He believed he could make every acre produce $65,000 worth of truffles annually and was actively scouting for investors and parcels.

When Griner sold Picart his acorns, something about Picart's quixotic vision—his bombastic sense that he could make black winter truffles not only grow for the first time outside their natural European habitat but also do so at commercial scale—must have delighted him.

When Griner arrived home, he seemed to have fallen under Picart's spell. Though no one had yet successfully harvested truffles in America, he told Hatch of his plans to retire on the money they'd make by planting Picart's saplings on land most famous for its illegal pot-growing operations.

"Why not?" Hatch said, considering their other options. At least his new agribusiness would be legal.

The men put in an order for a hundred of Picart's inoculated hazelnut trees, priced at roughly $12 each. Soon afterward, they planted. Griner tended to them like children.

—

About four years later, in 1987, Griner was out in the grove when he stumbled on a fissure in the soil. He didn't have a truffle dog, so he crouched down and put his fingers in the crack. When he felt the truffle's embrace, he shrieked. Startled, the neighbors—who lived about a hundred yards from the plot—came over to ensure he hadn't suffered a bear mauling or cardiac arrest. He stood there, wide-eyed. After removing some worms from the truffle's interior, he took a bite, as if it were an apple.

In the subsequent weeks, the men began noticing that more cracks—two to three inches long—were popping up in the soil. They resembled mole runs, and they took to sticking Popsicle sticks in the craters and periodically checking them. Most of them produced truffles "about the size of a woman's fist," Hatch explained.

Possibly for the first time, black truffles had been harvested outside their European habitat, and for a while the men who achieved the feat kept them for personal consumption. They placed their truffles in jars with eggs, the aroma carrying through the shells and infusing the eggs with flavor. They also made truffle butter this way. Steaks, pasta, omelets, fudge—everything became a vehicle for their new pungent treasure.

Griner began to experiment with cloning the productive trees, adding the cuttings to pots of sterile soil mixed with slices of the truffles they were harvesting. The process wasn't exactly scientific, but however amateur it appeared, the method worked. Griner also began trafficking in pseudoscience and superstition. During one season, he applied rabbit manure to the soil. During another, he dropped New Age crystals in different places throughout the grove. In the early years, with relatively little work, the men made about $12,000, or close to $25,000 in today's dollars, on a hundred or so trees.

Picart, meanwhile, fell off the truffle map: After a fateful and useless planting of more than three thousand truffle saplings in Texas, he dissolved his company and went on to expand his brother's French-based, American-style steakhouse chain, Buffalo Grill, into Florida.

<hr>

Word of the truffle's success in nonnative soil reached both France and New Zealand, where researchers were intensely interested in helping invert global truffle deficits. Small groups of mycologists from both countries flew out to examine Hatch and Griner's grove, hoping to glean insight into how the Americans had managed to do it. The men led them on tours through the grove, and if harvests allowed, they fed their guests with the spoils.

But having tasted success, Griner soon began to suffer from debilitating paranoia. He became convinced that the motivations of the visiting scientists were not purely based on research. He thought that at least some of them were spies, bent on stealing the secrets he had used to achieve production for their own self-enrichment. He came to suspect the New Zealanders were conspiring to poison the grove's production by clandestinely introducing an invasive fungal species that would outcompete his precious *Tuber melanosporum*. The already private Griner became even more withdrawn than usual.

When Hatch tried to talk some sense into his friend, to make him realize how far-fetched his theories were, he wouldn't listen. "He was his own worst enemy as far as propagating things," Hatch recalled. Even in a forest thousands of miles away from where Talon had first birthed cultivators' anxieties, the truffles, it seemed, had worked their dark magic.

In 1989, Hatch had a bad bout of diverticulitis, and his doctor recommended that he move somewhere closer to a hospital. He sold the property to Griner and moved south. He bought a vineyard and got married, leaving his truffle life mostly behind. But he kept in touch about Griner's progress and occasionally drove back out to the mountain to check in.

The grove was flourishing. The harvests grew each year. Eventually, Griner and a new tenant, Don Reading, were harvesting enough truffles to attract the interest of a local caviar distributor, which sold them to Jeremiah Tower's Stars restaurant in San Francisco and the Four Seasons in New York.

By 1994, Griner had grown so many truffles that *The Wall Street Journal* dispatched a reporter to the scene. Griner was netting higher yields than the French: twelve pounds with thirty-nine trees. "Across the Atlantic, truffle farmers swear it takes about 400 trees to produce that much," the reporter, Joan Rigdon, wrote. A French chef in San Francisco conducted a blind taste test with Griner's truffles and French truffles, and customers judged them equally delicious. Neither Griner nor Reading would tell Rigdon the secret behind their success.

All of the developments—the high yields and quality, the *Wall Street Journal* write-up, the secretive methods—could easily be turned into a sales pitch for an attractive private investment opportunity. Hatch thought more money would help his friend expand: more land, more trees, tractors to plow the space between the rows. He thought he had found a few financiers who might be willing to write checks, but Griner wouldn't even entertain the prospect of a meeting. "He was worried that they were going to take everything from him," Hatch told me. "He was really paranoid about that. . . . I've always found that it's better to get along with people and let things take care of themselves [than] always looking for the bogeyman."

Griner planted the property with hundreds more clones of the original productive trees and continued harvesting. But he became increasingly reclusive.

In 2008, Griner died alone on the property, at the age of fifty-eight, from a combination of pneumonia and sepsis. No one knew he had perished until a neighbor discovered him almost two weeks later. One of his six truffle dogs, Ace, stood over his corpse. Three pounds of truffles sat in his refrigerator.

The property gradually became overgrown, and the region's pot growers moved in.

Hatch is an earnest man not prone to excitability or grandiose pronouncements. He insisted on taking my call, even though he was driving—somewhere near his current home in Granbury, Texas—and then proceeded to navigate a flooded bridge as we spoke. He had a slow, mater-of-fact drawl, and his enunciation was garbled in a way that made him sound as if he had just finished putting a handful of large pebbles into his mouth. When I talked with him, it was clear that he was the kind of man that goes with the flow; nothing seemed to disturb him. If an asteroid were predicted to destroy the earth at midnight, he might brush his teeth at nine o'clock and then settle into a comfortable slumber. So when he went out of his way to call his old friend paranoid, you might take it to mean extremely, passionately, disastrously paranoid. When he says there's "an air of secrecy about all the people who grow truffles," you believe him. And when he complains about the quality of the truffles he's eaten recently, you listen intently, because eating truffles is about the only thing that precipitates a quickening of his speech.

"I bought some from Urbani just to see what was going on. Wasn't impressed with what they were selling compared to what we had. What we were using was like concentrated action compared to what these guys are selling.

"I know what the real stuff tastes like. Once somebody knows what the real truffle is, it's hard to pull wool over their eyes.

"If by any chance you come across some good truffle," he said, before getting off the phone, "let me know, because I'd love to buy some."

⚬

Truffle paranoia seems to pull growers and inoculators into its grasp, wherever and whoever they are. Even on the more professionalized end of the spectrum, truffle consultants and sapling suppliers guard against what they see as fishing expeditions for their data and proprietary methodologies.

Samantha Ellis, who leads business development for Mycorrhizal Systems Ltd., a worldwide truffle sapling distributor and consulting company led by the British scientist Paul Thomas, sorts through most of the company's client inquiries. In their business, they sell inoculated saplings and consulting services for would-be truffle growers. But Ellis regularly finds herself dealing with people she suspects to be data poachers. The email exchanges tend to begin innocently enough, with seemingly genuine interest in learning what the company can offer. And then the questions begin to get increasingly detailed. One Bulgarian company, "looking to create a serious investment in a truffle farm," requested the company's "valuable and professional opinion and co-operation." It listed eight questions about land selection, soil, types of seedlings, orchard management, and dogs but later expressed no interest in buying trees. "We've had people be 'in discussion' with us for years, and as soon as you mention any sort of payment—even something nominal such as £100 towards tests that can be refunded against a sale or a small deposit on the trees they are supposedly intending to order—then we get a huge reaction and a refusal to pay," Ellis said in an email.

Ellis has replied to seemingly serious questions about the suitability of the growers' land for truffle production, even going as far as preparing initial climate reports, only to have the conversations abruptly end after sending out answers. "I assume that a lot of these are data gathering as they are absolutely lovely in their emails and as soon as I confirm that yes, they do have suitable land, then we never hear from them. We apply no sales pressure whatsoever, so I don't believe this is a factor," Ellis said.

Other times, the interested parties don't want to be identified through email, so they leave voice mails and wait for return calls. When Ellis recently returned one of these calls, the person asked several rapid-fire questions about where the company sourced its truffles from, how the company prepared its seedlings, how to grow the trees, and what the ideal conditions for truffle orchards were. He then added that he didn't have any interest in purchasing inoculated seedlings from the company and hung up.

At times, it's difficult to tell whether growers are actually growers, perhaps trying to glean a little free information, or competitors conducting espionage. But the company has advised several potential clients about land and cultivation strategy who then, suddenly, went dark, only to be seen a few months later, launching their own truffle tree businesses on the web. The value of the company's data, which beams in real time from orchards in twenty-three countries, and the proprietary research advice the company provides, has driven Mycorrhizal Systems to ask all of its clients to sign nondisclosure agreements before it agrees to work with them.

Charles Lefevre thinks all this secrecy is ridiculous.

"It should be obvious to you that no one company or consultant has all of the answers right now," he wrote to me, "and I therefore regard heavy reliance on nondisclosure agreements mainly as a means of control over other people. The growers signing them are not receiving the secrets to cultivating truffles. If they were, there would be truffles to show for it."

Lefevre became interested in truffles in the 1990s, when he inadvertently picked up a phone call intended for Jim Trappe, then his office mate and mentor at Oregon State. The caller had wanted Trappe to help him grow truffles, and Lefevre, whose work was then focused on matsutake mushrooms, agreed to help inoculate some saplings with truffle spores. Not long thereafter, and with Trappe's blessing, he founded his own truffle cultivation consultancy, New World Truffieres, now considered one of America's most reliable suppliers of truffle saplings. He doesn't require his clients to sign nondisclosure agreements.

But at some point in our conversation, Lefevre got to talking about his inoculation practices. I asked whether he planned to sell saplings inoculated with *Tuber oregonense*. He said that he had already produced them, but he hadn't found a way to do it at a cost-effective scale for sale. I asked why it was more expensive.

Suddenly he stonewalled.

"I can't really describe to you why it's more expensive without giving you proprietary information," he said, laughing.

⬧

Though the black truffle has accommodated some level of understanding, the cultivation of the culinary holy grail, the Italian white truffle, has remained a complete mystery. No one, in Trappe's estimation, has come even close to figuring it out.

"An enigma wrapped in a mystery, as someone once said," Trappe wrote to me. "I am unaware of any progress in solving it. I know of several attempts at spore inoculation claimed in conversation to have succeeded, but I have not seen evidence of [actual truffles].

"No doubt many others have tried, especially in Italy, but I suspect if anyone has actually produced truffles they would keep it a deep, dark secret."

Scientists believe the white truffle may share some kind of unknown relationship with other plants besides trees. Attempts at cultivation have produced strange results. The formation of mycelium, but no truffles. The formation of truffles, but a hundred yards away from the inoculated tree. So far, in fact, that it was difficult to determine whether they came from the host tree at all. The white truffle seems to need a tree's roots in the beginning of its life cycle, but then, scientists suspect, it abandons them to feed off decomposing matter in the soil.

Because white truffle cultivation remains an impossibility, the world's supply comes from wild forests. But their discovery is so vanishingly rare that ideal white truffle territory is often protected, during short seasons, through brutal forms of sabotage.

# PART III

# THE FOREST · SABOTAGE

People talk sometimes of bestial cruelty, but that's a great injustice and insult to the beasts; a beast can never be so cruel as a man, so artistically cruel.

—Ivan, in Fyodor Dostoevsky's *The Brothers Karamazov* (1880)

# CHAPTER FIVE

# Disappearance of the Dogs

IN ORDER TO GET TO GOOD WILD TRUFFLE TERRITORY, YOU MUST leave Rome in the fall. You must drive away from the cool green Tyrrhenian Sea and the greenery that borders the city's edge. You must compose yourself on a highway with too many signs, and too many speeding cars, and too many tollbooths. You must cross a border between the loud somewhere and the quiet nowhere, into the region of Abruzzo, a place Italians refer to as a land of mountain people. You must take a dark, narrow road into some tiny village, at the foot of giant, skyscraping Apennine peaks, and then navigate an even slimmer road up into the mountains. But most of all, you must surrender yourself to the stillness of the forest and to the possibility of finding absolutely nothing at all.

To find a truffle in a field, a farmer might, like Billy Griner, get away with digging in the dry or bulging patches where the truffle steals the moisture from grasses and weeds. But here, in Italy, finding truffles among thousands of trees along this steep, rocky, and leaf-covered terrain, usually in the light of predawn or dusk, is impossible without a skilled and well-trained dog, one that can pick up on the faintest whiff of a truffle's scent and track it all the way to the source. Italian hunters select their companions with care. If they err in judgment or in training, they might never see a profit.

Some men become truffle hunters, or *tartufai*, for the money, others take up the hobby for the adventure, the hunt, the romance of finding buried treasure in the woods, but probably all hunters are, at some level, initially seduced by the prospect of working closely with a dog. A hunter and his truffle dog can find a special emotional symbiosis. The hunter comes to know his dog's movements—down to granular, undetectable details—and the dog comes to know his. They observe each other and often work without auditory signals, delicately dancing toward a shared goal. A hunter does not simply harbor affection for his dog's quirks; he understands and adores them. Over the years, and over many discoveries, the pair finds love.

◆

Before Luca Fegatilli even knew he wanted to be a truffle hunter, he wanted to be a dog owner. He dreamed of buying a British bulldog—a breed he'd come to obsess over. At €1,500 for a three-month-old puppy, though, he decided the breed was far too expensive. The price was roughly a full month of the salary he earned in a factory as an industrial aluminum painter in Abruzzo's Avezzano, and he needed to pay rent on his place in the sleepy village of Celano, about twenty minutes east.

Though Celano is only an eighty-minute drive northeast from Rome, along toll highway A24, the village seems a full universe away, completely detached from the frenzy of Italy's urban jewel.

The town (population: 11,018) is a gateway into the wider region of Abruzzo. Depending on isolation and elevation, and which bars you decide to venture into, accents are so heavy that other Italians find them difficult to decipher. Everyone knows everyone, and mostly rural folkways dominate.

One day, some time after he'd made the determination that he couldn't justify the expense of a bulldog, he accompanied his father on a work trip to a tiny village in Lazio, the region just to the west. His father, who performs odd jobs, had been dispatched to repair a hydraulics system at a house cloaked in oak forest. At some point during the job, the man who owned the property approached Fega-tilli and his father with his Border collie trailing close behind him. "Okay, I'm going to show you something," he said. Together, the group hiked about a third of a mile up the mountain.

There, the man broke with a tradition of concealing preferred truffle-hunting grounds (fathers don't even tell their sons about their secret spots until they're on their deathbeds), and the dog assumed its responsibility. She sniffed, trotted, and stopped; sniffed and sniffed; darted this way and that. Suddenly the collie dug its paws into the earth near the base of one of the trees, dipped its snout into the hole, and grabbed something with her teeth. The dog sprinted back to the group and allowed her owner to pry the dirt-mottled and slobbery fungus from her jaws. She had searched, dug, and delivered, and now she was trotting back out to another stand of trees to do it again.

Seeing the process, especially when the dog moved with little instruction, the whole ritual felt a little bit like magic, as if there were some missed sleight of hand. Search, dig, deliver, repeat. In that moment of witnessing the beginning of the truffle's journey from earth to table, Fegatilli fell in love with the rhythm of the search. It was difficult not to be magnetized by the fact that underneath the delicious white truffle tagliatelle at the *ristorante*, beneath the layers of kitchen preparation, scales, buying, middlemen, transport, and negotiation—all these human systems of economy and organization—the relationship sustaining this universe was a solitary one between a man and his dog.

＊

With a new subject of fascination guiding his canine interests, Fegatilli soon purchased his first dog, a floppy-eared, long-haired Italian Bracco, and brought him home. Fegatilli's father—who, as a competitive fishing world champion with more than thirty years of experience, wasn't as taken with the idea of truffle hunting—objected to letting the dog live inside their home, so Fegatilli set about finding a sliver of land to house him on. He found a secluded, wooded parcel where he could keep the cages and maintain a small vegetable garden. There were a few houses in the vicinity, but not much else. (Though unfamiliar to most American pet owners, the practice of housing dogs outdoors at a separate location from the home is quite common across Europe.)

Soon after spending some time with his puppy in the mountains, though, Fegatilli discovered that Macchia (Italian for "stain," or, more favorably translated, "spot") had little passion for sniffing out truffles. He was much more interested and skilled at tracking prey. "I mean, I cannot force a hunting dog to find truffles," Fegatilli explained at Gran Caffè, on the corner of the small main square in Avezzano, over the din of gruff, male Italian voices and an almost constant clanking of small espresso cups on their appointed saucers. "I'm not hunting, so I will keep him for affection."

Fegatilli is thin, lanky, and just shy of six feet four. He has dark eyes, pale olive skin, a stubbly black beard accented by a longish hooked tuft hanging off his chin, and a mess of curly black hair. He is reserved and speaks in a low, gentle voice. He doesn't have the dramatic singsong enunciation or excitability that many rural Italian men do. In a casual but stylish button-down and windbreaker, he looks a bit like a working-class hippie: rough around the edges, but rakishly handsome. His hardened exterior conceals a softness. He wears small, heart-shaped earrings, and his smile is big and sincere. When he's explaining something, he moves his hands, palms outward, in small circles, as if he were polishing a car.

After his difficulty training Macchia, he decided to shell out for a real truffle dog, his first Lagotto Romagnolo—a water breed from Italy's Romagna region, famed for its trainability as a master truffle detector. Buffo (Italian for "funny") was small and goofy, but after Fegatilli contracted a professional truffle dog trainer for a few lessons, he developed serious talent for digging up the fungus. Once he began hunting with Buffo, Fegatilli began to appreciate the nuances of the hunt. Suddenly his father became intrigued by the process as well and eventually dropped competitive fishing in favor of hiking out into the wilderness with the new dog.

Fegatilli received his second Lagotto, Kinder, as a gift. Immediately, the pair found a special kinship. He'd shared Buffo with his father, but Kinder was his own. He and Kinder lit out together and spent whole afternoons alone in the mountains.

Soon, Fegatilli began to feel that the male pack needed the grace and poise of a female, so he purchased another Lagotto puppy and brought her to the cages at the parcel. She perished after a fight with Macchia, but her sad passing proved somewhat fortuitous: Soon after, Fegatilli's girlfriend gave him another female puppy from the same litter named Sabatina, or Tatina for short.

"This female was phenomenal," Fegatilli said. At two months

of age, Tatina showed Fegatilli what a true truffle dog was capable of. As he was stuffing little plastic eggs with tiny pieces of truffle and burying them for Tatina to find, she darted away from the training holes and began digging furiously in the nearby forest. She had located real truffles, long before she was meant to. By three months, she behaved as if fully trained. By four months, she was competing with Buffo, who was already two and a half. And by seven months, she was beating out even the most expert dogs they encountered on the mountain.

"There are dogs who find the truffles for the master," Fegatilli told me. "To please him. And there are dogs who find truffles because it's their instinct. They're born to find truffles."

❧

Finding and training a top truffle dog is not easy. They need to be singularly focused, capable of tuning out all the sights and sounds of the forest. They usually need to come from a long lineage—preferably eight generations, on both the father's and the mother's sides—of success as a working dog. And they need to be highly intelligent. Lagottos, shepherds, and retrievers are the most favored breeds.

Each day, trainers begin by burying small pieces of truffle in a small, controlled environment. If the dog excels after a few weeks of practicing this first exercise, she will move quickly on to the next, which involves spacing truffles, of varying sizes, farther apart in a field. If she falters here, the trainer will patiently wait, sometimes for months, until she locates each and every piece of truffle before moving on. If she becomes frustrated, the trainer must allow a cooling-off period of a few days before attempting the exercise again. And if the dog senses frustration or impatience from the trainer, she will feed off the negative energy.

Once they've learned the scent well enough in a field, they begin practicing in the wild, where the truffle's scent can be more easily lost to the wind and to the distracting smells of wild animals. Usually these sessions begin with older, more experienced dogs leading the younger ones along. The ultimate goal is teaching the puppy, after about a year, to search and deliver truffles without commands. Realistically, this might take years of training, if it ever happens at all.

After a while, the most professional hunters can develop a pack dynamic. One dog might stay close, checking the hunter's immediate surroundings. Another can move farther out, to search within the hunter's field of vision. And the most experienced or skilled one might disappear, running hundreds of yards out into the forest, and return with huge truffles in its jaws. Together, the dogs can work concentric circles around the hunter. More territory covered means more truffles and a higher payout. But this strategy often turns out to be more of a dream than a reality.

For Fegatilli, though, this strategy worked well, and Tatina led the pack.

After a few years of routine hunts, he woke up one morning in February 2012, eager to get out to the craggy, limestone mountains above Celano. But the narrow roads around the village were clogged with snow. Icy gusts of Russian air had ripped through eastern Europe, sailed over the Adriatic Sea, and finally settled upon the Renaissance stone town, which is perched on a foothill above the flat and fertile Fucino valley.

The uncharacteristic weather pattern produced more snow than the country had seen in decades, halting traffic in Rome, forcing some trapped drivers to leave their vehicles on the side of the road, and compelling some citizens to lobby for the mayor's resignation. Even Pope Benedict XVI addressed the faithful from a window overlooking a white St. Peter's Square. "The snow is beautiful," he said, "but let's hope that spring comes soon."

Hearty and rugged, Fegatilli had a more muted reaction to the weather. The day of the big snow, as he remembers it, was enough to convince him of the impracticality of venturing to his preferred truffle-hunting grounds, high up in the forests of the southern Sirente range. But the high snowbanks in town were not enough to stop him from making the daily pilgrimage to visit his dogs. He drove his Jeep out onto the slippery roads. Without incident, he made it the kilometer from his home to his little parcel. When he arrived, he found that the high mounds of snow had already blocked access to the cages. As the white sky flaked, Fegatilli grabbed a shovel and dug a temporary exit path.

Once finished, he opened the gates, portioned out meals, and allowed the four dogs to bound around in the cold, snowy alley he had cleared. When the dogs had tired, Fegatilli put them back into their cages, walked back to the car, and drove off as they whined for him to remain.

A day passed, and the snow began to thaw, creeping down to levels that made the roads higher up on the mountain passable again. It was time to return to the forest and earn some cash, though cash wasn't the only thing on Fegatilli's mind. "What I like about going out in the mountains with the dogs, nobody tells you about this: the silence, the peace," he told me. "There is, of course, the beautiful landscape, but also this peace." Fegatilli drove his Jeep back to his small property. He walked toward the cages and found them empty.

His dogs were gone. He paced around the property in a panic, his heart pounding, hoping it was just that they'd somehow managed an escape and would wander back soon. But then he noticed that unfamiliar footprints scarred the snow. His concern turned to rage as he realized that Macchia—who still preferred chasing forest critters to digging up fungus—still whimpered in his cage. He knew this meant that someone had been watching him, that they knew Macchia wasn't a truffle dog, that they came to take Tatina, Buffo, and Kinder.

After the initial shock wore off, he phoned the small carabinieri station in Celano and told the responding officer that his dogs had been stolen from their cages. He needed detectives to come out to investigate. When they arrived, he answered their questions. They took down some notes for their official report. And then Fegatilli began to sense that the dognapping case wouldn't be handled with the sober and severe attention he expected. Beyond a perfunctory walk through of the crime scene, the team didn't seem to be particularly interested in collecting any physical evidence. When pressed about whether they'd need a record of the footprints, one of the officers plainly admitted that they'd forgotten their camera at the station.

Once the officers departed, Fegatilli went down to the station to file the unique identifier numbers for the microchips implanted in each of the three stolen Lagottos. If a veterinarian or Corpo Forestale dello Stato (State Forestry Corps) officer in Lazio or Molise logged a microchip number matching one of those filed, they'd be alerted that the dog had been stolen and could inform the authorities of the animal's whereabouts.

Days passed, and Fegatilli received no updates about the case.

He drove to the station again and asked to see the detectives. They told him there was nothing to update him on. Fegatilli's frustration boiled. "Do something! What are you doing?" he demanded.

"Yeah, yeah, we are," they said. "We are following it. Don't worry."

Fegatilli was persistent. This sequence repeated itself several times.

The lack of any substantive developments—and his somewhat mindless work at the factory—allowed him the time to ponder suspects, consider his own mistakes, and speculate. "At first, I suspected everybody," Fegatilli said, his voice solemn. "So I didn't suspect anybody. But for sure, it must be somebody close to me."

The fact that the criminals had left Macchia behind certainly meant that the dognappers had spied on him in the mountains. In 2010, when he first began seriously hunting, his naïveté about the business compelled him to do something no seasoned and characteristically tight-lipped Italian truffle hunter would ever do: He gave truffles away as gifts. His notion of the business, then, wasn't "egoistic." "It was me, my dogs, and that's it," he said, not realizing that advertising success would arouse jealousy among competitors. His dogs were still puppies then, but they'd somehow managed to locate a hundred kilograms, giving Fegatilli such a surplus that he had trouble selling and using everything before it spoiled. Even if his dogs were only finding the most common of the Italian species, the summer black, or *Tuber aestivum*, the market value for that kind of haul would be something in the range of €30,000, an extraordinary side hustle for the average Italian worker. And that was collected over several months of hunting just between his regular full-time shifts at the factory.

His distribution of surplus must have drawn the attention of unsavory operators. That kind of success, at such a young age, indicated the starting trajectory for master truffle dogs. Fegatilli believes the thieves were savvy enough to wait until the time the dogs had matured to peak value, around age two and a half, to strike.

A few months after his dogs disappeared, another truffle hunter he knew was also targeted. The man had a stroke of luck, though: His older dog was stolen as he trained a new puppy, which was showing more facility than his veteran. Fegatilli suspects the thieves targeted the older dog, and not the puppy, because they'd shadowed him in the mountains and saw that the older dog more frequently accompanied him.

Fegatilli believes he was tracked in a similar fashion. In his mind, the thieves practiced a rather sophisticated form of espionage. Instead of arriving in cars, as all the other hunters do, he believes they parked a distance away from his main hunting area and then hiked in without animals, to watch him and the other hunters in the area. They moved stealthily: Fegatilli would have noticed if his spies had followed him out among the trees. Like all hunters, he walked his preferred path alone, without disruption or interference from others in the area. Any break from this pattern, and he would have been suspicious. At a distance, perhaps through binoculars and dressed in hunting camouflage, his spies found cover and observed the mountain, trying to puzzle out which hunters and dogs were performing the best. They watched as he led Buffo, Kinder, and Tatina up and down the mountain. The other hunters, who came to the forest only occasionally, were disqualified. His frequent appearance on the mountain must have caught their attention. He wouldn't have been out there so often, they knew, if he didn't have skilled dogs and a high success rate. Over a period of time, they winnowed down their list of potential targets to him. They watched him as he left and walked back to his vehicle. They followed him to the parcel where he housed the dogs. Then they staked out his property to check for cameras, to figure out when he came to check up on them, and even established how useless Macchia was. "They do an investigation that doesn't last one day," Fegatilli said. "It lasts a long time."

He believes the Abruzzo region hosts a low-level band of thieves that is connected to an organized and sophisticated national network of dog traffickers. The wider network assists in moving the stolen dogs outside the immediate vicinity quickly so that the victim or one of his associates doesn't encounter the stolen dog out on a hunt. He imagines that there are secret region-to-region meetings where stolen dogs are traded and future deals are brokered.

Months passed, and his hope of reuniting with his Lagottos waned. But his anger fueled a stubborn determination to get out and begin truffle hunting again. He went out and bought three more puppies, Spugna (Sponge), Scooby, and Rosie. This time, he resolved to train all of the puppies himself, without any assistance from professionals.

At only five kilos, Spugna, a slight cream-and-brown Lagotto, quickly established herself as the leader of the pack. What she lacked in stature, she made up for in vigor, becoming known for digging like hell. Scooby, a mutt, performed well, too, and Rosie, another Lagotto, rounded out the team with a nose for white truffle, or *Tuber magnatum pico*. Fegatilli was there for each puppy's first, real discovery of a truffle, watching in the way a parent witnesses a child's first steps. As he trained them, he thought about the thieves. Fegatilli felt as if he were openly defying them, wherever they were, transforming his rage into a kind of perfectionist energy and attention to his dogs. It was a kind of revenge, showing these sad, little thieves that they couldn't touch him.

After the incident, Fegatilli also committed to shifting his public behavior: no discussion of the volume his truffle dogs were able to capture, no sharing knowledge about particularly fruitful spots. The 2012–2013 season proceeded nicely.

Before the busy period of the 2013–2014 season began, Fegatilli moved from Celano to Avezzano, to shorten the commute to his job. Because he now lived farther away from the parcel, his father and he split visits to the cages roughly equally. Fegatilli went between shifts, and his father visited in the evening.

One Friday in August, Fegatilli and his dad planned to meet in Avezzano. The elder Fegatilli, who may arrive ten minutes early to an appointment "but never late," made his son wait. Alarmed by the tardiness, Fegatilli called his father.

"Papa, where are you? What's going on?" he asked.

"Where am I?" he replied. "I'm looking for the dogs."

The truffle dogs were gone, his father said, and again Macchia was left behind.

<hr />

"So the criminals don't like the Bracco?" I asked.

"Doesn't produce anything, only love," Fegatilli's girlfriend interjected in Italian. "Only love, no money," she added in English.

When Fegatilli arrived at the parcel, he found the locks broken and the cages open. If the first theft inspired anger, the second produced sadness and recognition of his inevitable vulnerability. A formal police report wouldn't solve the problem, and neither would buying another set of hounds. The dog smugglers would study him, they would find an opening, and they would strike anyway. Because he'd trained this set himself, the sting was deeper too.

When Fegatilli and I spoke more than two years after the second theft, the pain was still in his eyes, and a sadness was still in his voice. He was angry at the criminals, dismissive of the police, and clearly damaged. He was sensitive and reflective and conveyed a clear love of his dogs. He was still in the process of healing and wavering on whether he had the strength to try to go truffle hunting again. He was still grappling with the uncertainty of what had occurred. As he told the Italian newspaper *Il Centro* not long after the second theft, "Dogs disappear into a kind of black hole."

His blond-haired and blue-eyed girlfriend, a local journalist, sat next to him, occasionally answering my questions or jumping in partway through his. She'd recently given him a cocker spaniel, hoping it might inspire him to return to the forest. She believes he's stubborn enough to start hunting again. "Giving up would be like they won," she said.

If a hunter in Abruzzo decides to enter the competitive industry, he must also have the willingness and financial wherewithal to protect his dogs and property. Some hunters sleep with their dogs. Others have paid for expensive security systems.

Often, hunters don't report or speak out against the thefts. There's a tacit acceptance of the dangers associated with the industry. If a hunter becomes a target for thieves, he'll move on, purchase new puppies, and start anew. Sometimes there are barbs thrown across the bar after a few too many sips of local wine, but they don't go further than that. For the most part, a silence hangs over the forest.

The statutes for truffle hunting are mostly procedural and niggling: periods of time when hunting is restricted, ceilings on daily collection volumes, and dimensions for the instruments hunters use to finish the jobs their dogs start. They don't specifically restrict some of the more significant and scurrilous behaviors truffle hunters must contend with. The laws hold hunters responsible for what seems like an endless list of rules and requirements but don't afford them protections in equal measure.

The acceptance of danger in favor of self-preservation, combined with a dearth of formidable legal standards, doesn't produce a vigorous pursuit of justice. Hunters view filing formal reports with the local carabinieri stations—which are largely disinterested in these types of crimes and never seem to report back on anything of substance—as a waste of time. When Fegatilli went to see the chief decision makers at both the local carabinieri station and the local Forestry Corps, the leaders admitted that they knew dogs were being trafficked out of Abruzzo and that they even had leads on potential suspects. But the intelligence they had wasn't actionable. A more thorough investigation would be necessary—the kind that would lead them to foolproof evidence rather than hearsay—and the will for such action simply wasn't there.

Fegatilli and his girlfriend have become unofficial advocates against Abruzzo's recent spate of dognappings. They hoped to spread the word, first, through journalistic channels: She wrote a piece about the thefts and condemned the secrecy that surrounds the crimes. Their hope is that more hunters will break the silence and speak out against the thefts and that eventually the thieves will back down out of fear of being caught. He dreams of a day when he can freely roam the mountain without fearing that a spy is not far behind.

Fegatilli wants to see legal change too. Dognapping is currently not considered a serious crime in Italy. By raising awareness about the issue, which receives little attention from Italian journalists (the couple was excited to talk to me, to have an American take interest), they hope there will eventually be some traction among lawmakers and law enforcement. To discourage the thieves, Fegatilli believes the crime should be considered a serious felony, punishable with a period of imprisonment.

If the interest did ever present itself, the couple believes, the Forestry Corps, and not the carabinieri, should be the body investigating these cases. The carabinieri, stationed in towns and cities, are removed from the secrets of the mountain. Because the Forestry Corps actually sends officers into the wilderness, the officers have a familiarity with corners of the forest where the men operate, know the faces and vehicles of the characters that rumble by on the mountain roads, and might have more of an interest in rooting out the problems that the natural treasure seems to attract.

At one point after the second incident, a friend called Fegatilli and told him to get to a nearby mountain. The man was certain he'd seen one of his stolen Lagottos. He arrived with hopes of catching the thief, but the dog wasn't his. "It's sad to say, but sometimes it's better if your dog dies, because you have a full stop," Fegatilli said. "When they get stolen, there is always this hope that you will meet them again, which is, of course, false." It's a depressing window of possibility. He has visions that he'll be up in the mountains one day, and his Lagottos will come running toward him, as if they'd never left.

He occasionally wanders the mountains alone. He knows his dogs are long gone, probably somewhere in the hills of nearby Lazio or Molise, or as far away as Umbria or Marche, perhaps with a hunter who was sold some pretty lie about their provenance and their training.

It's not so dissimilar from the way the larger industry has managed to manufacture an image of pure beauty and romance for its consumers. "They see the truffle on the table," Fegatilli says. "But before that, they don't know anything. They don't know the underworld."

They don't know that Macchia sits in his cage, while four surveillance cameras peer down at him. They don't know the pain truffle hunters feel when their dogs disappear. They don't know that when Fegatilli considers buying another set of Lagottos, he fears that nightfall will crack open another black hole.

The road to Sulmona, a little more than forty miles to the east of Celano, carves the shoulder of green foothills, accented by canopies of orange leaves. The rocky peaks above were topped with snow. After traveling through a few long tunnels, my translator and I drove off the highway and past a boulder of a mountain dressed in evergreen.

The president and the vice president of the Abruzzo Truffle Association, representing some sixty hunters, were waiting on the side of the road not far from the foot of an overpass, on the outskirts of town. The hunters invited us into the car, passing back neon-yellow hunting vests and dark green organization hats as welcoming gifts. They seemed to envision a tour of sorts, perhaps hoping that I would recommend the place—which is nowhere remotely close to any beaten track—to truffle connoisseurs.

The truffle business in Sulmona, and in Abruzzo as a whole, is also not remotely close to being renowned. (Sulmona, however, is quite well known for its sugar-covered almonds.) In the 2002 *Italian Truffle Guide*, carefully compiled by the Touring Club of Italy—"the country's foremost publisher of guidebooks for over 100 years"—neither receives mention in the index. It bounces from sights in Umbria and Lazio to the north and west right over the entire region to Molise, which cups Abruzzo's southern end. But this blank spot on the map produces a significant amount of truffles; it simply suffers from a lack of the sophisticated marketing that has made Alba, in Piedmont, and Norcia, in Umbria, well known. Renzo Ciuffini, the president of the organization, and Giovanni Grilli, the vice president, seem more than prepared to make a case to wayward truffle cartographers.

Ciuffini is older and sports a thick white mustache, tousled eyebrows above frameless glasses, a gray-and-blue argyle sweater, and a knit gray beanie, which covers his bald head and the tips of his pointy ears. He led the conversation with a deep baritone from the front passenger seat. With a weathered face and avuncular sensibility, he could easily have passed for a sea captain. Grilli, younger but also bald, seemed a faithful deckhand, minding the wheel and remaining mostly quiet; when he spoke, it was something that needed to be said. The serious, almost regal, tone of Ciuffini's voice telegraphed the pride he and his colleague had in running the organization: They felt it was their duty to act as sentries of the forest and to protect the truffle. "La guardia del tartufo," he said.

"To protect the truffle from?" I asked.

His voice quickened with excitement as he described the threats. The translator had to tell him to slow down. Meanwhile, the diesel sport-utility vehicle sped down the two-lane road into the valley as wind whipped against the windows.

"Most of the truffle business is black business," he said. Neither the regional nor the national laws provide clear instructions for tracking the sale of truffles, both in volume and in geographic origin, by hunters to middlemen, the first step in a byzantine supply chain. Because it would seem rather strange for a middleman to not declare *any* purchases, he usually registers a small portion, on which he pays a percentage of value-added taxes to the government, to make up for the hunters not filing anything. The hunters, meanwhile, are not required to declare anything and remain largely anonymous in this process, a pool of unaccountable supply.

"Because of this big amount of money, there are a lot of people who are going into the woods and digging without dogs, without thinking about the protection of the truffle," Ciuffini said. They walk aimlessly through the forest, ravaging the soil at the base of any tree known to associate with the fungus. Their slapdash use of shovels produces unripe truffles and disrupts the connection the fungal organisms have found with the tree's roots, decreasing the chances it will fruit again the following season.

Once out of the maze of Sulmona's narrow streets, we soon zipped down a country road. Ciuffini gestured out to the right, through a slight opening in the trees, at a field he owns. He used to keep three Lagotto Romagnolos—pedigreed, microchipped, and trained under his direction—at that spot.

On August 11, 2014, about a year after Fegatilli had his second pack of dogs taken, Ciuffini hosted a couple from Rome, to whom years before he had sold a puppy that had become a prizewinning truffle hunter. One of Ciuffini's male dogs played stud to the champion female. To ensure a litter, the couple wanted to leave their female behind in Abruzzo for a few days while they returned to Rome.

"Please, don't leave her here," Ciuffini said. "You never know. If something happens, I don't want to be responsible." Thefts had ravaged the area in recent months, and Ciuffini wasn't particularly anxious, but he didn't want to invite a high-value dog into the mix. Besides, there was another dog, a puppy Ciuffini had promised a friend he would train, already being kept in the barracks.

Though somewhat bewildered by the request, the couple agreed to take her home.

The next morning, at dawn, he brought a puppy along with him from his son's house, prepared to let an older dog coach the new. At a distance from the cages, he noticed that a gate was open. For a moment, he thought his friend's puppy had somehow managed to break the door. Then he realized his dogs, which usually went wild upon his arrival, were silent. As he walked closer to the open gate, he saw that the lock was broken and that the dogs were gone. As he drove home quietly, he was seized by sadness.

After he informed his wife, she wept. He almost wailed along with her. One of the dogs the thief had taken wasn't even capable of hunting anymore and needed a special kind of medicine to survive.

Later, when he recounted the story to me, there was a detectable rage in his voice. The day after the Lagottos disappeared, he called the couple back in Rome to advise them that their female's mate had been stolen. Had they not relented, their champion dog would have been gone as well. Perhaps they would've even suspected him of the theft. He filed a report with the police station, but nothing ever came of it.

Ciuffini, like Fegatilli, believes the trafficking networks are impressive in their breadth and organization; he goes as far as assuming they remove their implanted microchips after the thefts so the dogs can never be discovered. (A detective with the Forestry Corps told me this would be an unnecessarily complicated and expensive measure.) Ciuffini, again like Fegatilli, suspects that the thieves receive orders from other regions and that the dogs are trafficked out straightaway.

Ciuffini and Grilli are dedicated to removing the thieves and people like them from the business. Ciuffini is open to the notion of collaborating with law enforcement to this end, but the lack of coordination among the different provinces creates a critical discovery problem: Forestry police in Sulmona judiciously check microchips of truffle dogs moving through the hills with a special device, but agents to the south, in Molise or Campagna, don't bother, he claims.

The men believe that if they can successfully build an official truffle brand for the Abruzzo region, they can clinch a legal designation that would require hunters to file declarations of origin, volume, and dates for collected truffles that are then sold to middlemen, suppliers, or restaurants. Once this happens, they believe, much of the illicit profit will emerge into the light. They seem to hope that this air of openness and accountability might extend to the woods. By formalizing these market exchanges, they hope corrupt hunters might feel more exposed and less invincible.

After making a turn, we passed by a summer truffle plantation of roughly three hundred oak and hazelnut trees on a grassy hillside. The trees were young, stubby, planted in equally spaced rows. From a distance, the grove almost looked like a vineyard.

Soon the pavement turned to dirt, and the Mitsubishi truck was rumbling up and up, high into the mountains of the Monte Genzana Nature Reserve. We rose above the wide expanse of valley, and the peaks at the other side stared back at us. As we passed one particular thicket of trees below the road, Ciuffini suggested that if it were January, we would be surrounded by white hazelnut *bianchetti*, the small and much less expensive cousin of the *magnatum pico*. "Bad people" take advantage of the similar scent and looks and try to pass them off as the traditional whites, Ciuffini said.

A little farther down the road, Ciuffini advised us that we might meet a bear. Two Marsican black bears had been rummaging through this area of forest, occasionally dipping into the valley to eat hens, reminding people of nature's force. One of them was rifled down the year before, but one was still stirring up trouble. The truck struggled up the turns of dusty switchbacks, and a thicket of oaks hung above the roadside, some from the hill above and some from the hill below, forming a gently swaying tunnel of greenery that obscured the cloudy sky.

The road flattened a bit, and we entered a grassy clearing with leafless beech trees rising up, gray and skeleton-like, on hills to both sides. A swamp of tan-brown leaves covered the hill, drowning the bottoms of their parents' trunks. Two game hunters stood at the side of the road, which, at this point, had withered into nothing more than tire tracks worn in the grass. The men whistled in rapid succession, trying to lure a lost dog down from the hills and back to the car. After another minute up the hill, Grilli pulled the truck off onto the grass, and we opened the doors into the fresh, cold November air.

Grilli held out his wooden *vanghetto,* one of the only instruments permitted by Italian law for levering out truffles the dog cannot retrieve, and pointed at its metal end. Law prohibits the tips of the tools from exceeding four centimeters and digging where the dog has not signaled the presence of a truffle, he explained. As soon as he opened their cage, the Lagottos—small, kinetic—both bounded with puppy enthusiasm out of the cab, despite one being five months and the other five years old. "Hi, guys," I said in my goofy dog voice, chuckling at their panting excitement. Ciuffini had a wooden walking stick, curled like a cane at the top, and began venturing uphill. Grilli, in waterproof pants with large pockets and a bright orange hunting vest, followed as I trailed behind. The white and younger Lagotto, Argo, came up to sniff his left leg. The darker and older Lagotto, named, like Fegatilli's Bracco, Macchia, bounded up to Grilli's right, peering up over his snout into his eyes. Without his acknowledgment, the dog popped up into a turn on his hind legs and sprinted wildly up the leafy track. Argo followed, and soon the dogs were far ahead of all of us. At an elevation of roughly four thousand feet, our breathing became slightly more labored as we hiked up the gradual incline.

Finally, after the drive out of town and onto the dirt, higher and higher past parts of the forest where I thought we'd certainly stop, past the game hunters farther down the road, and now a little bit up the hill, Grilli told the dogs to commence their hunting ritual in this isolated pocket of forest. They slowed down a bit and put their noses to the dewy leaves and mossy trunks, as if they were processing the scents and sights of the mountain for the first time. Once the dogs were deeper into the copse, the only sound besides the rustling of leaves underfoot was Grilli's intermittent whistles. They bounced into the woody silence. I felt the same sacred stillness Fegatilli told me about.

As we walked farther up, Grilli explained that there *is* a way to detect the location of a buried truffle without a dog. You must learn to identify a flat little area where the gases of the truffle scorch the ground with tan discoloration and limit ground vegetation. But this technique only works with oaks and hazelnuts; the beech forest Grilli and his dogs were now traversing would not provide such obvious signatures.

One of the dogs panted more heavily than before. We passed some leaves covered in a very light dusting of snow. The rhythm of our footsteps on the brittle litter of the forest floor took on a meditative quality: whoosh, step, whoosh, step.

Roughly five minutes after the dogs had first put their noses to the forest floor, they signaled. There was a furious and frenzied scraping of paws at the leaves and dark soil, dirt whipping back behind hind legs, constant panting. The dirt came up at such high velocity that it looked as if it were being removed by a machine. "Hey!" Grilli shouted, advising the pair to take a slightly more delicate tack to the buried jewel. Grilli reached into the hole with a red-gloved hand and plucked out a small, black truffle. It was the *uncinatum*, or hooked, variety. The dogs loudly licked their chops as Grilli reached into his pocket for their reward: small pieces of ham. Before receiving them, the dogs wavered between sitting and leaping up to nudge their noses onto Grilli's gloves and jacket, tails wagging uncontrollably.

Ciuffini suggested we move farther into the forest. Grilli followed the dogs deeper into the bowels of the woods, closer to the hills at a distance from the worn track we'd been walking on. A few minutes later, they turned up another one. "Brah-vo!" Grilli shouted. The dogs' bodies bobbed in excitement. But the truffle wasn't worth much: The *brumale* smells, but that's about it. The dogs were off again, weaving between mossy trunks.

The most skilled truffle dogs remain close to their owners, retrieve the truffles from the ground, and bring them back. Grilli's dogs are not particularly skilled at any of those things, so he tends to chase them down, yell at them to stop, jostle and guide them as they're digging, reach his hand into the hole they've created to remove the truffle himself, or pry it from their mouths. But at least they know where to lead him and how to dig. This shouldn't be so easily dismissed: Training a dog to ignore the olfactory wonders of the forest, especially those of wild animals, and to focus instead on the singular musk of an underground object is difficult.

Several times, Grilli scrambled toward the dogs before they seemed to be making any indication or sudden movements: He knew the pattern of their movements so well that subtle shifts imperceptible to me were clear symbols of an impending discovery to him.

The dogs settled upon another gathering of leaves and began digging. "Dove sta?" Grilli said as they dug. "Where is it?" At one point, Argo's head was fully underground, beneath the leaves and the dirt, pawing back dirt with intensity. Grilli was on his knees, bending over both dogs, gently reaching into the dirt where Argo was focused. He put his dirty red glove over the far side of the dog's body and pulled him closer, then used both hands to lift him up and get him right on top of where he thought the truffle was most likely to be discovered. As he pulled Argo closer to the potential truffle, he pulled Macchia, who seemed a little less certain and concerned about the whole enterprise, toward him and away from where the other was digging. Grilli seemed to like managing the dig this way, hovering directly over the hole and making adjustments, like a dad overseeing his child's digging at the beach. But better-trained dogs don't need so much supervision. Ciuffini told us it was impossible that the truffle was down there, that the *uncinatum* doesn't grow so deep. Either it was so small they missed it, or it simply wasn't there. But soon the sour and earthy musk of another hooked truffle was in Grilli's hand, and he lifted it up to his nostrils. Even among the woody scent of the forest, the smell was bold and overwhelming. Grilli scraped the dirt back over the hole so another truffle could form.

Ciuffini hates the hunters who ravage the forest with shovels and leave it pockmarked with holes. The destruction can keep areas that are usually reliable from producing anything. During the summers, people from Lazio regularly venture into this part of the forest for summer truffles. Not too long ago, the authorities caught a group of six men digging with shovels; they'd split into three groups of two and were communicating about the best areas by two-way radio. Working without a dog also means finding less valuable, substandard product; dogs will only bring up truffles that are mature, and shovels bring up everything. This is one of the reasons why product from China, where they use rakes rather than dogs, has such a poor reputation.

At one time, Italian hunters employed pigs for the task as well, because they are naturally drawn to the truffle scent, even more so than dogs, because it matches that of the pheromone that the creatures give off during mating. But the process quickly turned cruel: Pigs rarely relent and drop truffles, preferring to keep them for themselves, and hunters used hooks to rip them from their jaws, sometimes piercing their faces. Other farm animals have been known to be attracted to the smell as well. Ciuffini once knew a shepherd who noticed his sheep were lingering underneath one particular oak. When he dug there, the shepherd found an abundance of summer truffles.

A delicate, light snow began falling. Ciuffini claimed that a heavy coating of snow could improve the dog's ability to detect the truffle, perhaps because it had a way of neutralizing all the other smells emanating from the forest floor. If the roads are passable, he makes it a point to venture up after a storm. One of his dogs always slides down the mountain while he's digging a truffle hole and then paces back up and slides again. We passed a bush of dog rose, which Ciuffini pointed out was incredible for the growth of summer truffle. A hunter might find two kilos of truffles underneath that kind of plant, he said. In the distance, Grilli was still whistling and scrambling and bending over the dogs. He'd found several small hooked truffles and several more *brumale,* but nothing big enough to sell.

"*Basta sui tartufi!*" Ciuffini yelled, addressing Grilli, who was somewhere across the forest. "Enough with these truffles!"

It was time to head back.

As Grilli led us down the mountain road, Ciuffini reflected on his relationship with his stolen dogs. He regretted keeping them on the parcel. He remembered feeling they were in a kind of symbiosis. He still feels that way. "When the dogs smell the truffle, we understand it long before they start digging," he said. His favorite part of truffle hunting is still this relationship, sharing the happiness of the discovery.

At the foot of the mountain, Grilli pulled off on the side of the road, near the back side of Ciuffini's property, and let us out of the truck. I followed Ciuffini onto the grass, between some tall bushes, and into a grove of hazelnut trees behind his son's house. The magnificent backdrop to the vista looked as if it had been ripped from the canvas of a Renaissance painting. Hulking white clouds hung in the azure sky, over the gentle slope of a weedy brown peak. Sun lit up pieces of bumpy limestone rock, and thick ribbons of maroon brown cleaved through the flatter sections. Farther down, the grays were marbled with splotches of dark green, which became more concentrated as the rock slid into the vegetation of the valley floor. In the distance, snow on the peaks down the range blurred in with the low-slung clouds. Amid this environment of light and beauty, perhaps it is too easy to take advantage of those not studying the shadows.

The deep browns and rusty reds of a vineyard rose to the left.

And beyond the grove, an empty plot of grass led up to the back of the house. Like the farmers in France, Ciuffini had planted the stumpy hazelnuts—which he purchased for €12 a piece—in several evenly spaced rows not far from the grapes. Leaves stretched out from them unevenly, in little crowns and clumps and skirts, as if we'd stumbled into a ballroom where the dancers had selected decidedly different modes of attire. Ciuffini began walking the rows. He pointed approvingly at the base of one of the trees, which hosted a browned, grassless patch. Here, death spelled fortune. Though the trees were four years old, he wasn't expecting black truffles until the following year. Other hunters in the area who had dabbled in cultivation had been robbed during the night, just like those back in Vaucluse. A few paces over, Ciuffini came upon a hole, which he inspected and seemed genuinely displeased with. A digging animal, he concluded. A raven squawked in the distance.

At one point, before walking the full length of the grove and into the field, he stopped for a moment in between the trees and looked out upon his little empire. As we walked over the grass, Ciuffini's voice broke into a gentle falsetto: He sang a country hymn ("la montana . . ."). The four dogs began yapping as they sensed our presence in the distance. When they finally saw Ciuffini, noses and paws went up on the fence and the barking was ceaseless: There was a clank of a metal water bowl on the ground and so many tones and intervals of woofing that it mirrored the soundscape of a young child stepping for the first time up to a grand piano. One of the four dogs in the cage was the one that Ciuffini had brought with him to the parcel the day he discovered that all his other dogs had been stolen.

Ciuffini opened the gate and retrieved a white four-month-old puppy, which he was training for a friend. Not far from the cage,

Ciuffini had hidden a black truffle and two yellow plastic containers with pieces of white in three separate holes in the grass. The puppy raced to each hole, quickly sniffing and sifting out the prize in each. The training regimen is simple: five minutes in the morning, and five minutes in the evening, Ciuffini explained.

For Ciuffini, these simple pleasures—the regimen, the dawn mist, the fellow hunters convening at the same bar for a drink, the anticipation after the dog paws at the earth—outweigh the evil. Perhaps Fegatilli, too, could one day find himself as weathered and certain in his philosophy as Ciuffini. Perhaps part of the beauty of truffle hunting is learning to function in darkness, to continue searching even when external forces seem bent against you. Despite the fact that guards are still necessary to protect local groves from known thieves at night; and the fact that a con man recently defrauded some local cafés out of sponsorship money for a fake truffle dog competition; and the fact that they haven't had much luck setting up a real competition because too many hunters fear spies; and the fact that the place where we ate lunch didn't even serve truffles; and the fact that poachers still use shovels to dig up the grove of oaks right across from the local police station, Ciuffini remains committed to improving the truffle-hunting community. By learning how to understand his dogs without using words, Ciuffini said he's learned how to be more observant and more empathetic in his interactions with humans. Some hunters—many hunters— have changed, he said. Not everyone. But the chief guardian of the Abruzzo truffle can still hope.

# CHAPTER SIX

# Poison

THE SABOTEURS WORK QUICKLY, USUALLY ON THE UNFAMILIAR CARS parked in dirt tracks or meadows next to the forest. They slash tires. They dent doors and hoods. They shatter windows. Sometimes, they open gas caps, stuff rags inside, and light the fringes on fire. They're gone before the gas starts leaking, before the doors blast open, before hoods slam into windshields, before the tires pop. They're gone by the time a hunter smells the smoke and the scent of burning plastic and upholstery, by the time he calls his dogs back and sees flames through gaps in the trees.

The saboteurs are locals. The forest and the truffles buried beneath it belong to them, they reason. This will teach them, they think. This is where their grandfathers first showed them how to truffle hunt. This is where their fathers disappeared on foggy mornings, carrying their satchels. These outsiders, from other villages and even other regions, don't belong. They have not worked their whole lives mastering the paths taken through these woods. They know nothing. The saboteurs work to protect memories of a quiet, untouched forest. They work to protect the money they earn each season. They work, maybe, just to prove to themselves what they are capable of.

They also feed on envy. How had that hunter or this one—someone they knew through family or at school or just by seeing him on the mountain—managed such a good day, when they found nothing?

But truffle hunters can repair slashed tires. Truffle hunters can fix shattered windows and dented hoods. Truffle hunters can even replace torched cars. The intimidation may give them second thoughts, but if the forest is rich enough, they'll return. The hunt is more important than a car.

Truffle hunters, after all, are brave men. They walk into the dark wilderness with hope. They know they might encounter snarling wolves or distressed bears, but still they trudge toward the incoherent noises in the distance.

When the saboteurs realize that their work hasn't done its job—when more hunters keep riding in and stomping through their territory—they fume. They realize that property damage is too dull a blade.

⚡

Before dusk on an autumn day around 2009, Gabriele Caporale, a short man with a tall forehead, put his cocker spaniel into his car and drove away from the hills of Perano. Away from the main piazza, with its old, weathered church and its friendly bar, the one where the same person who cleans the toilet also fixes the espresso. Away from his small truffle shop, where he works from a hulky desk in a corner by the windows, the scent of fermented earth flowing into his nostrils each day. The place where he buys from forty other truffle hunters like himself.

Caporale drove south on a winding two-lane road as the sun slipped behind the foothills. He passed the finger-shaped lake of Bomba, crossed over the skinny Sangro River, and veered into Molise, a region just to the south of Abruzzo, where white truffles were growing with abandon. He pulled off near the village of San Pietro Avellana, bumping along a dirt road to his special patch of woods, and parked.

Caporale was in his fifties, but hiking up the slopes in his camouflage coat and waterproof boots, he looked much younger. He had a dark mustache, a splotch of hair under his bottom lip, and the air of a high school teacher who wants to be liked by his students and somehow, despite the odds, is. His heavy mountain dialect, delivered in a low and slow staccato, is unintelligible to urban Italians but was perfectly understood by his dog, who had now run slightly ahead of him.

"Dove sta?" he called ahead, his voice telegraphing a command more than a question. "Where is it?"

Caporale had done evening excursions like this for more than a decade. He always hoped to find the massive, seven-hundred-gram white truffles his friend had taken to spinning tall tales about.

But he also knew, having driven in from Abruzzo, away from the forests of his own commune, that he was walking on enemy territory, of sorts. He'd never had any explicit disagreements with anyone on the mountain, but he'd returned to his car at least once to find his tires slashed. "If they love you, they only cut your tires," Caporale told me nonchalantly, as if he were talking about the type of ink his printer uses. The men of some villages and towns near the border of Abruzzo and Molise had perfected the art of intimidation and sabotage.

One of Caporale's friends had once returned after a hunt to discover that his vehicle was missing. Perhaps he'd misremembered where he parked it. He stumbled around the dark road in confusion, until he thought to look over the edge of a cliff. He saw it, tires up, at the bottom of the gorge.

Caporale detested this territorial behavior and was exasperated that hunters in certain villages had found ways of persuading their municipal officials to go along with it. Some village authorities had taken to granting dirt road access only to residents. Caporale had begun organizing a group of hunters from Abruzzo who met to discuss such concerns. Together, they would lobby against any local measure that violated the spirit of Italy's national legislation on the so-called free search for truffles on public lands.

Up ahead, Caporale's thirsty spaniel dropped his tongue into a pool of water that had collected in a large indentation of a log. Among the oaks, especially when it was dry, the spaniel always seemed able to find something to drink.

Several minutes later, the spaniel's interest in the hunt completely evaporated. The dog's breathing slowed and then grew labored. Caporale noticed something was wrong almost immediately. He picked the spaniel up and scrambled down the mountain toward his car.

The dog stopped breathing soon after he drove off. The veterinarian was clear: It was poisoning by strychnine, a colorless poison usually used to keep gophers and other small animals off agricultural land. It served no purpose in a wild forest, other than to kill competing truffle dogs.

The saboteur likely placed drops of it into each pool of water he encountered in the valuable patch of white truffle territory. Once other hunters had lost their dogs and stopped hunting there, he could cash in on the untrammeled territory.

Not long after, Caporale heard a story from his brother-in-law and one of his friends, who had gone hunting in the same general vicinity.

One morning, the pair caravanned out to the forest together. The friend brought along two dogs, but when he arrived, he decided to pull only one out of the back of his car for the hunt. The men took separate paths through the forest and met back up at their cars when they'd finished. They commiserated over a poor showing, and the friend put the dog he'd used in the back of the car with its companion. The men decided to hunker down and eat the sandwiches they'd purchased earlier, small consolations for a wasted morning. As they chewed, the dogs growled in excitement, playing and slobbering on each other in the back of the car.

But by the time the men were done eating, an eerie silence had crept in. The friend opened the back of the car to find both dogs motionless. With horror, he realized that the dog he'd taken into the woods had eaten something laced with strychnine. He hadn't noticed, and its kisses claimed the other dog too.

Caporale had already taken special precautions against poisoning when he lost his dog. The dog wore a hefty metal muzzle, designed to prevent him from eating a strychnine-laced meatball, which had lately been in vogue among the poisoners. By poisoning the water supply, the saboteur had thwarted the muzzle's design: though the dog no longer had space to bring larger baits into its mouth, it could still ingest poison with a swift flick of the tongue. For hunters who didn't employ muzzles, a careful and constant survey of the forest floor became imperative. Sometimes, the poisoners buried the baits in the ground to distract hunters who, during a fierce dig, expected that their dogs were on the brink of locating a white truffle.

In Ateleta, a village not far from San Pietro Avellana, hunters watched for meatballs stuffed with shards of glass. A few years after Caporale's dog died, twenty dogs consumed some form of poison there. (As local legend has it, at some point during Italy's history, the prisons in the area released their inmates. Instead of dispersing to other regions, they built their homes and settled in the village. Their criminal philosophy, the story goes, has not slackened.) Caporale refuses to take his dogs near that forest. In 2016, another nineteen dogs fell ill from poison there, sending men running down the mountain, clutching their companions in their arms. At least nine died.

But this problem wasn't unique to Ateleta or even to the thread of truffle forests on the border between the regions of Molise and Abruzzo. Caporale had heard of other spots where water was laced with antifreeze, capable of ravaging a dog's kidneys. Fegatilli, the hunter who lost his dogs to thieves, spoke of encounters with poisoned rigatoni. A hunter in the Marche region told me about booby-trapped chicken necks in the forest and a piece of poisoned sausage that was dropped on his front lawn. Lately, the poisoners seemed to favor salami, because the casing provided a stronger buffer against the elements.

---

By late afternoon, the small basement room in Asti—a city not far from Alba in northern Italy—smelled like piss, wet fur, and stale air. The white pointer, large black splotches on its head, stood in its cage and stared up with sad eyes. He would be released back to his owner, a truffle hunter, that evening or early the next morning.

The man had brought the canine in with the suspicion that he'd been poisoned out on the Piedmont region's hills, famed across the world for their white truffles. Dr. Remo Damosso confirmed his fears.

Some part of me hoped the stories I'd heard about poison were apocryphal—folklore perpetuated to demonstrate the courage of the truffle hunter, disappearing into a forbidding forest. Maybe it was intimidating puffery designed to keep men out of certain favored spots—the equivalent of putting a "Beware of the Dog" sign up without actually owning one. But looking into this dog's eyes and meeting Damosso made me understand that the problem was very real.

Caporale's stories weren't outlandish, or maybe even exceptions; they were privately considered part of the cost of truffle hunting in Italy's forests. Between January 2013 and March 2018, newspapers in regions throughout Italy reported at least 126 truffle dogs poisoned. Those cases likely represent just a small sliver of the real, unreported figure. Most hunters are unwilling or afraid to violate the trade's strict code of silence, for fear of shutting down the forest—as authorities sweep the area—and then falling victim to further retribution. Veterinarians in truffle territory, like Damosso, knew more about the shape and scope of this hidden cruelty than anyone.

Blood had poured from the pointer's mouth and anus. The vet, in his stained green lab coat, bent his ruddy face down to the lower cages and elevated his deep, raspy voice an octave and let out a rapid flutter of sweet nothings, as if he were leaning over a chubby baby in a crib. He put both hands on the head of another sick white dog and gently tapped his finger on the cage of the one who had ingested poison.

Damosso had taken me down to the cramped basement on the noisy elevator from the second floor, where he had a spacious office. Inside, there was a collection of tobacco pipes, a photograph of a Great Dane and a Chihuahua, and a kitschy painting of cats posing with a motorcycle at night. He spoke in a state of high animation, his voice a fast growl, his hands moving quickly back and forth, as he drew from a cigarette. The smoke filtered out of the open windows, which looked out onto a busy boulevard where traffic whizzed and merchants welcomed business.

The dog down in the basement was not an abnormal case for Damosso. Over his thirty-eight-year career in veterinary medicine, poisoned truffle dogs had remained a constant. The methodologies and toxins of choice had changed, but the motivations, and the consequences, have remained the same.

⚊

When he first started, the saboteurs favored the sponge. The killer boiled a sponge down until it shrank to a small, easily swallowed size. Once consumed, the material expanded inside the stomach, eliminating the dog's sensation of hunger and eventually starving it.

In the late 1970s, medical imaging for veterinarians had not yet been developed, so the problem was difficult to diagnose. But back then, it wouldn't have mattered much. Many of the sponge cases ended before Damosso even received them. Most hunters didn't notice something was wrong until too late. Nowadays, his clients bring in dogs at even the slightest disturbance or shift in behavior.

Saboteurs soon pivoted from the sponge to meatballs filled with shards of broken lightbulbs. If the hunter noticed early enough, Damosso compelled the animal to drink Vaseline oil, which would flush the glass out of the intestinal system.

Next, the saboteurs turned to strychnine. By the time the poison reaches the animal's mouth, the race is almost over. Depending on the breed and the dosage, the toxin can complicate breathing within seconds or minutes. If the dog is at a vet soon enough, though, it can usually be saved with anti-convulsion medication and can recover, over two or three days, without permanent damage. For the dog, it is either death or a return to normalcy. There is no middle ground.

The assassins have now turned to rat poison, which is more readily available than strychnine. Designed to give the rat enough time to travel back toward its brethren and poison its community, the toxin has a delayed effect. First, the dog's skin turns pale, and color drains from its gums. Drops of blood make their way into streams of urine. If the dog is presenting these early symptoms, Damosso can save it. The rat-poisoned dog's ultimate fate is the same as the dog who has consumed glass: internal bleeding. If blood has moved into the dog's lungs before reaching Damosso's office, death is all but certain.

Whenever a dog arrives, Damosso's biggest priority is triage: eliminating or alleviating convulsions, asphyxiation, and bleeding. When the animal is safe from the grip of death, he begins figuring out which medications might nurse her back to health.

Over the last decade, though, treating truffle dog poisonings has become less about cure-all antidotes. Rather than use typical poisons, the saboteurs have begun using intoxicants: industrial chemicals, like those employed in paint production. A normal poison works quickly and usually concentrates damage on a particular organ or organ system; an intoxicant works more gradually and is less partial to specific anatomy. It reaches into and warps all tissue and eventually produces a general malaise in the animal. This works to the advantage of the poisoner. The symptoms take longer to show, meaning that by the time a hunter realizes that something is off, it is almost too late to bring the dog to the vet. Intoxication is also more difficult to diagnose and treat; any number of natural ailments can produce similar symptoms.

Damosso detests the poisoners.

"It's a form of terrorism," Damosso said. "Because if your dog gets killed by poisoning, then you will not go to the forest anymore. Isn't that the point of terrorism?"

In 2008, the number of dog poisonings reached such staggering levels that Italian lawmakers introduced new legislation that placed heavier restrictions on laying baits for pig, deer, and wolf hunting, narrowing the language around what kinds of materials, what types of licenses, and what times of year were acceptable for the practice. These more specific parameters weakened any potential legal defenses of dog poisoners. The same law also established more thorough legal recourses for those who fell victim to the sabotage. It allowed city prosecutors to open public investigations into the reported crimes and for affected truffle hunters to collect reimbursement for their losses from municipal or provincial authorities.

In order to pursue an investigation into whoever perpetrated the crime, the hunter, according to the law, must first visit the veterinarian and receive a formal diagnosis on the ill dog. To qualify as a crime under the penal code, the chemical that led to the illness has to fall under a specific list.

From that point, the hunter must work with the local authorities and the mayor. "But the cases that go through this process are few, because basically truffle hunters prefer to deal with that within their community," Damosso said. "Not to spread the word, not to have authorities coming in and sniffing around and looking into each other's business." Less than 10 percent of hunters, the vet estimated, ever take more formal steps to follow up on the poisoning. Of those, the vast majority file general reports, listing no potential suspects.

Damosso remembered one case in which a truffle hunter pressed charges against a specific person rather than an unknown offender. The suspect's house was searched, and the authorities located the poison on the property. But the criminal was an old man, at least in his mid-seventies: not exactly the person a prosecutor wants to make an example out of or the kind of crime he wants to build a reputation on pursuing.

Damosso receives, on average, three or four poisoned dogs a week during truffle season. He said other veterinarians in the Asti area receive similar numbers. There are about fifteen of them, meaning, conservatively, hundreds of poisoned dogs move through the city's clinics each season. Damosso suspects that he probably treats the poisoners' dogs as well. Evil needs services too.

The worse the truffle season, the higher the number of incidents. The season I traveled in Italy was terrible for white truffles, which meant that the poisoners had more reason to do their work.

Damosso believes the sabotage is an intractable problem that doesn't respond well to even the most well-intentioned laws and skilled enforcers. For working-class Italian men hoping to enrich a humble existence, too much money is at stake. "They just don't give a shit about the consequences," Damosso said. Damosso recommends that his clients walk into the woods with salt and hydrogen peroxide, which can induce vomiting in case they encounter the traps of a saboteur.

Given all the blood, illness, and death Damosso had seen in

his facility, I was expecting him to explain how the truffle-hunting community needed to be upended through a series of legal and cultural reforms. But, with the exception of the poisonings, Damosso wanted to see the system, with all its financial shiftiness and secrecy, preserved. "This way the uniqueness of the truffle," he said, "especially from this region, can remain intact."

The State Forestry Corps, the military police unit focused on enforcing laws within Italy's forests and wilderness areas, didn't hear about the truffle hunters' poisons from any of the victims. Instead, they were looking for bears. There had been reports of black bear carcasses in the woods, likely targeted by local farmers ensuring the safety of their livestock. As they surveyed the landscape for bear poison, they also found other baits with curiously small payloads. The number of these smaller baits rose in early September, when white truffle season began. The truffle hunters they spoke to were tight-lipped, but the officers understood what was going on.

The State Forestry Corps decided to dispatch its team of five poison-sniffing dogs, trained in Spain, to the best truffle territories in Abruzzo, Lazio, Umbria, Marche, and Piedmont at the beginning of each season. When one of the dogs gets a scent, she follows it to the trap or bait, sits right next to it, and waits until her human assistant arrives to extract it. The dog trainers struggle to keep up with the diverse and ever-expanding inventory of lethal substances. When the teams feel they've made headway in removing one kind of poison, the dog assassins find a new type of chemical or a new bait—Gorgonzola, mascarpone—to conceal it in.

The corps officers bag the baits as evidence and transport them to the laboratory for analysis. Once active ingredients are identified, dog trainers refine their regimens based on the season's trends.

The anti-poison unit can consistently locate, by scent, meatballs with shards of glass, sponges, and snail poison, which can be obtained easily in any Italian supermarket.

·····

Carlo Console, the man in charge of monitoring truffle crime in Abruzzo's Gran Sasso National Park, works from a two-story brick building atop a hill that overlooks a green mountain at the opposite side of the valley. Visitors to the station must pass through an overgrown thicket of trees that slope up a long driveway. The vegetation hangs there boldly, as if to remind the officers that the wilderness they're charged with protecting never stands too far away.

The nearest town is Abruzzo's regional capital, L'Aquila. More than six years after a devastating 2009 earthquake, the streets were empty and the only discernible sound was the whirring of unseen construction equipment. Doors were closed; buildings stood abandoned; stone exteriors were pockmarked with cracks. Construction scaffoldings, gates, and nets graced almost every architectural surface. In the main piazza, the eighteenth-century Chiesa di Santa Maria del Suffragio's Baroque stone facade was concealed behind a canvas sketch of its former self.

In air already thick with economic desperation, and thickened still by the struggle of reconstruction, protecting the only opportunity for local wealth could make brutality seem necessary and even sensible. L'Aquila's dilapidation was extreme, but not unlike the economic depression felt in most towns and villages near truffle territory.

On patrols, Console senses the desperation as he enforces an array of regional rules governing truffle collection. Many of the infractions are prosaic: moving into the forest during restricted hours (six in the morning to six at night in November is acceptable, but the timetables shift during each month), using more dogs than allowed (no more than two per hunter), harvesting truffles before the official opening of the season, or harvesting more truffles than permitted (there is a five-hundred-gram maximum on the white, a one-kilogram max on the black winter, and a two-kilo max on the summer truffle). Console and his men frequently catch hunters carrying one or even one and a half kilos more than the limit for summer truffles, which are more plentiful and easier to find.

Slight and wiry with a gray mustache and a cleanly shaven head, Console looked stiff behind the large wooden desk in his white-walled office. The blazer, button-down, tie, and slacks were out of step with the lighter and more rugged uniform he dons in the woods of Gran Sasso National Park. He feels more comfortable there than in the office, amid his stacks of blue folders, a jumbled bookcase, and the bureaucratic churn. A map of the region he oversees hung behind him. He straddled the serious and jocose, allowing a breathy snicker here and a saddened, hand-to-chin glance there. He loves his job because he can leave these rooms and his tie behind, strap on some boots, and move as high up into the mountains and as close to the heart of the wilderness as he can get. "We're paid to take count of the deer in the woods," he said in a voice slightly higher in pitch, lower in volume, and more elegant than the truffle hunters I had recently met with. "To hear the calls of the wolves."

Though Console has had some success in curbing the more trivial truffle crimes, the dog killers had eluded him. He hoped he'd soon be able to catch someone using pesticide or fungicide; there are easily obtainable records of who has permits to buy those materials. Like Grignan's André Faugier, Console and his team installed cameras in sections of forest that attract the truffle hunters. Just recently, he saw footage that identified a potential suspect; it wasn't clear that he was laying baits, but his movements were suspicious enough to attract Console's attention. He would be watching this hunter closely in the coming weeks.

Part of the difficulty of arresting someone for the crime is the amount of time it takes to build a case. After collecting the poison, officers like Console have to wait for the lab to send back its analysis. If there's enough circumstantial evidence from the camera footage or witnesses, the State Forestry Corps must secure a warrant to search the suspect's home. In order to bring a strong case against the person in court, the officers must find a chemical matching the lab test somewhere on the property. Placing poison within Italy's wilderness areas is a serious offense and the punishment is stiff, but the burden of proof is high.

Unfortunately, the truffle hunter's culture of secrecy makes the crime almost impossible to investigate. Just that morning, he was administering a truffle license exam, when one of the test takers mentioned that his Lagotto Romagnolo had been poisoned only a few days prior. Console asked the man if he had filed a police report. "No," the man said. "I just went to the vet."

In the province of L'Aquila, hunters are supposed to report these types of crimes directly to the local police or the carabinieri. Under the ideal procedures, officials are then supposed to pass those reports to the mayor of the village, who is then required to shut down that particular area of the forest. The information should then be sent to Console's office on the hill, where the State Forestry Corps can call in a dog team and initiate efforts to clear the forest of poison and collect evidence. But more often than not, the forest remains open due to a problem at the beginning of the chain, a victim's unwillingness to make direct reports about his poisoned dogs.

In spite of the challenge of collecting intelligence from a community that has about the same affinity for disclosure as a drug-running organization, Console tries to remain hopeful about the possibility of making arrests. His secret weapon is a data set he and his team have been building since 2005. The spreadsheet holds details about the location and type of poison used in every incident report that has come to the corps for more than a decade. With the use of data analysis, trends and patterns begin to emerge.

The economic motive works to the investigators' advantage. "Because if someone put poison for this economic reason, he will do it again," Console said. "Usually, you only do it once when it's a personal problem." Similar data analysis helped them catch arsonists setting off fires in the woods. "A criminal is a criminal," Console said.

Even if there were enough evidence to bring someone to court for the poisonings, a conviction would likely not result in a very long prison term. Though the statute suggests a serious sentence, environmental crime is not considered a top priority among Italian prosecutors and magistrates.

And so, the saboteurs continue to operate with relative confidence. They know other hunters won't break the silence. They know that authorities won't vigorously pursue something that will be regarded as trivial and silly. And they also know that given the anonymity of the trade, with all its handlers and middlemen, a buyer will never know who they really are.

# PART IV

# THE MARKET · DECEIT

I've seen lots of funny men;

Some will rob you with a six-gun,

And some with a fountain pen.

—Woody Guthrie

CHAPTER SEVEN
# Middlemen

ONCE DISCOVERED, TRUFFLES ARE DRIVEN FROM FIELDS AND FORESTS overrun with thieves and saboteurs and are sold, after inspection, to a middleman. These sales are often not formally invoiced, so describing the full scale and number and quality of these transactions is a little like trying to characterize the murkiest depths of an ocean by studying the flotsam at its surface. Various estimates put the value of the European truffle market at €300 million, but the actual amount of cash that's exchanged for the product before it reaches a consumer's plate is largely invisible and unknowable. Very few farmers and hunters broker the final deal themselves.

On the smaller end of the scale, a middleman might be a collector, someone who lives in or drives into a village and visits each truffle hunter or farmer door to door, amassing as much product as he can, before driving it to the nearest regional dealer or company and making a sale.

A middleman might be a guy who owns a shop or cool-storage space the size of a bedroom but somehow pulls in hundreds of thousands of euros a year on the volume he sells directly to restaurants or private chefs. He might have a network of sub-middlemen who work the local truffle markets or nearby villages. That sub-middleman might prefer to work with a few of his favorite truffle hunters or farmers, who act as middlemen when they collect the truffles from all the other people in their village.

At the more organized end of the spectrum, a middleman might have a working agreement or contract with a larger truffle company to capture all the best truffles before hunters try to sell them directly to chefs themselves. Or a middleman might simply be a company employee, or even an executive, who meets hunters or regional middlemen at the receiving area and decides which pieces the company will purchase. Many companies, some worth tens of millions of dollars, must buy enough truffles during the season to ensure profit—through the production of canned product and derivatives—throughout the remainder of the year, when there are no valuable truffles available.

A middleman's job, other than making money, is buying and sorting through the raw product, blemishes and all, deciding which truffles should move forward and which aren't quite good enough for the fresh market. A skilled middleman filters out the bad and pushes forth the good. In theory, a middleman is the first line of defense against fraud.

In France, middlemen are called *négociants*. Pierre-Andre Valayer—the *négociant* who had 150 kilos stolen from a locked refrigerator by thieves who entered his storage space by rope ladder—buys from two hundred different farmers a week. He comes from four generations of men who have bought and sold the ingredient, during the period in which there was nothing else to do but prune their family's vines. When he started buying on the Richerenches market in 1987, there were only five other *négociants*, buying about one metric ton on the market. Now he competes with at least twenty others, and there are only half as many truffles to choose from.

The Richerenches truffle market takes place on Saturday mornings during the season, on a street lined with plantain trees and buyers' large vans and cars, their trunk doors open and facing out. One typical fall morning, throngs of sellers hoping to sell in bulk walked through the middle of the street, ping-ponging between the dealers' vehicles. No one took notice when three gendarmerie officers, military-style assault rifles slung across their shoulders, walked past. They were there to protect the dealers and farmers from the robbers interested in the truffles and cash—about €300,000 worth —moving quietly across the market.

When farmers walk up to the back of Valayer's Golf hatchback, he looks for size (with a preference for truffles above twenty grams), shape (whole and round rather than knobby or broken), structural integrity (holes from worms and other blemishes decrease the price), and maturity (usually marked by a dark chocolate complexion and an unforgettable scent). The exchanges happen quickly. A plastic bag is opened, a price is offered, a counteroffer is whispered, perhaps there's a quick debate about the details, and then a deal is, or isn't, made.

A fellow in a long, dark coat and beanie came up and offered six kilos at €500 per kilo. Valayer sniffed some of the product and handed it back. The man shoved the plastic bags into his gray backpack and stomped off, displeased that Valayer hadn't just handed over €3,000 in cash. "I bought them last week," he said. "And I'm not happy with the final work—I select, and I'm not happy. [I] look for ripeness." Later, the coated man found a willing buyer somewhere down the road.

The next farmer walked up with truffles in a jar. Valayer took them out, made small incisions in some of them with a knife, and inspected them carefully. He plopped them in a plastic bag, retrieved his wallet from the front of the car, and passed over €130 for 450 grams. Then he handed back the empty jar. "It's not a really beautiful truffle; it's not round," he told me. "But it's good for maturity."

As long as the truffle satisfies some of Valayer's requirements and the seller agrees, the euros are handed over, the product is placed into Valayer's trunk, and the seller walks on. After market, Valayer sifts through his raw quantities, eliminating the worst of the batch, and then brokers a sale with larger French truffle companies, like Plantin, the company that lost hundreds of thousands of euros to thieves who blasted through its warehouse wall.

***

That same day, Christoph Poron, the Plantin executive who bought truffles from Laurent Rambaud, the man who gunned down Ernest Pardo, wandered the market in Richerenches, glad-handing *négociants* and gleaning intelligence about the day's pricing. I had met him at the company's warehouse the previous afternoon—a squat building in the middle of the countryside so discreet that I blew past it several times before finding the driveway.

When we finally crossed paths in the middle of the commotion the next morning, he asked me if I wanted to see something. "We're gonna meet some farmers that we work with regularly," he said, pacing away from the open vans on the public market, as I followed. "We don't buy here because we don't want people to see exactly the quantities we're buying from them. Because . . . this market is about secrecy, you know? I mean, the more discreet you are, the better you are. These are the people to talk to. The truffles are very nice, and you'll see the quality as well. Really, really good."

"You follow me," he said, giggling, and then got into his Volkswagen.

·

We drove out of the town, through the traffic circle where Gendarme André Faugier's farmer-informants spotted the teenage thieves, and down a country road. Then we made a turn in to the gravel parking lot of a wine cooperative, across the way from a large vineyard full of rusty red vines and the beige grass of late autumn. The invitation felt lucky: I'd only been in France a day, and already I was on my way to an off-market exchange.

Poron wanted to avoid showing his cards to competing traders and companies. And his farmers presumably wanted to avoid the thieves who were rumored to attend the market to puzzle out who was thriving and worth following home. It seemed that there was also a degree of secrecy for secrecy's sake, or because this was how the market had always functioned.

Poron and I were the first to arrive.

"So, sometimes we do it here," he said of the rendezvous point. "Normally, we do it some other place. We change it a little bit. The big thing is, it's always better if nobody . . . we prefer people to imagine. Let their imaginations go."

Over the last four years, Poron and his selected farmers have developed a strong rapport under this secretive arrangement. "One of the guys brings a bottle of wine, they have ham, maybe Rhône sausages, and all this, so it's very friendly," he said.

I asked whether the farmers had any connection to the wine co-op, wondering whether this was some kind of designated turf.

"Just a rendezvous point," Poron clarified.

I characterized this as "shady."

"Pretty much, yeah. It's like drug dealing, you know?" He laughed heartily. " 'Okay, let's meet beyond the tree over there . . . ' "

He trailed off as he saw the cars heading in our direction. "And here they are." The timing seemed almost too cinematic.

A beige Renault Scénic pulled in to the lot, and four older men piled out. Not long after, an Audi drove in and parked behind our row, and a young couple—a tall fellow and a slender woman with dark hair—joined the group. The attire was jeans and winter jackets.

A greeting circle formed behind the vehicles; pleasantries were exchanged. Almost immediately, someone retrieved a bottle of French white from one of the cars and began pouring into plastic cups. It was a sneaky family affair, of sorts. The farmers seemed to delight in the fact that they were the ones Poron had chosen for a clandestine sale. At some point, Poron's brother-in-law pulled in, carrying his chubby-cheeked ten-month-old daughter in his arms.

One by one, Poron handed out envelopes, scrawled with names, to each member of the group as payment for the previous week's truffles. "See," he said, "we give Christmas gifts." Poron distributed roughly €20,000 in cash, right there in some country parking lot.

Soon, each farmer approached the back of Poron's Volkswagen individually, placing down bags full of truffles for his inspection. He rustled through them and selected a truffle or two near the top of each batch for a closer look. The specimens here were much larger and more finely shaped than the ones Valayer handled back in the village. By paying above market rate, Poron was taking the best diamonds off the market. Though these were trusted sellers, he still cut off small pieces to ensure they were black inside, a mark of full maturity. In a small notebook, he jotted down the name of each farmer, the quantity, and the price point.

After some quick reviews, Poron rejoined the conversation. The older farmers told him that he should get married soon, that, now in his forties, it was time. One of the farmers asked what I thought of the white truffle of Alba, the French truffle's more famous cousin. Of course, the farmer said, he prefers the *melanosporum* and finds the Alba truffle unjustly expensive.

One of the farmers said the price they set today was reasonable.

Poron disagreed, saying some of the truffles could have been more presentable for what they were charging. "I love them," he said, referring to the farmers, "but I *hate* them every week, you know?"

Poron's main challenge in buying truffles in bulk is not knowing what will actually happen once his crew reviews them back at the warehouse. At least with the farmers in the parking lot, Poron had some certainty that there wouldn't be any unexpected surprises: broken bits reassembled with toothpicks to resemble whole truffles, worm infestations, unripe specimens splashed with a synthetic scent.

The day before, I saw workers at the warehouse dutifully sorting through the dirt-mottled product. At some point afterward, it was fed into a machine called the brusher—which removes the gunk—in a hissing side room. The best truffles are sold to chefs and other clients fresh. "Of course, we try to sell the most possible fresh, because this is where we can get the most out of the truffle," Poron said. "The rest that's too damaged or soft or attacked by worms, we're going to preserve."

Finding a perfectly shaped, mature black winter truffle, the kind that ends up at a fancy restaurant, is actually quite rare. In early December especially, the returns on cash investments aren't great. "When we buy a hundred kilos, maybe we get about twenty to twenty-five kilos that we can sell fresh," he said. "The rest is not good enough." It ends up placed in a can with a tablespoon of water and dumped into a cylindrical steam cooker. The fresh business doesn't pick up until January, when more black winter truffles begin to reach their most mature and flavorful state.

In a cool refrigerated room at the warehouse, Poron fished a few hulking winter blacks out of a mucky bath of brown water in a white rectangular container on the cement floor. They were purchased that morning, at the market in Carpentras or some off-the-grid exchange outside it. One was broken and would end up canned, in the form of peelings. Another had been munched on by worms, with visible lines of entry. "This, I don't sell like this," he said. "I clean it up, and I want to make sure the worms are out of the truffle." He wouldn't sell another because it was far too white on the inside. He held forth another. "This one, we see, is nice and black." All of them had an alien knobbiness that would make them a hard sell to a Michelin-level chef, who seeks a finely rounded apricot. More truffles stood out on the tables on the main warehouse floor, awaiting inspection. "Our job is really going through all these truffles and sorting," he said. "What we are known for is our sorting. We are very careful to make sure that the customer gets a perfect truffle."

Back at the rendezvous, the young couple began walking to their Audi. "They're rich on truffle business," Poron said, pointing and breaking into a guffaw at his own remark. After the Audi pulled away, the older men piled back into the Scénic. Poron planned to return to the main bar in Richerenches to listen to the gossip and shake a few more hands, including that of a Michelin-star chef he'd done business with while starting Plantin's American presence in Manhattan back in the late 1990s. "It's interesting because at the bar now it's what we call the market of the liars," he said. "Because everybody is like bullshitting about everything." Perhaps how perfect their truffles were, how much they'd purchased, how much they'd sold.

But he was still thinking about how he'd agreed to pay the farmers too much for what he'd received. He gestured to his niece, who was wriggling in her father's arms. "I was hoping that she would manage to help me bargain the price, but, uh, it didn't work," he said, chuckling. "You know I was like, 'Come on, look at her! Look at her! I have to buy presents for her!' No, no, so she was useless."

In Italy, middlemen are called traders. The biggest of these is Urbani, the company once led by the man who fed Jim Trappe the best truffle dinner of his life. The second largest is Sabatino Tartufi, an outfit located just outside the small village of Montecastrilli, in the central region of Umbria, famous for its rich supply of wild white and black winter truffles. Its modern stone building sits in a remote valley of rolling green hills and delicate light. In the morning, wisps of fog snake through its ravines, and the air smells of pine and evergreen.

Federico Balestra, the company's CEO, works from the company's modest American headquarters in West Haven, Connecticut, surrounded by a collection of vacant lots, abandoned warehouses, and auto body shops. Federico first moved from Umbria to New York City in the late 1990s, not speaking a word of English, to launch Sabatino's American operations from his Fifty-Seventh Street apartment. He quickly captivated chefs with the quality of his wares and soon scored a distribution deal with a major supplier in the city. Distributors for other cities took notice. Since then, Balestra has been able to open offices in Los Angeles, Las Vegas, San Francisco, and Montreal. Now any fine restaurant and many supermarkets carry Sabatino product.

With short-cropped dark brown curly hair, cherubic cheeks, stubble, and light electric-blue eyes, Federico projects a boyish energy and a disarming innocence. Like Poron, whom he once competed with on his door-to-door sales pitches in Manhattan, he is almost always on the verge of a chuckle. He employs both his eyes and his eyebrows with skill. The way he moves them or flattens his lips often does more talking than the words that come out of his mouth. He speaks in a low, rapid mumble, emphasizing the most important words in a slightly higher pitch and punctuating them with a "you know what I mean." He telegraphs a tough rationality about the business, an allegiance to cold logic. But he does it in a way that encourages you to laugh along with his thinking, even if you're not sure you know what he means. At our meeting in West Haven, he applied some Sabatino truffle lotion to his hands.

These days, he only spends about a quarter of his time at the warehouse in West Haven. He's constantly on the move, meeting with importers and specialty food distributors, attending trade shows, making deals. Two days before we met, he was back in Italy. Two days later, he would be heading to Tokyo. He had come back to see his kids in Greenwich and to attend to business at the warehouse for a few days between trips. He would be back in Italy the next month, then to China, and then back to Italy. His relentless hustle for the company and his passion for his family's legacy, at a remove from the daily machinations back in Umbria, had afforded him a relative dispassion about his industry's crimes.

He first read about the death of a truffle thief at Laurent Rambaud's hands in an interview with a chef named Bruno, based in the southeastern French town of Lorgues and famous for claiming to serve four tons of truffles in his restaurant each year (a nearly impossible task that would demand serving 800,000 truffle dishes in less than four months). "Crazy people," he said. "Nobody I know—I'm in the business a long time—ever been shot for truffle. Dog has been poisoned, yes, but . . .

"I was reading his interview and I said, 'God. Bullshit this guy says.' . . . I think he's too embellished. I understand that embellish is part of the business. You need to embellish because people think it's more interesting, but you got to limit." He waved his hands wildly as he spoke, rolling his eyes and shaking his head at the absurdity of Bruno's dramatic portrayal of the industry. It was as if he were trying to squint the thought away, to press it out of his head.

"I don't tell you it's not a tough business. Don't get me wrong. It's a tough business. You go, you know, to buy truffles—it's like when you buy gold, same thing. You buy diamonds, same thing. . . . I think there is more dead in gold than truffle. The only dead is the one Bruno talk about.

"I think he's put many colors on the paint," he said. "Something that occurred once is not a normality, you understand what I mean? That's what I think. I don't think like they kill every dog. Happen? Yes. Happen to people I know? Absolutely. Happen every day? No."

One of Balestra's oldest truffle hunters had lost several dogs to poison. I asked whether he empathized with his plight. "I'm sorry for the dog. For the hunters, they understand these things. It's like a taxi driver loses his car. The truffles is the way to survive, to eat. What do you do? You need the dog to truffle hunt. That's why truffle hunters, they have multiple dogs. You lose one, you got a spare. If you have one dog, you're cooked."

His casual attitude about such brutality reminded me of a story Balestra had told me about his father-in-law when I first called him back in 2013, asking if there was some larger criminal organization at work, pulling strings from inside the industry. His answer was meant to be a parable, illustrative of how craziness could seep into any business, about how isolated incidents didn't speak for the truffle industry as a whole. That wars or larger conspiracies weren't as common as the press liked to make them.

Twenty or thirty years ago, his father-in-law worked in a New Jersey car dealership. One day, a deranged man drove onto the lot and shot his boss, the owner of the dealership, over his distaste with a car he had purchased a few weeks earlier. "That should not happen, obviously," he said. "But it doesn't mean every dealer is a crooked business." There were no behind-the-scenes Mafia ties; in fact, the owner was Jewish, Balestra said. All it meant, all it really proved, was that one guy was crazy.

Sometime in 2014, when he saw a red-carpet interview in which Oprah said that going truffle hunting was on her bucket list, Balestra instantly saw the marketing opportunity. He invited her to Italy for a tour. The company had supplied truffles to her private chef for years before they met. In the fall of that year, she and Gayle King spent three days at the facility. Sabatino managed to keep the visit top secret until they left. One day, they went black truffle hunting on the company's land, and on another they headed out into an undisclosed forest for whites. Oprah and Federico, who flew in for the visit, hit it off. Federico liked that she remembered people's names, that she maintained humility and normality despite her fame and fortune. At one point leading up to the white truffle hunt, she remarked to Federico that they were going to get rich. "Really, Oprah, you already are," he said. She appreciated his humor. Before she left, she signed the company's guest book. "Perfection," she wrote. After Oprah published photographs from her trip on Instagram, Sabatino was inundated with calls from the press. Federico and Oprah remain friends, trading text messages with each other regularly.

In 2018, Sabatino and Oprah's joint venture with Kraft Heinz, O, That's Good!, announced a deal to promote Truffle Zest, "an all-purpose seasoning," that contains summer truffle. This was only a more formalized recognition of Oprah's relentless promotion of Sabatino. She put the Zest on her 2016 and 2017 "favorite things" lists (other Sabatino products have enjoyed similar treatment), and her 2017 cookbook contains no fewer than eight recipes that call for the ingredient. She added it to her eggs while cooking on *The Late Show with Stephen Colbert*.

Federico has also directly supplied truffles to Billy Joel, Celine Dion, Jimmy Kimmel, and the Obama White House. The relationships usually begin when restaurant chefs shift to the private-chef trade and continue to call on Sabatino after they've begun work with a high-profile client. People trust Federico, and the way Sabatino carefully and reliably delivers its product, but the Balestra family's path toward the truffle business did not follow a simple or clear trajectory.

In the early 1880s, in the hilly farmland outside the village of Montecastrilli, there were two types of people: the barons and the workers. The barons owned the land, and the workers tilled it. The laborers weren't exactly slaves, but they were compensated with only enough of the land's spoils to feed themselves and their families.

But the barons had a problem.

Three outsiders, a band of roving builders specializing in the restoration of churches, had ridden into town from their home of Tuscany. Each year, the brothers, carrying the surname Balestra, traveled to a new village, painting and repairing a crumbling place of worship. When they stopped in Montecastrilli, they liked what they saw and decided to pull in and settle for a time.

Over the years and through their travel, they had developed something of an enlightened outlook on the world, a set of principles that the average laborer wouldn't have dared to impose on power. It didn't take long for them to notice that the working conditions on the local farms weren't humane. They presented their thoughts to the landowners and encouraged the farmers to do the same.

"The big landowners, they didn't like them so much," Balestra said of his great-grandfather Sabatino and his great-great-uncles. The barons began to stew over their new irritants, wondering when the brothers might finish their business and take their idealism elsewhere.

One night, a local merchant led his horse-drawn carriage down one of Montecastrilli's main dirt roads, when a man bolted in front of him, brandishing a knife. He demanded that the merchant hand over his cash and valuables. The merchant refused. During the ensuing struggle, the robber slit the merchant's throat. The criminal was able to slip away before the local authorities were alerted. When they followed the footprints from the bloody scene, they were unable to locate any promising suspects.

The gentry saw an opportunity in the tragedy. They ordered the local police to arrest the renegade Balestra brothers. "At that time," Balestra said, "a landowner control the judge, control the police, control everything. . . . They say, 'It's the right excuse to put them away.'"

Sabatino, though, had a clear alibi. His wife had given birth to a son, Federico's grandfather, the same night. The police arrested the pair anyway. The doctor who had delivered the baby the night of the murder could hardly contain his disbelief. "I was there," he told the police. "He was with me. It's impossible."

Despite the facts, the court sentenced one of the brothers to twenty-five years and the two others to thirty.

The Balestra brothers wasted away in the damp cells on Elba Island, off Italy's southern coast. In 1908, long after the brothers had given up hope of reprieve, the real killer confessed on his deathbed. "That was me," he said, "it was not them." The village government had no choice but to overturn the charges and release the Balestras from prison.

Their beards had grown long and scraggly, and they had fallen ill. One of them had gone blind.

By the time the brothers returned to the village, the original landowners who had accused them of the crime were no longer living there, and the village government, feeling a sense of guilt about the harsh injustice, resolved to issue the brothers a general business license and a plot of land as a form of apology. At the time, only the wealthiest of the country's citizens were able to secure the expensive permits.

In 1911, less than three years out of prison, Sabatino Balestra and his brothers used the new opportunity to open a small store in the center of the village, in front of the church. Employing their skills at restoration, they set about rebuilding their lives. They sold bread, olives, olive oil, and other Italian staples. "That's how everything start," Balestra said. "Until then . . . we didn't own anything." The same government that robbed the Balestra family of their freedom provided them with an opportunity that would lead to four generations of success. By the 1950s, Sabatino's small shop had grown into a successful medium-sized supermarket chain. "One day, I'm going to make a movie," Balestra said.

---

But by the 1980s, larger, forty-thousand-square-foot stores began moving in, pushing the smaller mom-and-pops out. The Balestras realized their stores would fail in competition with the conglomerates, so Federico's father, in close consultation with his family, made the difficult decision to sell the supermarket component of the business and pivot elsewhere.

The family still owned the land that the Montecastrilli government had gifted them in 1908. The plot actually ended up being quite valuable: It produced substantial quantities of wild black and white truffles. Until the 1980s, the Balestras had merely dabbled in truffles: They sold what the land produced wholesale to restaurants and companies. But knowing good opportunities when he saw them, Federico's father decided to turn the small truffle operation into their main business. "We're familiar with the problems," Balestra said. "We were selling for many years. And it came natural."

By that point, Urbani, just over the mountains to the east, had already been a commercial truffle giant for more than a hundred years. There were many other companies as well, but Federico pursued new clients with rare humility. "At that time, we were so small that anybody else was so big," Balestra said. "If I see now other companies that at that time I thought were huge, now we do in a week what they sell for a year." After some key American distribution deals, Sabatino overtook Plantin and became one of the best-known truffle brands in the world.

⚬⚬⚬

Before Sabatino's truffles end up in the hands of Oprah or Michelin-star chefs, though, the company's raw product must pass through the back doors of a modest and quiet building outside the village of Montecastrilli. And all of it must first pass through the inspection of Federico's sister Giuseppina or someone she has closely trained. She has dyed blond hair and her brother's expressive blue eyes. It wasn't the only similarity. "He's just like me, but with trousers," she said.

He calls her almost every day, at around 1:00 p.m. Italian time, as he makes his morning commute from his home in Greenwich to West Haven. Sometimes, Federico's wife jokingly says, Giuseppina knows things before she does. The other three Balestra siblings work at the company too, one sister at the Sabatino factory in Italy and then another sister and brother at the headquarters stateside.

Giuseppina's voice is gentle and syrupy, and she breaks into laughter with the same frequency as her brother. She is exceedingly friendly but also exceedingly tough, unwilling to stomach bullshit.

When she first began buying truffles from the company's hunters, she was underestimated in the male-dominated sphere. "Oh, it's going to be a piece of cake dealing with her," the hunters would say. But over the years, the buyer and her sellers have developed a mutual respect. A few days before we met, she had stood with four grizzled truffle hunters in front of the office espresso machine. Sabatino's commercial director walked past. "*Mamma mia*, look at you, one lady and four fellas," he said. He turned and looked at the hunters. "The person who is in danger here is you four." The hunters all nodded in agreement.

She meets the hunters downstairs at the back door or upstairs in her office. She has a roster of three or four hundred of them, and they drive in mostly from other towns in central Italy, but some of them come down from Piedmont, the northernmost region. She's married to the notion that the best truffles come from Umbria, even though Piedmontese white truffles are more expensive and better known.

They bring bags full of truffles. Giuseppina sorts each one into a grade, and both she and the hunter must agree on a final price. Many of the hunters object to her decisions, usually citing precedent on other, similar truffles they have sold her in the past. They haggle and disagree, but she considers the hunters family, and all families argue.

"What's important is this continuity of this relationship that we have with our hunters," she said. "We need to have hunters that will bring us truffles, but it's also equally important for them to know that there's going to be somebody willing to buy what they find." When they see each other in town, she'll join them for an espresso, and they'll tell her about the christening of their sons. If the market prices have dropped one week, she won't gouge them; she'll respect their morning hikes and pay a fair amount. "And good, honest people will remember that," she said. "So truffle hunters that are worth their salt will recognize the way they've been treated."

She sees what she does, and what the company produces, as artisanship, not as industry. "Our aim is to concentrate on quality, not quantity," she said.

She knows each hunter well and scrutinizes each bumpy specimen, spotting the suspicious and rooting it out. She's more comfortable permitting other staff members to buy summer truffles because there's not as much nuance, but she insists on being one of the main decision makers on whites and winter blacks.

Still, wily hunters will find a way to slip through the doors. Some hunters will bring in batches with very few quality truffles and tell her they had a bad day. She'll still purchase the ones with deformities and make sure they're marked for use in the company's oils or sauces. But if the hunter comes in again and explains that he's had another bad day, she'll begin to question him. A standard haul will include a few beautiful truffles, a few average ones, and a few gnarled ones. If the mixture consistently leans toward the ugly, the hunter has likely plucked the best ones to sell directly to restaurants and is only offering the chaff to Sabatino. "The first time you forgive them," Giuseppina said. "The second time you warn them. The third time you show them the door."

Other hunters mask imperfections with clumps of dirt and mud or fill holes with a small pebble and some soil to boost the truffle's weight. Giuseppina knows these ploys and studies each truffle to ensure that it's only covered in the amount of soil that would naturally cling to it after it was pulled out of the ground. "Earth, I buy in hectares, not in grams," she said. She scrapes off excess mud with little picks and knives, and the hunters look at her as if she were a man grabbing their wives. The guileless ones brush off the dirt before they bring the truffles into the factory. The guileful are subjected to interrogation.

"What's this?" Giuseppina will ask tartly.

"Oh, I didn't see it," the hunters say, as if small stones made a regular habit of burrowing themselves into truffles. "Fancy that happening."

She loves catching a deceptive hunter red-handed, especially if he is not one she normally gets along with. Giuseppina laughed in a highly amused manner when she spoke of these deceitful exchanges and then swung abruptly back into her tough, no-bullshit lilt.

Her vigorous reviews discourage her hunters from attempting more daring forms of deceit. They know that if Giuseppina will not even fall for a truffle with too much dirt on its surface, she will surely detect a laundered truffle, a specimen whose geographic provenance is misrepresented upon sale. They could be black winter truffles advertised as Umbria's finest and offered at €900 per kilo but in reality purchased from a Romanian, Bulgarian, Serbian, Albanian, or Croatian dealer at a rate of €500. Or white truffles from Piedmont, offered at €2,000 per kilo but actually sent in from Croatia, Hungary, or Slovenia, at a rate of €1,000. The eastern European truffles are identical species, but expert traders like Giuseppina who value the specific aroma that the Italian *terroir* imparts can detect the difference and won't pay Italian prices for an inferior product. The final bouquet depends on humidity, rainfall, soil type, host tree, and even depth—small changes in any of these could produce notes at odds with the scent of Umbria's truffles. There are other tells too: A truffle that has been discovered locally that morning will have moisture on its surface. If it has sat in a truck for days, there might not be any. A hunter trying to sell Romanian product might suddenly offer much larger quantities than he's ever able to hunt or collect himself. Romanian suppliers won't usually allow single-kilo purchases. Giuseppina is a master of all these subtleties.

Not all buyers are as rigorous or ethical as Giuseppina. The number of "Alba" truffles sold globally each year far outpaces the region's—and even the entire country's—estimated supply. There are simply not enough truffles in Alba to account for all the truffles and truffle products that are presented as having originated there. One key Romanian dealer, whom I briefly spoke with as he was traveling for business in the U.K., referred my questions to an Italian shop called Alba Tartufi, one of his best clients, and then proceeded to ignore all further communications. The shop doesn't advertise any Romanian truffles on its website. But actually catching a seller for this graft is almost impossible; it would involve tracking single pieces of truffle all the way to the anonymous hunters at the start of the supply chain and proving that the final actors deliberately mislabeled or otherwise misrepresented their geographic provenance upon sale.

The most serious frauds involve a counterfeit species. This type of deceit is far more lucrative but riskier from a legal perspective. With geographic frauds, the hunters and traders work on higher margins, but they need boatloads of cash to buy the still-expensive product. Cheap, impostor species offer a more compelling economic incentive. The two main Chinese truffles species—*Tuber indicum* and *Tuber himalayensis*—cost as little as $30 to $100 per kilo and appear nearly identical to the expensive European black truffle. One trader told me they smell and taste about as good as a battered tennis ball. But when mixed into bags of *Tuber melanosporum*, *Tuber indicum* takes on the luxury scent. Too much reddish Sichuan soil, though, could expose the con before it begins.

Desert truffles, members of the *Terfezia* genus, that grow in the sands of Morocco, Tunisia, and Libya, cost about as much as Chinese truffles and look enough like white truffles, *Tuber magnatum pico*, and *bianchetti*, *Tuber borchii*, to dupe an untrained nose. Most Italian traders refuse to even use the word "truffle" in relation to the desert fungus. The truffle deceits began as early as the nineteenth century, when, in 1876, *All the Year Round*, an encyclopedia-like journal edited by Charles Dickens, called desert truffles a "poor tasteless sham." Identifying and plucking out the inferior product from large batches become much more time-consuming and expensive than a reasonable truffle trader or company can afford. Even though the impostor species hold relatively little monetary or culinary worth, they move into circulation with relative ease. Sabatino is one of the few companies that conducts spot checks, using microscopes and, if suspicions are aroused, DNA analysis.

Neither desert truffles nor Chinese truffles can be legally sold for consumption inside Italy. But one or two nodes on a vast, unregulated supply chain can slip them into real batches to make a huge illicit profit while denying the end consumers the pleasure they're paying for. Producers of carpaccios, sauces, and oils can use whatever truffles (or, more likely, none at all) they want and label them as the finest Alba whites and Umbria blacks. There are no truffle regulators to ensure the sanctity and purity of the product that ends up on plates across the world. All the industry has is its trusted middlemen, who often provide their buyers with an invoice that lists the truffle's scientific name and place of origin. But sometimes, even they can deceive themselves with fanciful logic.

When I asked Giuseppina if they'd ever encountered Romanian truffles that were rumored to be flowing in bulk throughout Italy, she was certain that they weren't a problem at Sabatino. "That's the difference between an industrial company and an artisan company," she said, implying that these were other companies' problems. Only Urbani Tartufi is larger than Sabatino.

Finding a large, round white Italian truffle is among the most delicate matters Sabatino and other quality buyers undertake. Giuseppina's hunters go into the woods knowing they'll recover a few black truffles, perhaps of less value than *melanosporum* (*Tuber uncinatum, aestivum,* or *brumale*), but whites are much harder to find and generally more difficult to keep intact. A dog that hunts for white truffle must be trained to resist the urge to dig and scoop and instead point to its location with its snout. Otherwise, the fragile white, which is usually found deeper in the earth, cracks or breaks into smaller pieces inside the dog's mouth. "Not all dogs are suitable for white truffle hunting," Giuseppina said. "A good truffle hunter will train dogs to do both. The [dog] that's not so good will just do black." The white truffle's rarity, especially in full form and from the most renowned regions, is what makes them so expensive. Some sellers have set prices at as much as $7,000 per kilo.

Broken pieces of white truffle are not nearly as valuable. In that way, pricing a truffle is not unlike evaluating a fine artwork or jewel, checking the canvas or surface for structural flaws. The cut matters too: the more round and the less bumpy, the better. A perfect two-hundred-gram white truffle sells for much more than its imperfect five-hundred-gram counterpart. Giuseppina refers to the misshapen ones as *tartufi al cervello,* or "brain truffles."

An adept buyer like Giuseppina has more than just integrity, savvy negotiation skills, and an art buyer's eye; she also has the nose of a master sommelier. What might look like a perfect truffle from the outside may lack the olfactory qualities that make it transcendent at the table. Giuseppina can shut her eyes and identify whether there's something off about the specimen she holds. Her taste for cigarettes—she stepped out of our meeting for a jolt of nicotine—might have weakened her lungs, but it hadn't thrown off her scent. "My nose is good," she said. Training someone to see with her nose can take years.

No one had managed to describe the scent of a white truffle quite so poetically as Giuseppina. "The white truffle is like a primary color," she said when I asked her about the scent. "It's like nothing else. It's like saying, 'What does red look like?'" The winter black truffle could be compared to the smell of the woods or mushrooms, with a hint of chocolate. But the white is different, she said. "It's the king of kings."

The difficulty of finding even a small one with a nice shape was why, when a Sabatino hunter called Giuseppina in 2014, saying that he had unearthed a perfect, round nearly two-kilo truffle, he was a bit nervous. The dog who discovered it was quite young. The night he found it, he took it home and sleeplessly guarded the fridge until someone could drive it to Sabatino. "It's not NASA," Giuseppina said, noting her amusement at the security protocols the hunter had established. Neither Giuseppina nor any of the other staff had seen something so large. There was legend about a two-kilo truffle that was discovered in Umbria a century ago, but it seemed apocryphal. Seeing this one made everyone at the warehouse a bit emotional; it ended up weighing in as the largest white truffle ever to be discovered in history.

Giuseppina arranged for its shipment to headquarters in the United States. She and Federico decided to auction it off and give the proceeds to charity. Two truffles, each less than half this one's size, had sold in 2010 for $330,000 to the Macau casino tycoon and truffle lover Stanley Ho. Some observers, including CBS, suggested this one might attract bids as high as $1 million. But, for whatever reason, a bidding war never began. In an auction held at Sotheby's Manhattan offices on a Saturday morning, a Taiwanese buyer secured the winning bid by phone and shelled out a disappointing

$61,250, a mere $30,625 per kilo, for the pleasure of shaving it over plates at what was surely a lavish dinner.

—

Downstairs on the factory floor, we stood around a table where four women, who wore Sabatino hats and aprons and lab coats over their civilian clothes, worked scrupulously to brush off small fresh whites, which they plucked from a traditional blue, red, and white Italian cloth. The women had the same stern focus of sculpture artists putting the final chisels into their marble masterpieces. They stared down, picking and brushing and turning the truffles until the dirt was reduced to crumbs and dust in buckets and on paper mats on the metal table in front of them. The strong scent of garlic and mountains rose from the table into the cool air as they worked. But there was something else too, some quality that defied description.

One of the women was concerned that given the amount of dirt on a particular portion of the truffle she was holding, there was an unsightly hole underneath it. Giuseppina peered down at the truffle intently, picked off some dirt, and concluded there was no cause for concern. She compared the delicate process to the restoration of a fine painting. In a way, they were brushing the dirt layers off the truffle to give consumers the highest experience of the art. The women were gentle in their work; an overzealous pick could lop off hundreds of euros in value.

On the floor behind us, a Willy Wonka–esque machine produced bottles of truffle cream. Another contraption pasteurized truffles, a process that would allow them to be stored for at least four years. A new machine, wrapped in plastic, was designed to wash finished product.

Surveillance cameras tracked our movements. When night

fell, alarms would be set throughout the property. Giuseppina was hesitant about photographs of the specific machinery because of the risk of leaking trade secrets. Most of the machines are custom-made for Sabatino because machine manufacturers don't generally produce machines tailored to truffles.

Despite all the modern machinery, the truffles must first pass through a traditional evaluation process that is probably not much different from the one her great-grandfather Sabatino subjected hunters in the area to more than a hundred years ago. "The worms are still worms," she had said earlier as we looked at one of the company's first vehicles and an old cash register that had been used at the grocery store that was the family's start in business. "The stones are still stones."

"It's an unusual world," Giuseppina remarked back upstairs, at the long wooden conference table facing the hilly forest where truffle hunters were likely at work. "Because it's a world that doesn't have an official market." Many of the hunters, traders, and smaller companies operate in the shadows. "In life, there is always a short-cut," she said. "The companies who want to pass on their work from father to son have to do things the right way." Otherwise, she said, "how long can they last?"

In the land of the white truffle, in northern Italy, the first middle-man I was scheduled to meet left me with his brother, a champion truffle dog trainer, because he had to race off in his black Mercedes to sell a 1.5-kilogram white truffle at a market across the border in Nice. His brother later explained that he accommodated the whims of oligarchs who flew in for lunch on helicopters from Monte Carlo. Fabio Capello, the renowned Italian soccer coach, was also a client.

Perhaps more mysterious than the man in the Mercedes or, for that matter, any other middleman was someone the veterinarian in Asti, Remo Damosso, mentioned in passing: a white truffle trader who supposedly dominated the northern Italian restaurant market. At first, Damosso refused to give my translator and me his contact information, but eventually he agreed.

We arranged to meet the middleman at a combination bar, pizzeria, and truffle shop he owned in a parking lot at the center of Asti. The night was cold and thick with fog, making street and building lights eerie orbs in the indecipherable distance. The bar resembled something of an old-style diner or deli; there was a counter taking orders in one room and a row of tables under an arched ceiling with plastic siding in another. The garlic undertone of white truffle wafted through the air. Sandrino Romanelli, the middleman, sat down with us at a table soon after we arrived. The structure was quite clearly designed for more temperate weather; wind slipped right through the crevices, but he seemed content sitting in the cold.

Sandrino had a beer belly, a clean-shaven face, and blue-brown eyes and wore a black neck warmer as a hat over a mop of gray hair, which had a tinge of yellow left over from his younger blond days. He was fifty-one, and he struck me almost immediately as someone operating somewhere on the moral periphery. Part of it was the bluster of the hustle: He always seemed in a detectable state of slight distraction, thinking or talking or texting about business matters at his bar, or at his restaurant, Tartufo d'Oro, a few blocks away, or his truffle trade, which seemed to follow him wherever he was. He spoke brashly, the volume and tone of his bellow constantly suggesting that he was the only one who could be right.

He slouched back, with one arm resting on the back of the chair beside him and the other hand sloppily gesturing as he spoke. During the course of the evening, he openly tugged at and caressed more than one woman who was trying to talk to him. He didn't care about the image he was projecting in front of a reporter, his employees, or his customers. Maybe he didn't need to. He was one of the most powerful and important white truffle traders in Asti, if not the whole region of Piedmont. The vet attested to this fact, stories in the local press confirmed it, and Sandrino himself made this clear from the outset. As he drank, his confidence slipped into arrogance and then gradually slithered toward cruelty. Occasionally, he made what seemed like an earnest remark, but it was almost instantly punctuated by several other pronouncements that didn't comport with widely accepted truths of the trade.

When he was twenty-one, his girlfriend gifted him a puppy, which he soon took to the woods. By his own characterization, he became a talented hunter. He used money he had saved through his hunts to open the bar, which was nothing fancy but enjoyed good foot traffic and was conveniently located for someone who wanted to do business at Asti's open-air market. The bar allowed him the cash flow to enter the truffle trade as a middleman, and his success in the trade eventually allowed him to open his restaurant.

Sandrino was clearly proud of the American connections in his portfolio: He sold truffles to Robert De Niro, and almost immediately upon our meeting he name-dropped his longtime connection to Tony May, the Manhattan restaurateur who became well known for his management of the iconic Rainbow Room, San Domenico, and most recently SD26. Tony was how he'd found his way into the high-profile American export market. He was flying to the septuagenarian's birthday party in Marrakesh the following weekend; they had been good friends for many years.

American kitchens don't care what kinds of truffles he provides them; when they call, all they ask for is truffles. Not white truffles from Alba or Piedmont, the most expensive and best tasting according to local chefs and hunters, or black winter truffles from Umbria's Norcia, the most famous place for Italy's wild winter blacks. Just *truffles* so they can satisfy the prerequisites of a luxury establishment and please their wealthy, and perhaps image-conscious, clientele. The origin and quality of the truffles are secondary to possessing them. In Italy, the truffle is something you savor. In America, he suggested, the truffle is a status symbol you procure for the enjoyment of your tablemates. He counts the Trump restaurant chain, among others, as clients.

Urbani Tartufi, the world's largest truffle company, doesn't have the connections that Sandrino has, according to Sandrino. The larger, industrial companies are more focused on volume and profit, which means they're most concerned with their derivative products: oils, butters, and creams. This leaves an opportunity for people like Sandrino to deliver fresh, whole truffles to American restaurants that need them and don't want to deal with the administrative back channels and added costs of a corporation. American restaurateurs and chefs know they can call Sandrino directly and get a comparatively cheap and reliable three kilos of white truffles quickly.

Sandrino works with three favored traders, or sub-middlemen, who have networks of hunters they call upon, but he also buys directly from the hunters who meet him at the bar or his restaurant. To keep costs down, he does not serve white truffles at his restaurant; he reserves them for his trading and export business.

Where his Alba white truffles actually come from is something Sandrino considers irrelevant. He is of the mind that an Alba truffle, defined as a truffle found in the foothills outside the famous truffle city or in the wider region of Piedmont, could actually be purchased from southern Italy. This loose definition, of course, puts him at odds with honest hunters, traders, and chefs who believe that truffles from the northern region boast a magnificent advantage over those of other regions. They believe that it contains something—some special essence—that cannot be replicated in other Italian soils. Italian law backs their belief: A trader cannot misrepresent the regional origins of his truffles. Philosophically, this makes Sandrino something between a conscientious objector and a huckster, perhaps a characterization that depends mostly on the ethics of the beholder. Sandrino finds the regional distinction hollow; if it were the same species, *Tuber magnatum pico,* it could be sourced from anywhere in the country, he told me. "In Italy, all white truffles are truffles of Alba," he said. However, given years of regional marketing combined with what hunters believe is a more sophisticated smell and taste profile, truffles from Alba simply cost more, which weakens his argument considerably. What Sandrino was suggesting was not unlike selling Napa Valley wines from Virginia. It would not sit well with customers, even if they were unable to discern any difference in taste. To hunters in Piedmont, who believe that something from the *terroir* makes these white truffles more spectacular than ones found in other regions, it is fraud of the highest level. Italian authorities agree, and they pursue regional mislabeling with verve.

But he believes the pursuit of this kind of regional fraud is borne of ignorance. And he takes his twisted logic a step further, to a place of delusion. A good truffle from Croatia, he said, could beat a bad truffle found in the Roero hills outside Alba, as long as it is not waylaid for too long in the back of a van's freezer. A white truffle is a white truffle. But even if that is so—and many Italian hunters, law enforcement officials, and chefs would argue that it's not—why, then, not sell it as a white truffle from Croatia rather than misrepresent it as a white truffle from Alba? If Croatian truffles are so wondrous, then why not become an evangelist for them by calling them what they really are? That's where Sandrino's logic begins to falter. The prices are different for a reason—valid or not.

Sandrino doesn't believe traders should be hassled over the regional origins of their truffles, but he's not against legal traceability, as long as consumers are educated that not all truffles grown in Piedmont are actually the most flavorful. "I want exact, true information spread," he said, except, that is, for the true origin of his truffles. He wants to see other myths dispelled as well. Traders are not fat cats who simply profit off the backs of hunters. Purchasing quantities of raw product from truffle hunters is a very expensive proposition; traders spend large amounts of their money simply purchasing their wares. If the cash on hand goes to financing an expensive lifestyle, there's nothing left to pay hunters enough to persuade them to keep coming back. Traders do not become millionaires, he said; though, it's easy to see how myths like this get started: Sandrino's own wallet is stuffed, to the point of over spilling, with a wad of euros thicker than his forearm.

Executives at companies like Sabatino and Urbani, the ones that specialize in derivatives and whom he claims he can sometimes outcompete on fresh truffle sales, are the ones who sell enough volume to become rich, he said. But, he admitted, the traders who, like him, sell to these companies are the ones in the supply chain who generate the largest rates of profit.

Most of the truffles Sandrino buys are unearthed in the foothills and valleys in the province of Asti. Some come from other areas of Italy. In the past, he has purchased from Croatia. He always looks for quality and usually that comes down to specific patches of forest and the hunters who work them. One spot in Asti can produce a perfect white truffle; a stand of forest a hundred meters away can produce foul ones. Quality, not origin, is what matters to Sandrino.

The true fraud, according to Sandrino, comes in the form of selling poor-quality truffles or cheating customers on weights. His opinion on this matter became clear when I asked him about the case of Dario Pastrone, a trader at the Asti market.

In 2007, Pastrone was driving on a narrow mountain road between Chiusano and Asti, when another vehicle tailgated him, then pulled so tightly against his side that he was run off the road. Three men identified themselves as police officers before asking where he was storing his drugs. Confused, he acceded to their search, and before long the "police" had stolen €2,000 worth of white truffles from his trunk, pummeled him, and left him at the side of the road. I had assumed that Pastrone was a victim, clear and simple. But then Pastrone refused to talk to me about the incident, saying that he didn't want to reflect back on the traumatic episode. A provincial police officer told me that it was a simple theft, and there wasn't too much more to the story than that. He added that Pastrone was not a very attractive-looking man, and when he saw him at the Asti market after the incident, "he was even uglier."

Sandrino had an even less charitable view. Though at first he didn't want to say anything about a rival, he explained that Pastrone had developed a reputation for selling bad truffles, both of poor quality—unripe, soft—and of fraudulent weight. "He's a piece of shit," Sandrino said. Violence at the market was rare, but Sandrino implied that Pastrone's continued deception had inspired the revenge attack. Sandrino showed absolutely no sign of sympathy for the man's misfortune; it was clear that he believed Pastrone got what he deserved.

When he was done telling me this, Sandrino invited me to join him for dinner at his restaurant a few blocks away.

Tartufo d'Oro, the Golden Truffle, was supposed to be the nicer of Sandrino's two spots. But it was an average kind of place, the kind of just-above-seedy restaurant that you might imagine a guy like Sandrino would run. There was a bar at the front, a framed newspaper clipping about Tony May on the wall, and holes in the ground for toilets in the back restrooms. It had a 3.5-star rating on TripAdvisor, based on eighty-nine reviews.

Not long after we took a seat at a table near the back of the restaurant and Sandrino insisted I order a pizza, two truffle hunters walked through the front door. There was an air of forest and hope about them. I figured that Sandrino would conduct his truffle trading in a more private locale, but it soon became apparent that he planned to do the deal right there, at the front bar. The middle-aged hunters held two bags of white truffles forth, and Sandrino called behind the bar for a scale. The first truffle, round and large, was unwrapped from its paper towel sheath, and Sandrino set it on the scale. It weighed in at just under 100 grams. As soon as he registered the weight, he pulled his wad from his pocket and handed the man €260. The second man handed Sandrino another bag, and Sandrino gingerly placed each of the six or seven smaller truffles on the scale. One of them had a large hole, the result of a burrowing worm. Together, they weighed in at 140 grams. He put them back in the bag and handed it back. The hunter flashed Sandrino a look of disappointment, and then the men turned to leave just as quickly as they came.

Back at the table, Sandrino explained that a collection of smaller truffles was useless compared with the larger, nicely shaped one he had bought. He alternately drank red wine and beer and ate a risotto with clams. "Is good pizza for you?" he asked, in a vaguely menacing manner that enforced polite affirmation and gratitude. As the night wore on, he became even louder and more imperious. He always commanded attention when he spoke, but the alcohol seemed to make him bask in the power of his domain.

After eating and a fair amount of drinking, an old, wrinkled, red-haired Ukrainian woman dressed in a dark overcoat and sweater walked in and doddered up to our table. She sat down in a chair that was pulled up to the side, looking exhausted and slightly wary of the impending exchange.

She had discovered truffle hunting in a most curious manner. As a nurse for an eighty-year-old patient, she accompanied the man into the woods for truffle hunts in the last weeks of his life. When he died, she adopted his dog and took on the trade herself. Now she is a nurse by day and a truffle hunter by night.

She pulled out her white truffles, wrapped in aluminum foil and paper towels, and placed them on the table in front of Sandrino. There were five small ones, a couple larger ones, and a broken piece. He again called out to the waitstaff for a scale. In the meantime, Sandrino weighed them with his hands and breathed in their scent. He handled them in a delicate but hurried way. He seemed uncertain in his determination of their quality. He passed them to one of his buyers, who had joined us at the table. And then they were passed to me. They smelled potent, of garlic and forest air. The wad of cash reappeared.

The woman advised him that they weighed 151 grams. Sandrino said 148.

The scale arrived: 173 grams. The haggling began. He tried to hand her a few bills, around €280, and she slapped the money back at him and scowled. She shook her head at the thought of accepting the offer. Her Italian was limited, so she didn't have much leverage. Sandrino's domineering personality was only amplified during the one-sided negotiation process.

"Come on," Sandrino said. "Have a glass of wine. Have a drink, a piece of cake. You don't like it? Go." He suggested, arrogantly, that she keep both the money and the truffles and decide which she wanted to give back when she came into the restaurant the next time.

With the money on the table, she reconsidered the offer. Sandrino was her only middleman, and certainly the only one whom she could meet late at night, after work. If she didn't sell them to him, she likely wouldn't sell them at all.

Finally, she relented, picked up the cash, and walked out into the fog.

# CHAPTER EIGHT

# Detectives and Fraudsters

WHEN ROBERTA UBALDO, AN OFFICER IN THE STATE FORESTRY CORPS, reported to the organization's gated beige compound on the edge of downtown Asti, Italy, in 2012, the memo had already arrived from Rome. The top commanders had ordered an investigation to ensure that sellers at agricultural fairs across Italy were adhering to financial requirements governing the purchase and sale of foraged goods. In Piedmont's Asti province, officers quickly focused on checking middlemen's declared purchases against the quantities of truffles they were trying to sell.

Commander Renato Diodà, the Forestry Corps's leader in Asti, tasked Ubaldo—a petite woman whose oversized gray military regalia draped around her frame like a quilt held for warmth—with reviewing the financial documents that flooded in during the course of the checks. She combed through the files carefully, peering through brown-framed glasses to search for oddities. When her thin eyebrows rose, she called the middlemen to request further information and secured search warrants to evaluate documentation held at local notaries and the chamber of commerce. She had received her degree in forestry sciences and worked as an academic researcher before joining the corps, so she was comfortable burying herself in mounds of paperwork and skilled at divining meaning from numbers. She was at ease with the quiet, but even from the start the paperwork seemed to scream that something was off.

Early in the investigation, Diego Grizi, one of Ubaldo's colleagues, approached several truffle traders in plain clothes at the main truffle fair in Asti, posing as an interested buyer. During the course of his rounds, he noticed one man who had not set out tags listing the origin of the Piedmont white truffles he was selling. Though prepared by the sellers themselves, the origin tags introduce at least some degree of accountability to the process, because they can be checked against dealers' purchasing paperwork. Grizi, an athletic man with dark eyes, short-cropped hair, and a stubble beard, asked the trader for some kind of confirmation that the truffles were really from Asti's foothills. He didn't have any.

"Who are you?" the trader asked. "What do you want from me?"

Grizi and his partner identified themselves as investigators with the Forestry Corps and asked him for the "self-invoices" he was required to prepare on behalf of the truffle hunters he purchased from. The Italian system makes it the responsibility of the middleman, as the buyer, to document the Latin scientific name of the truffle species, the corresponding Italian name, the location of origin, and the quantity purchased from truffle hunters.

The man fidgeted, covered up his truffles, and hurriedly packed them into a bag. As he was preparing to leave, Grizi asked for the documentation again. The trader shoved one of Grizi's colleagues out of the way and sprinted down the street. Grizi and other corps officers pursued him on foot through the streets of Asti.

Panting, they ran after him for about a mile. Before they could catch up, he hopped into a car and escaped.

Back at the corps's offices, the reason the trader fled gradually became apparent as Ubaldo and the team worked through the financial documents. What began as a check to ensure adherence to basic administrative rules quickly developed into a full-scale fraud investigation. The Asti truffle market had been plagued by systemic deception.

Officers interviewed witnesses. They tracked paperwork. They examined the activities of at least a hundred different companies. Finally, after months of investigation, Ubaldo and the rest of her team found that roughly 75 percent of the white Piedmont truffles moving across the Asti market originated in Italian regions far away from the famed territory, including the central region of Umbria and the southern region of Molise. As soon as the truffles arrived on the tables of the Asti middlemen, though, they "became" truffles from Piedmont. They remained that way, of course, until they reached dining rooms. Roughly 15 percent of the Piedmont whites in Asti didn't even originate within Italy's borders: Traders bought them from hunters working on Croatia's Istrian Peninsula. Altogether, more than 90 percent of the truffles didn't come from Alba's famous soil, making wholesale prices among suppliers much cheaper than what hunters working the local hills would have accepted, and the profit margins for dealers much steeper.

Together, during the course of the investigation, the companies included in the dragnet bought and sold more than €5 million worth of product. But truffles have a way of disappearing, into company trucks, onto international markets, and into eaters' mouths. Despite the immensity of the fraudulent activity they detected, the Forestry Corps was able to physically seize a mere thirteen kilos of truffles after traders were unable to show any formal documentation proving where the products came from.

⬧

Many traders in Asti knew the international value of the Alba and Piedmont names, and for years they had capitalized on it by selling the same species from less renowned regions and countries. Buying an authentic, whole Alba white truffle allows an aristocrat to demonstrate that, contrary to belief, wealth *can* buy some measure of happiness, as long as sensory ecstasy and experiential beauty are what you desire. This is something rich people like, and pay, to think. But the rich who pay to think such things can also be unwilling to ask questions that rip them from a predetermined understanding of what money makes possible. In recent years, the volume of truffles found in Piedmont has declined precipitously because of rising temperatures, declining summer rainfall, and the expansion of grapevines and other crops to previously foraged landscapes. White truffles are simply scarcer in Piedmont than in other lesser-known regions. No amount of money can will more of them into existence.

Yet despite the dwindling supply, at restaurants across the world, white truffles are almost always marketed as being from Piedmont or Alba. "Do the math," Ken Frank, an American chef who runs La Toque in Napa and has been working with truffles since the 1970s, said flatly. "They can't all buy truffles from Alba."

Asti truffle hunters believe that the truffle found in their region is the best in Italy and therefore the world. But they know local traders who sell one to three kilos at a time directly to restaurants from Dubai to New York City often don't care where their truffles actually come from and often buy the cheapest possible supply, meaning the most honest hunters can often be left without willing buyers. The market parking lots are filled with cars with license plates from southern Italy, Tuscany, and Acqualagna. No matter where the truffles come from, the traders always sell them at the official price, set by Asti's chamber of commerce. Unless the middleman or chef personally knows the hunter he's buying truffles from and knows the area he hunts in, there is no way to verify any white truffle they sell or serve is from Italy, let alone Piedmont.

To buy the best of an already extremely rare product, you must submit to the suspension of disbelief. The allure and romance of the luxury have a way of erasing objectivity. The truffle middleman sells a product, but he also sells a story, the one that places the buyer on a hill, in a thicket of oaks that sprawls toward the Po River. Those who can afford to buy white truffles often do so without interrogating the architecture of this narrative.

Ubaldo's checks with the chamber of commerce revealed that there were at least two shell truffle suppliers that had never registered with the state. Italy's tax office had no record of the companies' existence. The phantom firms shipped in Croatian truffles and sold them off the books to middlemen in Asti, leaving about the same trace as a hunter would, even though their total sales came in at around €2.5 million.

One of the companies had ties to Romania and had an office near Rome, an area not well known for its wealth of truffles. This company was providing middlemen in Piedmont with truffles shipped in from Ukraine. Not enough evidence was assembled against the executives at the Romanian supplier to file criminal fraud charges.

During the siege, the investigators also came across 550 kilos' worth of *Terfezia*, or desert truffles, that had been smuggled across the Mediterranean from Morocco. Moroccan truffles cannot be legally sold within Italy, but their import is authorized for private consumption and for preparation in derivatives, like truffle oils, which can then be exported to international buyers. One trader had paid suppliers about €6.50 per kilo for the desert truffles and then turned around and sold some of them as *bianchetti*, or *Tuber borchii*, to a few upper-class restaurants in Milan, where customers are willing to pay rates of €500 per kilo.

The Italian scientist Gianluigi Gregori, who has served as an expert witness in court proceedings for fraud involving the North African species, says one easy way to tell them apart is their hard surface. "If you throw it at a wall, the wall will break down," he said. The other tell is the lack of an extraordinary scent profile, something he compared to "an orchestra"—or, in the case of the *Terfezia*, something closer to a high school garage band.

In 2004, Gregori attended a conference in Rabat. There, the king of Morocco led him into a sandy forest where he had a chance to watch a completely different kind of truffle hunting than he'd observed back home. Groups of women flitted about the sand, carrying large sticks. They gravitated toward the places where white-and-yellow desert lilies sprouted from the ground. If the stick moved down with ease, the women kept on. If there was resistance, they stopped and dug.

Soon, the women had filled several large bags with their spoils. Gregori asked one of the women where they would take the bags.

"To the airport in Casablanca," she said.

"But where to?" Gregori clarified.

"Italy," she said. "Acqualagna."

The truffles were bound for a company based there, called Marini.

The fraud lasted two or three years, before the Italian government made it harder to get *Terfezia* truffles past customs. Marini remains in operation today.

When we spoke, Gregori and I were dining at a restaurant near Acqualagna that stood at the foot of forested mountains filled with wild truffles. At some point, I noticed that Gregori, a man who had devoted his life to the study of truffles, had opted for pasta topped with porcini.

❧

The restaurants in Ubaldo's investigation advertised the Moroccan truffles on the menu as Piedmontese *bianchetti*, but investigators were unable to determine whether the chefs and owners knew they were fraternizing with a fraudster. Portions of the 550-kilo shipment, apparently advertised honestly as desert truffles, were sent to companies in Germany, Spain, and Austria.

By the time I met with Ubaldo at her office in November 2015, the trader had paid administrative fines for selling Moroccan product within the country, but his trial on fraud charges—of actually passing it off as *bianchetto*—was still ongoing. She suspected that the Romanian company they caught smuggling in Ukrainian truffles was still providing its wares to Asti middlemen. None of the major traders charged had been previously convicted, and none were effectively shuttered because of the crimes. In fact, all of the traders and companies investigated were still actively operating when we spoke.

By the end of the Forestry Corps's work, it had sent the names of fourteen middlemen to the prosecutor's office, with evidence that they had profited from fraudulent mislabeling. I later discovered, in reading about the trials in the local press, that one of those men was the middleman I had dined with: Sandrino Romanelli.

Investigators discovered that Romanelli, who was identified by local newspapers as the most powerful trader charged, had sold at least seven kilos of Croatian and Molise truffles to Asti's own municipal government and at least two more kilos to restaurants, including at least one in Manhattan. Given his relationship with Tony May and the fact that he was honored as a special guest at a truffle dinner held at SD26 during roughly the same time period as the investigation, those unknowing guests might have been eating Croatian truffles marked as Italian. An Italian truffle news site, which posted about the trial, published an old photograph of a younger Sandrino—white truffle in hand—leaning in between Robert De Niro and Andrea Bocelli, the renowned Italian opera tenor.

In a court appearance in June 2014, Sandrino's defense attorney, Maurizio Lattanzio, questioned the then-retired forestry commander Renato Diodà about the investigation. "Truffles have no license plate," Diodà told the court, explaining the difficulty of building a case. "Ours was a job on the basis of accounting and descriptions made in the bills." Having seen Sandrino buy truffles and knowing his philosophy on geographic differences, I found it hard to imagine that he kept a vigorous accounting of his purchases. When he bought the truffles at the restaurant, he ate, drank, mingled, and argued. He did not take any notes.

But in March of 2016, the court acquitted Sandrino and six

other middlemen and hunters on fraud charges. Lattanzio had convinced the court that when Sandrino sold Alba truffles, he was simply using a commercial shorthand for Italy's white truffle and not referencing the truffle's actual provenance. Because every trader sold Alba truffles not from Piedmont, the label, he argued, had become legally meaningless. This might explain the confidence with which Sandrino spoke about his misleading business practices. But the actual statute and the law enforcement officials who continue their thankless jobs in enforcing it don't agree with this high-flying legal analysis.

In the years since the investigation's conclusion, Ubaldo became the commander of the Asti province. Past a first-floor waiting room with illustrations of different types of fungi hanging on the walls, her corner office on the second floor looks out into the canopies of towering trees on a lawn at the back of the building. A framed poster read, "Funghi garanzia per il bosco." "Mushrooms guarantee for the forest." On the L-shaped desk, a small journal, with flowers and a butterfly on its cover, sat next to a stack of paperwork about the criminal investigation.

Her love of the environment and her desire to protect the earth drove her to the job, but her smiles of amusement seemed to indicate that the wiliness of the con men was what intrigued her enough to stay. Since the crimes, the Forestry Corps has completed major media campaigns to warn Asti buyers about the possibility of deceit at the markets and to check tags of origin and scales before agreeing to buy product. Of course, there are food safety implications for being able to trace products to their origin; contaminated or otherwise unsafe foods must be traceable to help prevent illness outbreaks. But Ubaldo was particularly concerned that geographic truffle fraud hurt the hunters and traders who spend the time and money to comb the local landscapes and markets looking for the rarest of the rare. The fraud also endangered the reputation of the true taste of the authentic Piedmont truffle.

She believes that if the trade relied less on all-cash deals (current rules do not subject cash sales under €1,000 to tax-reporting requirements), it would drive more transparency about how much and what kinds of truffles people were actually selling. It would be difficult not to draw attention from authorities if sales figures could be checked against claims of origin; there are only so many Piedmont truffles available for foraging each year.

Ubaldo and her team continue to do patrols at the market, often in full uniform, to remind traders that they are being watched.

All this investigation of small-time truffle dealers might seem like a lark, but European food fraud is a quickly expanding phenomenon, often linked to the interests of organized crime. NAS, the carabinieri's food and health crime division, investigates food fraud the way the FBI investigates terrorism. In thirty-eight different offices throughout Italy, with more than a thousand officers, the organization works tirelessly to catch fraudsters and remove counterfeit food from the shelves. They often receive approval for full-scale surveillance operations: They tail suspects with cameras, track trucking routes with GPS devices, plant bugs, and monitor email wiretaps. When they raid warehouses and manufacturing facilities, they carry guns.

The fraudsters they attempt to catch are organized and dangerous. When Sergio Tirrò, a former major on the force with dirty blond hair, a serious stare, and the air of a European cosmopolitan, once arrived at an olive oil factory somewhere in southern Italy, dressed in his black and red military fatigues, he and his three colleagues thought they were prepared for what they would discover once inside. When they breached the doors, they found ten men, all unwilling to surrender. They began to attack. "They do not have any problem in facing the police," Tirrò, who now works at Europol, told me. Everyone at the warehouse was arrested.

The men were participating in a fraud that had overtaken the world's olive oil supply. They purchased large batches of cheap sunflower oil and transformed it into something resembling extra virgin olive oil using a mixture of chlorophyll, carotene, and food dye. The resulting product would sell for twelve times its worth.

Olive oil is only one of many conventional Italian food products that has attracted the interest of organized crime groups. The buffalo cattle breeders for *mozzarella di bufalo* are under the surveillance of the Camorra Mafia. When NAS officers arrive to take samples of blood, milk, or hair, to ensure the animals are healthy, intimidating men have grabbed the samples right out of the officials' hands and shattered them on the ground. Near Naples, the men who transport trucks of wine and olive oil are known to carry pistols.

Organized crime groups have created fraudulent, mirror supply chains for Italian and French champagnes and wines. They create the beverage; manufacture or broker deals for bottles, foils, and caps; hire designers to manufacture counterfeit labels; build external distribution teams to get it into international grocery stores; and suddenly they're selling fake bottles of Moët & Chandon, Bocelli Prosecco, Veuve Clicquot, and Brunello di Montalcino, among many others. Tirrò showed me a trophy case full of seized counterfeits in NAS's basement.

The criminal groups have even manufactured a counterfeit

ham stamper for Prosciutto di Parma. On one raid in 2012, the carabinieri seized 6,144 legs of ham stamped with the fake imprint. In a few seconds, the syndicate was turning cheap, conventional ham into some of the world's finest.

Over the last two decades, as Italian food became an ever-more-marketable good in the international marketplace, the Camorra, the 'Ndrangheta, and the Cosa Nostra Mafias began to see an easy way to produce illicit revenue. As with cocaine and heroin, the prices and demand were high. But unlike cocaine and heroin, the risks of detection were low. The Coldiretti, an Italian association of farmers and other food producers, estimates that each year criminal organizations, or the *agromafie,* make about $27 billion on counterfeit, mislabeled, or otherwise manipulated food and beverages. Law enforcement officials believe the revenue flows into and out of other illicit activities, including drug and human trafficking.

"We are talking about industries, not just a few people," Tirrò explained, after apologizing profusely for his garlic and onion breath, obtained from an authentic lunch with officials at Rome's Chinese embassy. He popped a mint into his mouth. Some countries don't view food labeling as seriously as the Italians, he noted. If mislabeling is discovered, national authorities might subject the fraudsters to an administrative penalty and demand label adjustments. But Tirrò doesn't understand this logic. "You cannot adjust crime," he said.

Truffle fraud does not require any of the counterfeit labeling required of other food frauds: The truffles normally ride unmarked in plastic bags, satchels, and paper towels and are often sold unlabeled, after inspection and negotiation. There are no lot codes, dates of harvest, or even paperwork about their origin, until a middleman prepares a self-invoice for a hunter. Unlike famous cheeses, hams, butters, vinegars, wines, and other Italian food products closely associated with specific regional histories and *terroir*, the truffle is not subject to protected designation of origin controls. Despite its cultural value, the truffle has never been an official good, with an official history and market, and its production isn't protected by the consortia, rules, and laws that govern products like Brunello wines or Parma ham. The geographic origin and scientific species of a truffle are the origin and species a seller can convince the buyer of. Unless the buyer happens to have Giuseppina Balestra's nose, fraud can only be detected with review underneath a microscope or by genetic analysis.

The Camorra could easily move in, but there haven't been any clear indications of their presence yet. Interpol suspects that organized crime groups are becoming increasingly interested in luxury food fraud because of the ease and low criminal risk of misrepresenting something only a real connoisseur would know was fake. In 2012, along with thirty tons of fake tomato sauce, around seventy-seven thousand kilograms of counterfeit cheese, nearly thirty thousand counterfeit candy bars, and various other goods, Interpol and Europol's Operation Opson ("food" in ancient Greek) received reports from various law enforcement agencies about two tons of fake caviar and truffles.

Various proposals from truffle-hunting associations about enforcing a more formal system of traceability, perhaps using hunters' license numbers—which correspond to the region they're permitted to hunt in—have been floated to the Italian Parliament with no result. This would make passing off foreign truffles more difficult, but like most other suggested solutions to criminal problems in this business, the industry power brokers have little interest in seeing it happen.

◆

Just as Ubaldo began working through her paperwork in 2012, one of Tirrò's NAS subordinates was beginning his own investigation 175 miles to the east, in the sleepy suburbs of Bologna. Some discerning truffle eaters had tipped the NAS unit off about a few restaurants in the area that were serving *bianchetto* truffles that didn't taste like the real thing. The commander of the unit assigned Paolo Fasciani to the case.

Fasciani, a portly, cheery fellow, smiles often and often for no particular reason but to signal his enjoyment of life. He can often be found in the back of the most traditional of Italy's restaurants, sampling the chef's pasta, forking over the extra money for the pleasure of fresh truffles shaved atop. He dresses nicely but only to a point. He wears a dress shirt, tie, sweater, slacks, and silver timepiece but finishes his outfit off with a quirk: tennis shoes. He has silver and black hair atop a jowly face and brown eyes. His hands are small, especially when held in comparison to his trunk-sized thighs and chubby midsection.

His personal email address starts with the name of a seasoned Jedi master: Obi-Wan. He speaks rapidly, with words bumping together at a clip that makes it seem as if his voice has trouble keeping up with his mind. He has an intimate understanding of the criminal system and can spot vulnerable crevices where he can collect useful leaks. What he lacks in physicality, in the ability to chase or disarm, he more than compensates for with instinct and wit. His commander speaks in slow, deliberate sentences; Fasciani speaks in paragraphs.

After college, Fasciani decided to join the academy at the carabinieri, with the intention of working either in the force's crime scene investigations unit or at NAS, where he could indulge one of his greatest passions: food. Before he could work on complex food investigations, though, he had to spend seven years as an officer doing mundane street work. When a spot in the course to become an investigative inspector for NAS opened up, he enrolled, and once he passed, he was assigned to the office in Bologna, where he began his first round of food fraud investigations.

He spoke with criminals, restaurateurs, diners, and food suppliers, always searching for the next big tip. Sometimes they came in anonymous emails or phone calls; occasionally, people walked right into the office. Fasciani wouldn't tell me where the tip about the truffles came from, but recently, he said, after a few high-profile frauds with products as prominent as Prosecco—Italian diners had become surprisingly savvy.

In supermarkets, people looked at labels and carefully evaluated prices. The information coming into the Bologna office must be pretty solid to warrant an investigation. Fasciani's investigations don't often get approval for wiretapping or video surveillance. Usually, the prosecutors in the area only provide that investigative privilege to pharmaceutical matters or if there's solid information about a serious risk to human health. The truffle case wouldn't get those kinds of approvals, but Fasciani decided to look anyway.

Fasciani paid a visit to the restaurant, in a small village in the province of Bologna, and asked the manager to see the truffles they were serving. When Fasciani looked inside the bag, a whiff of the *bianchetto*'s earthy perfume rose into his nostrils. But when he took one of the truffles out and allowed it to sit for a few minutes, the aroma evaporated. The restaurant was unable to identify the region that the truffle had come from with a set of required self-invoices.

All the restaurant owner could tell Fasciani was the name of the company, based in the province of Pistoia, that had sold him the product. Without being able to look at any paperwork, Fasciani and his comrades were forced to seize all of the restaurant's truffle product.

Fasciani and his team drove to another restaurant, this one closer to the heart of Bologna's city center, and found the same product in the kitchen. The product had come from the same source, a company in Tuscany, and both restaurants told Fasciani that they had paid the market price for *bianchetto*, anywhere from €100 to €500 per kilo. When the company representative brokered the deal, he asked the kitchens that they not prepare self-invoices recording the sale. Often, the company man would reduce prices and throw in other products, including other wild mushrooms or olive oil, to sweeten the deal.

After bringing the truffles back to the office as evidence, Fasciani contacted Alessandra Zambonelli, a mycology professor at the University of Bologna who is widely acknowledged as one of the world's leading experts on truffles, and told her that he needed help in identifying what these curious-looking truffles were. She conducted a genetic analysis.

The results proved the tipsters' hunch. They were not Italian *bianchetti* (*Tuber borchii*), as advertised on the menu, but belonged instead to the genetic species *Tuber oligospermum*, a type of desert truffle that thrives in the sands of the drier regions of the Mediterranean. In Tunisia, buyers can find one kilo for as little as ten cents. In Italy, they are not considered of any culinary value and are therefore banned from sale.

After further chemical analysis, Fasciani was notified that the scent he had taken in when he initially examined the bags was derived from a petroleum-based essence, likely bis(methylthio)methane, a product harmful to human health.

In coordination with another office of NAS, Fasciani secured a warrant to travel to Tuscany to perform a search of the small Tuscan company the restaurants had bought the truffles from. The team recovered one kilo of what appeared to be the same product they'd found back in Bologna and paperwork that indicated the product had come from Tunisia.

The company told Fasciani and the other NAS officials that it was not the only enterprise in the area hawking the Tunisian product. Many restaurants, even sophisticated ones with unblemished reputations, the owner said, were serving the Tunisian fungus. He knew because he had negotiated with the Tunisian smugglers who agreed to travel there, buy the product, and exchange it with him near the Italian border. During these meetings and subsequent dealings with others in the industry, he had become familiar with other movers in the illicit trade. He agreed to Fasciani's offer to become an informant. "Sometimes the small fish feels trapped," Fasciani said, "and then he starts speaking."

Fasciani followed the new intelligence to another restaurant in Bologna that the company said was selling the same smuggled product. There, the team discovered two jars filled with preserved, presliced *bianchetto*. As soon as Fasciani looked at it under good light, he suspected that the raw product had come from the North African desert. Uncapped, the jars had the same overpowering synthetic scent Fasciani had breathed in at the first restaurant; it was a clear tell. They seized the jars and provided them to Zambonelli, who confirmed the pieces had been sliced from a desert truffle.

People at the restaurant provided Fasciani with invoices to a company with an address in Bologna. It did not exist. The shut-tered company, they later realized, had changed its location and name. When they finally tracked it down, the proprietor provided them with the first real lead to the big fish. The jars of sliced truffle were produced by a much larger truffle company, based not in Bo-logna or Tuscany but on the Adriatic coast in the city of Fano, in the northeastern region of Marche.

Fasciani and his commander wouldn't reveal the identities of any of the companies, citing European privacy laws (the cases were proceeding through the courts when we spoke), but, they assured me, the one in Fano was "very well known."

When the NAS investigators arrived, they uncovered three hundred kilos of jars filled with sliced Tunisian truffles. The company was preparing to load the packages, filled with roughly €150,000 worth of mislabeled product, for an international ship-ment to Brazil. Officials at the company in Fano told NAS that there was still another company, based back in Bologna, that helped them import and export the Tunisian product.

The timing of the investigators' arrival was truly lucky. Pre-served and packaged truffle was rarely held in the warehouse for very long. When an order came in, it was fulfilled and shipped out. The manufacturing process—the arrival of the raw product, the slicing, the jars, the false labels—only lasted about two days. And they arrived on the day that it was to be trucked out of the factory, meaning the full scope and motives of the fraud were clearly vis-ible: Expensive labels had already been slapped on the worthless product. If they had come any sooner, when the raw product sat out or was still being sliced or jarred, a capable attorney could have batted the charges away.

How the larger company was able to smuggle the truffles

through customs was more difficult to pin down. It likely employed multiple smugglers, and the product likely came concealed in larger shipping containers filled with other miscellaneous goods. Border officials in Italy are trained to spot weapons and narcotics, not odorless desert truffles. It took Fasciani months of working with Zambonelli before he was able to grasp the subtleties of the industry or the differences between *Tuber borchii* and *Tuber oligospermum*. Only a small percentage of the containers receive any degree of serious scrutiny anyway. And even so, technically, as long as they are not mislabeled as *bianchetti* or white truffles upon their entrance, the import of desert truffles is not prohibited.

NAS froze the transport and sale of the Tunisian tubers at all four companies.

❦

Once seizures are made and a fraud is made public, other companies actively participating in the same fraud tend to back off. Perhaps they give up the game all together, or they prospect for another con in the business. After a series of seizures of *Terfezia*, companies and restaurants, for the most part, stopped trying to pass it off.

The risks of operating a criminal enterprise in the truffle industry remain low, though. Self-invoicing allows a motivated fraudster to declare that he purchased the fraudulent *bianchetti* from an anonymous hunter and not from a Tunisian courier. A company could invest very little and have huge returns, as long as it chose its collaborators wisely and weeded out snitches. "What other kind of product can cost €5,000 per kilo and that you find under a tree?" Fasciani asked.

Whenever an elite or luxury product is made affordable to the masses, Fasciani suggested, authenticity begins to erode to the point where the original product becomes almost irrelevant in comparison to its name. Fraudsters know the truffle's true taste or smell doesn't exist in the minds of people who've never actually shelled out the kind of money needed for fresh shavings, instead of often artificially flavored oils or creams. As truffles have exploded in popularity over the last decade, making truffle fries and truffle pizza a common sight on the menus of even the most decidedly non-luxury restaurants, so, too, have the possibilities for con men to cash in. People's abiding interest in buying the appearance of wealth will continue to pave the runway fraudsters need to thrive.

Fasciani told me he was actively developing another truffle investigation, speaking with informants and working in consultation with Zambonelli. The companies Fasciani had already caught weren't the only ones buying Tunisian product. He couldn't reveal specifics, but he claimed his leads were promising.

The truffle frauds haven't slowed down. Across Italy, vans and trucks are regularly pulled over, carrying loads of undeclared eastern European truffles. In 2017, the Guardia di Finanza, Italy's financial police, discovered a €66 million tax fraud among truffle producers, including some of the country's largest. In 2018, an Italian citizen was arrested in Turkey and held on more than €100,000 bail for attempting to smuggle twenty-six kilos of *Tuber borchii* out of the country and into Bulgaria. The truffle fraudsters operate boldly, as if they know people like Fasciani and Ubaldo have other investigations to pursue. They also understand who their target market is: diners looking to buy truffles for what they represent—class, wealth, refinement—rather than for what they really are.

# CHAPTER NINE

# The King's Ascent

AS OWNER OF THE OLDEST, LARGEST, AND MOST SUCCESSFUL TRUFFLE company in the world, Olga Urbani must manage her time carefully. She can't meet with just anyone. Unlike with Plantin's Christoph Poron and Sabatino's Federico Balestra, whom I communicated with directly, getting to her would require working through an intermediary and then an attaché.

Olga is the daughter of the late Paolo Urbani, once known throughout Italy as *re del tartufo*, or the "Truffle King," and the granddaughter of his father, the late Carlo, the man who showed the scientist Jim Trappe the company's armed guards in the 1960s. She manages the company's operations, legal and corporate affairs, public relations, and corporate image from international headquarters outside the small Umbrian village of Scheggino.

As the face of the company, Olga made a very public splash in 2012 on CBS's *60 Minutes* as one of the main sources for a program about fraud inside the industry. She accompanied the program's host, Lesley Stahl, on a truffle hunt on the family's property and later complained to the cameras about deceitful hunters and middlemen who try to pass off worthless Chinese truffles, or *Tuber indicum*, which cost as little as €20 a kilo, as valuable black winter truffles, or *Tuber melanosporum*.

She spoke with a strange, aristocratic affect, had a dark tan despite the cold, and wore a gigantic fur coat. Though she looked like the Italian version of Cruella de Vil, CBS casted her as a knowledgeable and earnest source.

⬧

Urbani's headquarters in Italy looks like any other corporate office, except that it sits above a two-lane road in the middle of a remote valley in the middle of nowhere. The large windows of its executive offices overlook the Valnerina valley's bright green fields, forested hills, and mountains of jagged beauty, which, when I arrived in late November, had been dusted with the season's first snow. Across the road, the Nera River runs through a lush tunnel of greenery. A giant Urbani Tartufi sign, with the company's signature truffle hunter–truffle dog logo, spun in circles against the slapping wind.

When I got to the front desk, I was introduced to Sylvia, a young and attractive attaché whom Olga had appointed to show me around. Before I'd have the opportunity to meet Olga, I'd have to go on a tour. I'd have to understand the family's legacy.

First, we accompanied an Urbani hunter as he sifted through one of the company's 123 acres of truffle orchards and forests. Luna, his dog, worked like a machine with few verbal instructions. The hunter said his favorite part of truffle hunting—besides having a quick, self-directed dog like Luna—is finding a lot of them. This seemed a perfect answer for someone who worked at a company that controlled a self-professed 70 percent of the global truffle market.

Next, Sylvia drove me on a narrow road to the tiny commune of Scheggino (population: 460) for a history lesson at Museo del Tartufo, which Olga opened in 2012 to honor the memory of her father, Paolo, who died in 2010. Sylvia, who, like most others who grow up in Umbria, ate the truffles her mother prepared for her once a week during the winters as a child, unlocked the doors to the stone building and darted around flicking on lights. The company's very first processing facility had operated here. Back then, in the mid- to late-nineteenth century, it was a small, single room, with just enough space to wash the truffles discovered earlier in the day up in the rocky forests.

The company had come a long way. The museum seemed a gem of contemporary marketing. In the front room, the team had decaled the floors with maps of Italy's different truffle regions and stocked Urbani's newest products for purchase on wooden shelves.

"So here we have a small store," Sylvia said, in her delicate, polished English, but with the characteristic melodic ups and downs of an Italian accent. She spoke in an exalted manner that I assume all of Olga's employees use when they talk about the company. "Would you like to try a chocolate truffle with truffles?" she half asked, as she handed them over. "This is black chocolate with black truffle, and this is white chocolate with white truffle. . . . The white one is most intense."

They tasted like chocolate.

"We have preserved truffles; we have sauces, different types of sauces, different ingredients, different truffle percentage. We have oils, we have sweets, we have honey, pasta, we have tortellini, tagliatelle, salt . . . polenta—which is traditional here in Italy. . . .

Then we have rice. Oh, and also barbecue, ketchup, chili, curry, mustard, mayonnaise with truffles. Butter, cheese. Yeah . . . Pretty much everything," she said, giggling. I wasn't sure why anyone would want truffle barbecue sauce, but it felt somehow sacrilegious to challenge the concept inside Urbani's sacred space. The company produces six hundred products in all and ships to seventy different countries. At my local Italian grocery store back in California, you can buy one pound bags of dried Urbani porcini mushrooms for $47.

Constantino Urbani, a farmer in the valley, was the first Urbani to see money in truffles. His realization probably came somewhere deep in one of the red oak forests in the hills near his parcel, when his sow recovered more than he'd expected on a wild truffle hunt. He founded the company in 1852, shipping the black winter truffles he—and other hunters he recruited—found to the market of Carpentras in southern France, where demand had exploded and the French truffle merchant Auguste Rousseau had just begun his experimentation with cultivation. It would be the beginning of a long-running relationship between Urbani and French truffle merchants.

The operation then was simple. In the early days, the women sorted the best black winter truffles into baskets, which they carried down to the banks of the river. They washed them in the bone-chilling rush, before packaging them in crates and handing them off for shipping. Because it was a single room and the work was menial, every so often the women would swap duties with each other for a change of pace.

Taking over after Constantino, Paolo Urbani Sr. pursued an aggressive expansion into markets outside France. Because the extremely delicate and perishable product often spoiled during its rough transport by horse-drawn carriage and locomotive to its clients farther afield in Europe, one of the company's first challenges was finding an effective mechanism for preserving the product long enough that it could survive trips to far-flung customers.

Sealed cans satisfied the company's requirements for many years, but Paolo senior, the company's first true marketing visionary, wanted to deliver his truffles to customers who had never cooked with them before. He realized that compelling an early twentieth-century chef to buy a foreign product he had never used and couldn't even see through the can was not a winning strategy. "If you're buying something that is not part of your culinary tradition, you want to know what it looks like," Sylvia said.

After visiting Carpentras to learn Rousseau's bottling technique, Paolo senior developed an airtight bottle that would provide chefs and other customers a full view of the lumpy black diamonds they were being asked to put serious investment in.

Inside the museum, full of old tools and telegrams, Sylvia pointed to one of the original bottles: The truffle inside, she told me, was at least a hundred years old. His solution "was extraordinary," Sylvia said, evincing the awe of someone who'd just learned about the big bang. With the shift in packaging, the company began shipping out more truffles than ever before.

Instead of waiting for chefs in international markets to discover truffles themselves, Paolo senior started sending representatives to pay them visits and demonstrate the product's culinary power. In 1946, the next leader of the company, Carlo, began working with an American nephew named Paul, who was interested in establishing a more serious foothold for the company in the United States. But almost immediately, he found it more difficult than he expected to introduce his family's old-world business to American kitchens. "He was desperate in the very beginning because people did not know what truffles were," Sylvia said. Those who did were already using those of French origin.

The company always understood the importance of standing out in the crowded food market, so its leaders ensured that each truffle tin and can the company sold had a brilliant, colorful label and was translated into English for the British and American markets. Even in the company's infancy, there was a clear enthusiasm for appearances and branding. The Urbanis seemed to be creating a demand for truffles as much as they were serving it.

Coordinating an international expansion from the small town of Scheggino was not an easy task. Sometimes there were long delays in communication between the small-town headquarters and the company's one-man operation in the United States. But Carlo continued to encourage his nephew. He was certain he could convince Americans of the truffle's culinary promise.

In 1951, Paul at least appeared to be succeeding at generating press. He explained some of the basics of his family's operation in Italy to June Owen of the *New York Times*. Because very few white truffles were found near Scheggino, he told her that he had recently traveled with one of the company's buyers up to Piedmont. "The truffle hunters would know the day we were to arrive in town," he said. "They came to meet us, bringing baskets of the fungi just as they had been dug from the ground. Since we paid according to weight, we had to be careful that there weren't a few stones hidden in among them." Paul also told Owen of Aunt Olga, the contemporary Olga's grandmother, and of her skill with truffles in the kitchen: combined with ground veal, placed inside omelets, and turned into sauces. "There's a truffle sauce for spaghetti, one for chicken and an especially good concoction to go with the trout that flourish in the mountain brook that runs by the Urbani doorstep," Owen marveled.

By 1970, the *Times* had sent an admiring Craig Claiborne all the way to the tiny hamlet of Scheggino to report on the company's firm international reach. "Mr. Urbani's product is consumed throughout the free world; indeed, there are few luxury restaurants anywhere whose dishes have not been garnished and flavored with his wares," Claiborne wrote.

"What's more," Carlo told Claiborne, "they're good for you. My father ate truffles all his life and lived until he was 90. And his father, a truffle eater, lived to be 100." Claiborne reported that Carlo and his wife resided "in a mansion that, for all its many rooms, is actually a modest place."

In the intervening years, Paul had made some significant inroads into the Manhattan market, delivering truffles to the Four Seasons, Windows on the World, and Giambelli, among other restaurants. He also carved a space for Urbani at the city's gourmet food stores, including Dean & DeLuca and Balducci's. Around the same time, the Urbanis began building a monopoly: They bought Giacomo Morra's Alba-based Tartufi Morra, a company that specialized in white truffles and one of their only Italian competitors.

Back in Italy, the older of Carlo's sons, Paolo, assumed the lead role in the management of the company in the early 1980s. He continued the international expansion that his father famously began.

It was also under Paolo that the company sent eleven hundred pounds of white truffles to President Ronald Reagan, hoping to build brand awareness and interest in the foreign ingredient.

In fact, Paolo borrowed this idea from Morra, who selected Rita Hayworth in 1949 as the first high-profile recipient of truffles; he followed soon after with shipments to Harry Truman, Winston Churchill, Joe DiMaggio, Marilyn Monroe, Dwight Eisenhower, and Alfred Hitchcock.

The Urbanis were relentless promoters: They wined and dined chefs, they made the rounds at all the truffle fairs and food shows in Europe, and Paul kept pushing as hard as he could in the United States. Eventually, the brand became widely recognized as the global leader in the industry.

Paolo was the king, recognized throughout the industry for his creative genius. That made his daughter, Olga, the princess and, as his only child, the rightful heir to his throne. She represents the fifth generation of the family involved in the business; her sons represent the sixth.

The company still presents its product in ways that it believes target customers will understand. Recently, truffle carpaccio designed for placement on sushi rolls and truffle soy sauce have gained traction in the Japanese marketplace. Everyone who has any connection to the truffle industry knows the family's name.

"How was the chocolate?" Sylvia asked.

"It was very good," I answered.

We walked out of the museum, and Sylvia locked the front door behind her.

The wind whipped our faces as we headed back to her car. She said that we'd be eating lunch at the company's "truffle academy," a modern, all-glass structure back at headquarters. She had the easy smile and eagerness of a fresh and loyal recruit. As we drove back through the narrow valley, she explained that she commuted thirty kilometers each way to get to the office from the former industry town of Terni but didn't mind it. "It's always different," she said of the drive. "It's beautiful."

Soon I sat in a conference room of the main operations building, one teeming with all sorts of different Urbani product. By this point, hours after my arrival, I still hadn't even caught a glimpse of the person I had come to meet. The tour had a propagandistic shine, and I was beginning to wonder how much time I would actually get to spend with the executive herself. Then, suddenly, Sylvia provided some reassurance. "Ms. Urbani is coming," she said.

Not long after, Olga walked through the door. She wore a long, poufy black gown, with ruffles at the sleeves; elegant, dangling earrings; and a white necklace that was probably worth more than Sylvia's car. Her dark brown hair was pulled back into a ponytail. Her teeth were impeccably white, bright against her darkly tanned skin. Her voice was soft, delicate, and a little bit cartoonish. She greeted me with warmth and projected an authenticity I hadn't quite expected. It immediately became apparent that as strange as it was, the CBS appearance wasn't performance or self-caricature; it was simply who she was.

Olga is a master of charm and public relations. Soon after she had sat down, she asked me which other companies I had visited. I said I had only been to Sabatino thus far. "Only Sabatino?" she asked, in a manner that suggested there were so many other places to go. There were at least two hundred truffle companies globally, she said. "There are companies in Asia," she said. "There are companies in Bulgaria and Slovenia. They are all over. In France and Spain. We have a lot of respect for all of them."

When I finally asked her for her opinion of Sabatino, she

refused. "I never give an opinion of my competitors," she said. "I think it's more serious. I do have one, but I never say one word. . . . All competitors say terrible things about Urbani, so I leave them to talk about us, but I never, never say one word about my competitors. Not me, not my family. I think that there is a space for everybody in this world, and I just hope that everybody does business fairly."

But, it seemed, Urbani recognized an inherent level of temptation and vice in the world she commands. The company works with hundreds, if not thousands, of hunters and middlemen across the country, and some have closer relations with the company than others. "This is so hard," she said. "Because the truffle is the easiest world in which you can become a thief. Because young people with a lot of cash money on their hands, for sure they become thieves in a few months. First of all, you have to choose humane people, simple guys. Guys who want to help the company, who want to work hard. Who believe in the name of Urbani and in the truffle world, but in a serious way. They're very few. I hired one yesterday, and I was looking at him very carefully.

"Because in a certain way, I'm the one who is ruining a lot of people. Because when I hire them, I'm putting these people in a situation of risk. Because I'm putting them in a world full of money, full of cash, full of possibilities of becoming a bad person, if they don't have brain. I was talking to this guy yesterday and saying, 'Listen, it will be very easy for you to steal my money. But it will be very easy for me to understand when you will be starting to do it. I will be keeping you for a while because I will be needing you. But, at a certain point, I will fire you, so you know that, I told you. So, please try to have a serious behavior, because we can continue for a long period of time. We can do a long piece of road walking together. We can have satisfaction together.' But it's hard. Sometimes people understand the message. Sometimes, they are shocked by the money and the value.

"Also, the kind of customer you are dealing with can make you crazy in a certain sense. Because you sell truffles to Madonna, to Obama, to all these people or to three-Michelin-star restaurants. You see the big world . . . for me, it's not a big world. The big world for me, it's the truffle hunter that loves me in a real way. These very VIP people . . . they don't give a fuck about me. There are many young people who are very fascinated by this empty world, in my opinion.

"Our life is a sacrifice," she explained. "It's a beautiful life, I'm not complaining. Our life is completely dedicated to the company. There is no difference, there is no limit between private life and the life of an entrepreneur. It's the same. You work and you live; there is no separation. Sometimes, this is happy, sometimes, I'm sad. Because I don't recognize my own real life. I ask myself, 'What am I really . . . ?'" She trailed off. "Because if I stop being Urbani, what am I? Nothing."

For Olga, delivering truffles to the market is an identity. She's particularly fond of the mission of the museum she designed, perhaps because it helps remind her just how important her family legacy has become. She told one Italian publication that it "is dedicated to those who are able to innovate themselves without forgetting where they came from. It is a place of memories, the finest and dearest possessions of all, holding deep inside the hope of turning nostalgia of the past into positive energy for looking toward the future."

But there is one troubling part of Urbani family history that the Museo del Tartufo doesn't display. One part of the company's story that Olga can't easily separate herself from. As the company's modern innovator, it's also the part she conveniently chooses to forget.

# CHAPTER TEN

# The King's Betrayal

IN THE EARLY 1980S, TWENTYSOMETHING ROSARIO SAFINA WAS JUST starting a career in advertising and direct marketing in Manhattan. As an assistant account executive, he worked on materials for Merrill Lynch, the United States Mint, Gevalia coffee, Wisconsin cheese, and Depend adult diapers. He had long swept-back hair and was highly intelligent, loquacious, and in possession of a photographic memory. The firm's work wasn't boring, but it wasn't enough to keep the fast-talking, quick-thinking New Yorker occupied. He was on the lookout for a side hustle. Soon, he had saved enough money to buy an Italian food and wine catalog—more of a glorified pamphlet than anything—and pulled the trigger. It advertised pastas, canned tomatoes, biscuits, and other requisite staples. He bulked it out and renamed it *Rosario's Commestibili,* or "edible" in Italian.

One day, Safina thumbed through an issue of *Gourmet* and landed on an article about truffles. He immediately tried to include the ingredient as an item in his offerings. But Liberty-Ramsey, the specialty food importer he worked with at the time, was always out of stock. The representative at Ramsey suggested that he look up the guy listed on the label of the product. He was a septuagenarian near Princeton, New Jersey, by the name of Paul Urbani, nephew of Carlo and cousin to Paolo and Bruno, the heads of Urbani Tartufi back in Italy. When Safina called, Paul complained of the sluggish pace of the company's domestic distributors. He hadn't generated good sales figures since 1981, two years before Safina's call. The constant delays of his domestic distributors, Paul said, had set off a 300 percent drop in sales. "I've got plenty of stuff here in my basement to sell you," Paul said.

Safina began buying it directly from his basement storeroom.

Recognizing the Italian American kid's entrepreneurial spirit, Paul decided he wanted to introduce Safina to his Italian family. The following year, he arranged for Safina to meet Paolo, then in his early fifties, in Manhattan at an international gourmet food show held inside the New York Coliseum.

The men found an instant kinship. Paolo saw Safina's youthful charm and enthusiasm for truffles as a potential boon to the company's struggling American operations. Safina appreciated Paolo's generous smile and country simplicity. Apart from the distributors, the company's struggles in the American market could be partly attributed to Paul's age, which made him slightly more interested in retirement than in busying himself with the day-to-day machinations of growing sales in the market he had been trying to build up since 1946. Paolo decided to tap Safina as Paul's replacement.

"Why don't you just take over the business from Paul?" Paolo asked, over what became one of many regular international phone calls.

"Sure, why not?" Rosario said. "Show me the number."

The Urbanis sent over the domestic sales figures, and Safina agreed to handle the company's products on the American market.

"That's where it took off," Rosario told me. "I'm not going to do the catalog business anymore. I gave up advertising, and I feel good and that felt right."

At the age of twenty-five, after just two years of advertising work, Safina became exclusive licensee and head of Urbani Tartufi's product in the United States.

❦

Paolo Urbani had the same unaffected air as his father, Carlo Urbani. The Umbrian soil seemed to coarse through his blood. He did not graduate from high school, but he worked hard and was preternaturally perceptive. He was deeply loyal and protected his people, including the hunters and middlemen he purchased from. Everyone in the industry and in the small town of Scheggino adored him for this commitment and his humility. No matter how successful the company had been or how much his fortune had grown, he never assumed anyone else knew who he was. "If he ever met politicians or really, really smart people or lawyers or big businesspeople," Safina told me, "he would always say, 'I'm Paolo Urbani. I own Urbani Tartufi.'" To emphasize his pastoral roots, he always asked the elite to speak slowly and to avoid using fancy words, but the people who knew him well supposed this kitschy portrayal was by design. Perhaps he wanted to see how important people reacted, how they treated a simple man.

Safina picked up on this early. "He's definitely no country boy," Safina said, thinking back. "This guy is a smart-ass man."

Paolo taught himself French and learned how to persuade and charm the truffle traders and companies located in France. The Frenchmen were dazzled by his expertise. He seemed to have better contacts and a better handle on the French market than even Plantin. He knew the quality of truffles at small markets throughout the country and which *négociants* purchased the most. When he heard that certain French traders were selling directly to Parisian chefs, he hired them. He was regularly buying about 40 percent of the truffles moving across French markets, leaving smaller French companies to pick up second-rate remainders.

Knowing that France had been struggling with its truffle production, he also persuaded the Frenchmen to buy his supplies of wild Italian black truffles for nine times their worth and did so in such a way that they felt they were getting an excellent deal. "You should sell insurance," Safina told Paolo, after watching how he negotiated. "You could sell a blank page. You could probably sell the same blank page to ten different people." Safina felt that he'd landed a rare opportunity to serve as an apprentice to a master salesman. "He was like Tony Robbins," Safina said.

Safina was roughly the same age as Olga, Paolo's only child. Paolo came to view Safina as a son, and Safina looked up to Paolo as a father figure from whom he could learn every aspect of the business. "I admired the guy through the roof," Safina said. At the time, Safina ran the business with his brother, Andrew. "I love you two boys," Paolo would tell them. "I wish I had boys."

Their familial relationship was more than an empty managerial cliché. "He was the most caring, kind person I ever met in my life," Safina said. At some point early in Safina's Urbani tenure, Paolo asked him to seriously consider the prospect of improving his Italian-language skills, which, around then, were average.

"That way we could become better friends," Paolo said, "and we could understand each other better." Safina agreed. "Why don't you take six weeks off from work, have your brother run the business in the summertime, when it's slow?" Paolo said. "I'll pay for it, and you'll learn Italian." The offer sounded fantastic, but Safina didn't have anyplace to stay while studying in Italy. "Don't worry," Paolo said. Safina could crash at Olga's apartment in Perugia; she had finished at the university there and was no longer living in it. When Safina arrived, Paolo began sending him 500 lira (the Italian currency until 2002) a week for meals. "I don't want you cooking in the apartment," Paolo said, "in case you burn the place down. Just go out to eat every day."

During the early days, Olga, then in her twenties, and Gianluca—Paolo and Bruno's nephew of roughly the same age— befriended Safina. "We grew up together," he said. As young adults, they traveled across Italy and partied in Rome. Safina met many of Olga's friends and later became close to her husband. "Olga and Gianluca and myself, we were the three musketeers," Safina told me. "It was a really nice time, you know?"

＊

When the Safina brothers ran behind on payments for their merchandise, Paolo told them not to worry. He allowed them to run up the debt, having confidence that Safina would pay the money back and, in the process, help the company translate the brand to an American audience.

"I want you to grow the business," Paolo said. "I want you guys to get big. And when you have the money, pay us."

With assurances from Italy about the credit, Safina was able to expand and hire salespeople on the West Coast. Safina's phone bills during this period of Urbani U.S.A.'s growth regularly ran up to $500, much of it connected to his international calls with Paolo. Part of these conversations revolved around business, but a good portion of the time was spent "just shooting the shit."

Paolo even took Safina on vacation, wherever Paolo and his girlfriend, Tina, decided to luxuriate next. "I'd see these people in their sixties, they'd be so in love," Safina recalled. Riccione, a resort town on the northeastern coast, was a favorite. "They treated me like I was their son," Safina said. "They were really, really good people. They were really, really good to me. I will always remember them for that."

Like any obedient son, Safina even introduced Paolo to the girl he thought he would eventually marry. Paolo approved, encouraging him to propose soon. After she broke it off, Safina felt hopelessly inconsolable. At the time, Paolo was making an appearance at a food show in Cologne, Germany. When Safina reached him, Paolo told him to buy a ticket and get on the next plane to Cologne. "I will give you money for the ticket when I see you," he said. "You can sleep in my room while I'm on the sofa. I don't want to see you go through this. Get on the plane now; come hang out with me at the show."

Later, Safina learned that Paolo had called the woman, pressuring her to reconsider. "You're making a big mistake!" he told her. "He's going to be big one day! I guarantee it. He's with me. I don't hang around with losers."

⬧

Two to four times a year, Safina flew to the Urbani headquarters outside the sleepy town of Scheggino. Paolo always treated him to the best dinners and the finest wine, even though he never poured any for himself. Safina enjoyed the sense of community and family that Paolo and Bruno had fostered. Everyone greeted each other in the mornings at the designated café in Scheggino. And at

3:00 p.m., the warehouse workers took a collective breath of fresh air and an espresso. When Safina and his brother tried to walk the mile or so from the warehouse into the village along the valley road, they didn't get very far before cars stopped and insisted on giving them rides.

During much of the 1980s and 1990s, Paolo, Bruno, and the rest of the senior leadership looked to Safina for insights about what kinds of products Americans wanted.

"Hey," Safina told Paolo, on one of their calls in 1986. "We got big trouble now. There's this thing out there called truffle oil."

"Oh yeah, we know about it," Paolo said. "Don't worry about it. People will get tired of it. Nobody wants that stuff."

A year went by, and nothing changed. Chefs were calling and practically pleading with Safina to carry the product.

He finally nudged Paolo over the edge by explaining that other Italian competitors were already selling it. Later, he dreamed up the concepts for truffle butter and truffle carpaccio, among other American favorites. Safina and his team relentlessly marketed the company's fresh truffles and its new line of products on a national scale. By the early 1990s, almost every American restaurant kitchen that prepared truffles knew the Urbani name. It was the company that had been in the longest: Doing business with it felt like buying into a long and authentic Umbrian family legacy, one that came with the best ingredients and the highest level of service. Safina had done what Paul struggled to do: He made Urbani matter to more than just Manhattan's rarefied culinary elite. "They wanted to conquer America," Safina said, "and we conquered America."

⁂

And then, gradually, the image that Paolo had so carefully crafted began to fray. Sometime around 1994, Safina began to notice that something was off about Urbani's black winter truffles, but he wasn't sure exactly what could explain it. Occasionally, the fresh truffles arriving in New York from Italy each week, seventy or even eighty kilos of them, didn't give off that indescribable scent. Instead, when Safina leaned over the table to sniff, he got nothing. He also noticed that headquarters was shipping more black winter truffles in than ever before. Hunters' discoveries had skyrocketed, with seemingly no explanation as to why. He called Paolo to check in.

"I don't smell anything," Safina said, looking, hopefully, for an explanation. Paolo gave him the equivalent of a verbal shrug. "Depending on the *terroir,* some seasons they're very aromatic, some seasons they're lighter," Paolo said. "I don't know," Paolo said. "We buy them in huge quantities. We can't check every one."

Safina trusted Paolo. "I just took their word for it," he told me. "Nobody ever really complained. . . . They had red soil on them just like the soil in central Italy."

—

Unbeknownst to Safina, long before he noticed this olfactory shift, Paolo had been approached with an attractive offer from the French. During excursions in the remote forests of China's Sichuan province and the Tibetan Plateau, morel mushroom foragers working for a French food supplier had come across two interesting fungi not far from the surface of the soil. When they showed the specimens to their client, the supplier recognized them as truffles and tipped off a French truffle merchant.

Paolo's incessant courting of French suppliers had finally paid off. The merchant, who was buying a good deal of product from Urbani during this time, called Paolo to inform him of what must have seemed a lucky and most unlikely development for their supply chain: bulk quantities of black truffles—one called *Tuber hi-*

*malayensis* and another called *Tuber indicum*—that looked identical to French and Italian black winter truffles, or *Tuber melanosporum*, and only cost about a quarter ($25 to $30), or even less wholesale, of the price. It was the equivalent of finding a fully functioning currency printer abandoned in an alleyway. It would be extremely illegal to mint new dollars but irresistible to those with greedy impulses. The only problem was that the Chinese truffles lacked the black winter truffle's signature woody chocolate scent, and many of them—harvested with rakes—were unripe and held no real flavor. Even so, banking on their appearance, Paolo and the merchant hatched a "big scheme." They worked together to find a German broker's company that would agree to import metric tons of the stuff, pile it into trucks, and then drive it over the French and Italian borders to the companies' warehouses. Some of it moved directly through France and then into Italy.

"They had this two-level thing going to throw me off and their nephew off," Safina recalled. "They were very, very secretive about it." At first, Paolo instructed his workers to mix seven hundred grams of real black truffles with three hundred grams from the new shipments. The Chinese truffles would absorb the musk, and they could generate significantly more profit with the mixed batches. But eventually, Paolo resolved to put even less of the real thing, maybe two hundred grams, in the bags. Finally, the number of real black truffles in the shipments Paolo was sending out dropped to zero. To disguise the fraud, Paolo ordered them sprayed with a synthetic scent used in the truffle oil that the company had begun producing. The Chinese truffles with lighter, more brownish skin were dyed with black food coloring before they were placed in Urbani cans.

Though some of the shipments during this period seemed off,

there was no smoking gun. "Unless you have a microscope or a mycologist, it's very, very hard to tell what it is." Safina would become an unwitting accessory to the largest-scale truffle fraud ever perpetrated in history.

The black winter truffle dishes served at many of America's finest restaurants during this time, especially those that used canned product from Urbani, were more than likely piled with counterfeit Chinese truffles.

New York kitchens began to spot differences in the fresh European truffles they were buying in the winter of 1995. In February of that year, Florence Fabricant, a food reporter for the *New York Times*, reported that chefs at tony restaurants around New York City were being "ambushed" with Chinese truffles—specifically a species called *Tuber himalayensis*—mixed in with the bags of French, or *Tuber melanosporum*. "Right after Christmas I started getting some truffles that I thought were overripe at first," Daniel Boulud, then chef and owner of Restaurant Daniel, told Fabricant. "They were very dark and had very little veining. They smelled of benzene and tasted like cardboard. Then I began hearing about the Chinese truffles." Back then, Boulud sold sea scallop appetizers with black truffles for $21; he charged $35 to $40 for a salad or baked potato with black truffle shavings. European black truffles sold for "around $400 a pound." The value of a pound of Chinese truffles hovered around $100. Boulud wouldn't tell Fabricant which of the four suppliers he used furnished him with the counterfeit ingredient. Another of the chefs Fabricant spoke with "compared serving Chinese truffles without identifying them to 'selling American paddlefish caviar for Russian sevruga.'" In the piece, Fabricant noted that none of the fresh black truffles she tried at Balducci's,

Dean & DeLuca, or Urbani Truffles appeared to contain the Chinese counterfeit.

What no one knew then was that Urbani's explosive growth had not only been a function of Paolo's marketing and sales genius. It depended on his ability to charm everyone well enough not to notice his invention of a massive, innovative fraud that would plague the industry for decades to come.

One of the people Safina recruited to work for him during this period of American growth was an Urbani customer named Roberto Saracino, a Turin-born *chef de cuisine* at the glitzy Armani Café in Boston (in 1994, "Best of Boston" wrote that the restaurant had "refined the alfresco lunch to high art"). Saracino had decided to move back to California and accepted a sales position working under Safina's brother, Andrew, at the company's Los Angeles office in early 1997. He sold to Piero Selvaggio's Valentino, Madeo, and a majority of the other celebrity-teeming Italian restaurants in Los Angeles. He regularly supplied truffles to the luxe pleasure palaces of Las Vegas: the Bellagio Hotel and Casino, Le Cirque, Circo, and Julian Serrano's Picasso. During this time, he recalled, two of the restaurants inside the Bellagio were purchasing two to three cases of "winter truffle peelings" a week, at a price of more than $11,000 in today's dollars. The product seemed to move itself.

Global business was thriving too, thanks at least in part to Safina and his team's brand-building efforts in the United States. By this point, frozen and canned exports to international markets had transformed the former one-shop operation into a multimillion-dollar empire. *Panorama* magazine, Italy's equivalent of *Businessweek*, put Paolo Urbani on the cover and named him the country's man of the year. In 1997, while Urbani's truffle exports were undergoing an outlandish spike, Italian truffle hunters experienced only an average season. The company's expansion more than likely had nothing to do with the Umbrian product supposedly at its core.

Upon the release of the *Panorama* issue, a ripple of unease moved through the company. Everyone at headquarters knew that the high-profile visibility would draw more scrutiny. *Panorama* was known to land on the desks of the Italian business elite and the men who investigated them: the detectives at Italy's financial police, the Guardia di Finanza.

"Those guys, they see the magazine that sits on their desk," Safina said, "and they look at it, and they go, 'This guy can't be paying taxes.' That's the first thing they always say, because they're really, really bad about it in Italy."

❦

In the winter of 1998, not long after Paolo's cover hit the newsstands, the Italian carabinieri's food division, NAS, working in collaboration with the Guardia di Finanza, raided Urbani Tartufi's Scheggino warehouse. The provincial police assisted with the search, wearing bulletproof vests and arriving in black cars, sirens blaring. The officers discovered that the company was storing forty-seven tons of Chinese truffles on its premises, purchased for a price of only $20 per kilo. (The entire country of France produces about thirty tons of truffles annually, and back then European blacks sold on the U.S. market for around $400 per kilo.)

Both Paolo and Bruno Urbani were questioned. The NAS investigation was the first Safina had ever heard of the scheme.

When Safina was able to get in touch with Paolo to find out what was going on, Paolo played up his guileless bumpkin role. "It wasn't my fault," Paolo told Safina. "I was buying them from France. I trusted my broker. I'm just a country man—how am I supposed to know the difference? I always did a lot of business with him.

"Don't worry," he added. "If I have to pay any fines, I will pay my fines. I just won't do it again. I'm sorry, it's very hard to control this stuff. We'll get it straightened out. If there's some damage, it's my responsibility."

Safina didn't press him further. In fact, at the time, he was "100 percent" convinced that Paolo was telling the truth because the master had always delivered on the promises he made to his apprentice. "And you know what? Who the f knows? *Maybe* he was telling the truth, maybe it was a setup. I don't know." Given the support and affection Paolo had always shown him, it wasn't really his place to interrogate. "I was a good son," Safina told me, with a palpable measure of certainty.

The U.S.-based business suffered after the news, which made headlines across Europe and even in some American publications, including the *New York Post*. In the meantime, Safina became frustrated with his operation's finances and somewhat less credulous when it came to his dealings with Italian headquarters. "We're here trying to build up the business, and they're over there getting in trouble," he told me.

⁂

Back in Los Angeles, Saracino, who had been supplying restaurants across the West with $200 cans of Chinese truffles marked as black winter truffles, had, like Safina, assumed the product he was peddling was authentic. "I was not in charge of buying the product," he told me. "I was only in charge of selling it. We were selling it for a ton of money," he said, "something that today is worth [only] about $15 or $20. . . . Never knew the difference." In fact, he hadn't even known what *Tuber indicum* was until the crackdown.

"My gosh," he said, in disbelief at the audacity of the fraud. "That is a ton of money for something that's worthless. Somebody made a lot of money." If they had successfully mislabeled all forty-seven tons, it would have amounted to roughly $18 million in fraudulent profit. And no one could know just how much had already shipped in previous seasons.

A few months after the scandal, Saracino decided to leave Safina and the Urbani family and start his own food import business, Liaison West. He made sure to pay regular visits to his new truffle supplier, Trivelli Tartufi in the Marche region, to ensure he was receiving the quality product he knew he needed for his clients. "When you meet somebody . . . you have a gut feeling . . . whether they're going to be honest people," Saracino said. "I don't know if it was triggered by the fact that Urbani had all these Chinese truffles in their house, but it definitely, you know, when you're talking a lot of money, you're buying fifteen kilos of white truffles a week. I wanted to be safer. I wanted to be a little bit more protective than just opening a box and finding out that half of the product, I cannot sell it." Even then, Urbani's reputation seemed to precede it. Trivelli claimed to have known "for quite some time" that Urbani was selling Chinese truffles.

"When I ended my relationship, and you start seeing what's on the market, what the real thing is on the market, then you put one plus one together and you're like, okay, there is no way to . . . There is not that kind of money in this business. If you do things on an honest level, you don't become superrich when you're working on 10–15 percent. Obviously, when you do those kinds of things, then it's a lot easier."

By 2001, Saracino's import business had carved out such a significant slice of the West Coast's truffle distribution market that he received a personal phone call from Olga Urbani herself. Despite having done business together by proxy, they had never met or spoken to each other.

"We are learning that you are an important distributor. The Cavaliere wants to meet you," Olga said, using only the honorific to refer to her father, Paolo. ("It's like a noble term, when somebody becomes so important they're the Cavaliere," Saracino told me. "It's one of those titles that they gave back in the days.")

"We want to come and pick you up at the airport and take you to the castle," Olga said.

Knowing that more product could mean more profit, he initially agreed to the meeting. But in transit to Italy, he had time to mull over the company's previous exploits. He decided to call and cancel.

"I'm not interested to meet anybody," he told Olga. "I'm happy with [whom] I do business with. Have a nice life."

A few years after that, he received another call from an Urbani representative. This time it was a man who was more direct. He wanted Saracino to distribute the company's product on the West Coast.

"Look," Saracino said. "I'm not interested in buying the product from you. I don't want to buy product from you."

"Why don't you want to buy from us?" he asked.

"I don't trust you, and I don't want to buy product from you," Saracino responded flatly.

The man had an aggressive riposte prepared.

"Well," he said, "it's only a matter of time before I'm going to take all your customers away from you."

"Okay," Saracino said, "that's fine. America is a big country, and there is opportunity for everybody, so go for it."

Saracino hung up, aghast at the man's ego.

＊

As Safina walked closer to the villa he'd rented for a vacation on Mustique in the Grenadines, he noticed a note taped to the door. After spending the better part of the day at a tropical beach, with friends, his wife, and his son, he found it posted there, fluttering in the wind.

It was March of 2001, a few years after the Urbani Chinese truffle scandal, and he was taking a much-needed respite from work, where nothing seemed to be going his way. He had almost weathered the drop-off in sales, but he was struggling to manage cash-flow problems. What Safina needed, just then, was a lucky break.

Instead, he got a surprising scrawl of ink, in a place where he was not meant to be troubling himself with business.

"Urbani has been arrested," it read. "Please call Florence Fabricant," the *New York Times* reporter.

"Holy shit," Safina thought. "What the hell did these guys do now?"

Having no notion of why the Urbani brothers had been arrested, Safina began to panic. His wife tried to soothe his nerves before he returned Fabricant's message. "Stay calm, relax, call her up," she said. "Just tell the truth: 'I don't know anything about this.'"

He picked up the phone and dialed.

"Did you know they got arrested?" the reporter asked.

He told her that he was on vacation and had only just learned of the news from her message.

The Guardia di Finanza had finally come for the Urbani brothers on account of large sums of unpaid value-added taxes on their truffle purchases. "This was news to me," Safina told me. Though he always agreed with Paolo and Bruno's philosophy that truffles did not deserve to be categorized at a higher tax rate than an agricultural product, he did not realize that they were rigorously practicing their beliefs. Or that those beliefs translated into paying zero.

After he hung up with Fabricant, Safina called Paolo.

"Don't worry," Paolo said. "I'm here at home. I have an ankle bracelet on. I'm not going to jail; Bruno's not in jail. We just have some financial issues now. They exposed all the accounts."

A few days later, Safina boarded a plane for Italy "to see what the hell was going on" at Scheggino headquarters. Paolo greeted him at the entryway of his castle, wearing an ankle bracelet. He made it clear that Urbani Tartufi— which did roughly $18 million in business each year—desperately needed money to pay off around $9 million of back taxes and fines and had already begun asking all of its clients to send in payments immediately.

Later, when he visited the office, the place was crawling with Guardia officers, rifling through desks, piling papers into boxes, and wiring computers into the company's servers. The investigation eventually concluded that there was simply too much canned and derivative truffle product on warehouse shelves compared with the amount of truffles the company had officially purchased and reported. "Well, that stuff has to come from somewhere, doesn't it? It doesn't mystically appear growing underneath your garage," Safina said. "That's why these guys get in trouble. How can you have €17 million in inventory and your records only show you bought *X* amount in fresh and you sold most of it fresh? How'd you make the stuff in the can? How'd you make the stuff in the jars? How'd you make the stuff in the bottles?"

Safina understood the basic mechanics of the fraud because he'd heard about many other truffle dealers who practiced the same strategy. When the hunters came in with their fresh discoveries, the dealers paid in cash and then later memorialized the exchange for the tax authorities with a self-invoice listing the amount purchased. But because there were no electronic records of the transactions and the dealers owed a 22 percent tax on every purchase, the dealer could claim to have only bought half or a quarter or even less of what he actually acquired. "You write one [invoice], you don't write one," Safina explained. "You write one, you don't write two. You write two, you don't write three." Fresh product moves within days, enjoying a degree of invisibility. But Urbani was a large company producing large quantities of oil, sauce, and other truffle derivatives, which are shelved for long periods and can easily be discovered during a search by authorities. The inconsistencies were glaring.

At some level, Safina could see the appeal of Paolo's logic. He believed that he needed to take care of all his employees and allow them to feel a sense of job security. There was very little turnover on the Scheggino crew; people stuck around for twenty or thirty years. The whole town was practically employed by the company. He felt a sense of real responsibility for the community. "It was like Detroit, the '70s, you had a job for life," Safina said. He viewed the government's hefty 22 percent tax as an unnecessary burden, especially when paying it meant he could employ fewer people on the production line. It was the Robin Hood defense. Though the tax evasion was less shocking than the Chinese truffle fraud, it was more personally distressing for Safina, who was already struggling with cash-flow issues.

Then Safina's problem grew only more serious. When the World Trade Center fell the following September, Safina's largest account went along with it: Windows on the World, the swanky restaurant on a top floor of the North Tower, bought, on an annual basis, roughly $800,000 to $1 million worth of Safina's imported product. Accounting for the gap was not easy, especially as Manhattan struggled through a recovery and truffles seemed like an unnecessary expense.

Despite the precarious financial spot his American operation had found itself in after 9/11, Safina slowly began to settle the debts with Urbani. "It was one whammy after another," Safina said. The situation was obviously urgent, and Safina soon began to realize that he'd be unable to satisfy the family on the kind of timetable they were demanding.

What made this all the more troubling was a report, by the Italian newspaper *Corriere della Sera,* that some of the shell companies the Urbani brothers used to doctor invoices were connected to the Camorra Mafia.

⁓

For the first time, Safina began to have serious doubts about the company's generosity. For one, he learned that Paolo and Bruno had openly suggested that their nephew Gianluca, then just a salesman making roughly $35,000 a year, act as the fall guy and claim that he had come up with and perpetrated the tax fraud in isolation. If he went along with it, he would serve four years in Italian prison and the fines would be reduced. But Gianluca balked at his uncles' pleas, reminding them that he was still a comparatively young man. They tried to guilt him into it by suggesting that he wouldn't want to see his poor uncles in jail, but he still refused, on the simple principle that he had not been involved.

Neither uncle was pleased with his defiant behavior. When he left the family in a fury, they invented a false narrative, telling colleagues that he had a drug addiction and could no longer be trusted. In fact, he married an Estonian model and settled, for a time, in her home country. He never looked back. (Now, as a sign of his continued estrangement, he buys truffles for a competing fine food distributor in Milan.)

Meanwhile, the U.S. bank handling Safina's business accounts discovered that he was purchasing product from a company under tax investigation by the Italian authorities and canceled his line of credit. This exacerbated an already intractable cash-flow problem.

When the Urbanis realized that Safina was not going to be able to pay them quickly enough, they called him back to Italy.

Safina knew something was afoot when he walked into the conference room to find three previously unknown American relatives of the family, hailing from Pennsylvania, seated at the table. Until that point, he had only dealt with one person based in the United States: Paul Urbani, who had once said there was no one else to hand the American part of the business to. "I was like, 'Mm. This does not look good,'" Safina said. "Paolo was sitting there; he did not look happy. He did not say a word. And *Olga* did all the talking." The company needed cash, Safina couldn't provide it, and they wanted to keep the business within the family, she said. Olga was by then the director of the company, and she made the decision to cut him out of the exclusive licensing deal. "I have never had *anything* bad to say about Paolo," Safina told me. "Olga was the one who steered the company in different directions that didn't want to include me. But I couldn't say anything bad about Paolo. He had an excuse for everything with a smile on his face."

There were further delays in the negotiations between the two parties, and eventually Urbani Tartufi filed civil lawsuits against Safina's company, Urbani Truffles, to collect debts and halt the use of its trademarks. In April 2003, twenty years after he placed his fateful call to Paul Urbani, Safina was forced to settle with the company in federal court.

"We didn't want to arrive to this serious point with Rosario, but we were forced by his 'un-understandable' behavior, years of shipments without any payment and unfaithful competition while my family treated him as a son," Olga told *Gourmet News* after the settlement, with her typical public relations bravado. "He was for me like a brother, and we have built together very much during the years . . . life is hard to believe sometimes." In a separate statement released by the company, Olga said, in part, "Rosario's clinging to the URBANI MARKS speaks volumes about the importance of those marks and our family's proud tradition so closely associated with the truffle." The American portion of the business was handed to Lee Urbani, one of the relatives in attendance at the meeting back in Italy. The company settled with the Italian government over the tax case, without admitting liability.

"I look back, and I got to say one thing: It was great being with them," Safina told me, clinging inexplicably to his fondness for Paolo. "It was so nice to be part of that culture. At the end of the day, business came down to business. They had to do what they had to do. I had to do what I had to do. That's that.

"I was never happy with the games they played and the press releases and all that and slandering her cousin like that—which is basically her brother. Everybody makes those types of life decisions, and all that shit eventually comes back."

—

Perhaps the most absurd part of the Urbani saga was the victimized tone Olga Urbani took in her interview with Lesley Stahl on CBS's *60 Minutes* in 2012:

> URBANI: Prices of winter truffles is about $1,000 a pound. A pound of Chinese, maybe $20, $30. There are many people, bad people, who mix them. So maybe they put 30 percent of Chinese, 70 percent of . . .
>
> STAHL: And they think you won't see it?
>
> NARRATION: On the day we were at the Urbani factory, sorters found a number of Chinese truffles mixed in with that day's purchases. They were separated out into specially marked red baskets. More and more, Chinese truffles are slipped in with the good French or Italian strains. Experts say it's like cutting flour into cocaine.
>
> STAHL: But look, your own farmers or middlemen are putting the Chinese in with your truffles.
>
> URBANI: Yes.
>
> STAHL: You're telling us you have to be on guard, not from the Chinese, but from your own people.
>
> URBANI: Yeah, I know.
>
> . . .
>
> URBANI: This makes us crazy. This destroys all the tradition of the truffle. It's an entire life that goes in the garbage. It's unbelievable.

Of course, what Olga Urbani and CBS failed to mention was that it was not farmers, hunters, or middlemen who first brought Chinese truffles into the Urbani warehouse; it was her own father.

Roberto Saracino was infuriated, as many others were, when he tuned in. "I'm like, that is just a lie in itself, because in Italy, as you know, the Chinese truffles are not allowed," Saracino said. "In Italy, it's impossible to hunt a Chinese truffle that are not there. So how does a truffle hunter bring the truffles . . . ? How they can deliver Chinese truffles is beyond me."

Plenty of hunters have attempted to conceal imperfections, increase weights, or even pass off a few unripe truffles. It's the kind of irritating, small-scale deception that sucks up a company's resources but rarely trickles down to the level of the consumer. But geographic or species fraud at scale, of the kind that the Urbani family had been accused of, was clearly not the work of the small-time hunters the company relies on. Problems like that demand significant organization and capital: They demand commercial infrastructure.

"Even though they were caught with an unbelievable amount of Chinese truffles in their property, they're still in business: They're still trying to find buyers," Saracino said. "Again, the strongest company in the world, obviously, and they're able to bypass the system."

Sabatino's Federico Balestra watched the program online after it aired. When I first asked him what he thought about it, he asked me to move on to the next question. But after a beat of performative rage, he came back to the subject. "It's fantastic," he said, with heavy sarcasm. He couldn't believe that CBS or anyone else would believe Olga or what she said. Inside the industry, people couldn't stop talking about the curious way CBS had presented its source.

"It was a pretty joke," Balestra said. "If you know the truth, you know how it is." The hypocrisy, he said, drove him to drink.

Plantin's Christoph Poron was still amused by the dainty, made-for-television symbolism of red baskets for bad product from communist China, given the company's past. On my own trip to the Urbanis' warehouse, they were notably absent. "Let's put it this way. Urbani, I'm not going to say it's a good or bad company. I don't want to speak about something I don't know. I hear stories. Stories are sometimes a bit exaggerated."

But Poron also remembered that everyone was laughing after the program aired, and he was surprised that such a tony journalism program was so thoroughly reeled in. As I was gathering my things to leave his office, he offered a harsher critique of the quality of CBS's sourcing. "It's like talking about crime with the Godfather," he said.

At our meeting, Olga Urbani admitted to me that the company had been accused of Chinese truffle fraud, but she claimed that the company had been targeted because it was the biggest name in the business. "Of course, when there is a scandal, they come to Urbani for sure," she told me. "We were very tranquil because we knew what we were doing. After one year, they made an analysis on all our things, and they discovered that there was no mixture."

The Chinese truffles that they were selling to American consumers, she said, were correctly labeled *Tuber himalayensis*. However, people selling Urbani product at that time say the cans were labeled "winter black," and only ingredient lists revealed the deception. At the time, no one in the United States even knew what the Latin names for Chinese truffles were. "We don't deal with Chinese truffles anymore," she said. "Because it is very difficult to import them, so we forgot about them really." Importing Chinese truffles into Italy is difficult because they cannot be legally sold inside the country. It is rumored that Urbani is actively lobbying, behind the scenes, for a repeal of the law.

※

Carlo Console, the forestry officer who tracks truffle crime in Abruzzo, seemed convinced that the Chinese truffle problem was never truly solved. Companies simply found more compelling methods to conceal them. Many of the truffle creams, oils, and other derivative products coming out of Italy still contain Chinese truffle, he said. The number of truffles in Italy was simply not high enough to sustain the amount of truffle product that large companies were exporting to the international market. "With the whole truffle, you can understand the species," Console said. "When it's transformed, it's only their honesty: the good conscience of who prepares them."

Console suspects that the Chinese product comes in through Italy's ports in large containers packed with other products. He believes the Chinese have Italian agents on the ground to get through customs.

"For sure, Urbani built an empire on truffles," Console said. "For sure, they had the intuition to create the brand of the Umbrian truffle. It's a merit of the family. The thing is that for all the quantity of products they make, they're taking probably truffle from all over the world. . . . If every product of Urbani was with Umbrian truffles, they would need . . . tons and tons of truffles."

※

If a truffle company like Urbani wanted Chinese truffles, they wouldn't have to look very hard. They could contact someone like Oliver Chang or one of his many competitors.

His truffles come from the pine forests in the mountainous

regions of China's Yunnan and Sichuan provinces. He has a network of hunters and farmers who sell to village collectors who pass their product on to county dealers. County dealers pass the best of the supply to prefectural dealers. And the prefecture heads drive the truffles to Chang's facility in the city of Kunming. In particularly important areas for truffle production, he has made arrangements directly with the heads of villages.

Chang sells the two truffle species that set off the Urbani scandal—*Tuber indicum* and *Tuber himalayensis*—but roughly 95 percent of the stuff flowing to his clients is the *indicum*, which is much cheaper. Between August of 2016 and March of 2017, he moved 13,000 pounds, or around 6.5 tons, to companies in Germany, France, Japan, and the United States. Once the goods are inside the European Union, they can move freely to other member countries. His shipments can arrive in Europe in less than thirty hours, and they take two to five days for arrival in New York or Los Angeles. Since 1999, Chang has sold more than 200 tons of the ingredient: 80 percent of it to the European market, 15 percent to Japan, and 5 percent to the United States.

He wouldn't share his price points or the names of his largest clients. When asked specifically if he currently sold—or had ever sold—to Urbani, he said no. His competitors in China also ship directly to Europe and the United States.

After the messy split from Urbani, Safina remained in the business. He now runs daRosario Organic, which produces one of the few USDA-certified organic truffle oils available in the country. Fraud on the truffle market, he says, is still rampant, especially among producers of truffle oil, sauce, and butter. And Urbani is only one of many companies—he estimates there are around thirty-five large companies—that mislabel, misidentify, or otherwise misrepresent their products. "All those guys are the biggest crooks in the world," he said, who produce "artificial and fake and completely illegal" product. The truffle oils he must compete with contain no truffle. They are produced with a synthetic chemical called bis(methylthio) methane, which the truffle companies buy from chemical companies like Sigma-Aldrich, owned by the global pharmaceutical company Merck.

"The FDA won't do anything about it, because it's a small business," Safina told me. Indeed, the FDA makes no distinction between different types of truffle species, even though they can be of vastly different monetary and culinary value. The only existing labeling standard for canned truffles is that the product be "Fruit of the truffle." One of the officials he's bothered at the agency about the issue admitted that she knew there was a significant issue with truffle mislabeling, but stricter controls could only be introduced when "someone gets sick or until someone dies." "The FDA is a reactive agency," Safina said. "They can only be proactive on controlled substances like medical devices, medical equipment, and medication."

For now, the best protection is reading labels and ingredient lists carefully, which very few retail stores, including Dean & De-Luca, Whole Foods, and other high-end independent specialty food shops, care to do. "They're all culpable in this situation," Safina said. "It's all about the money. Who has the best deal?" Respectable manufacturers will list the scientific name of the truffle used. Smart customers will avoid more general descriptions or references to "truffle essence" and "truffle aroma," which are signifiers that the product actually contains flavor chemicals, like bis(methylthio) methane, rather than the valuable fungus. "All you got to do is check the label, read the ingredients, and you'll say, 'What the hell's going on?'" The ingredients list for Urbani's White Truffle Oil includes the real thing at ".1%" and "aroma." It costs €8.40 and probably costs about $0.10 to produce.

Much of the truffle butter found in the United States is manufactured at one facility in Texas and contains the same ingredients. "It says olive and umami protein extract," Safina said. "Excuse me, what the fuck is umami protein extract? It's boiled-down bones, spinal fluids, and brains and all that shit." No one sends truffles down to the butter plant in Texas. The butters all share similar lot codes.

"There are all these easy shortcuts because there are no standards in this country, and nobody knows anything about truffles," Safina said. "It's very hard to get away with it with a chef. But in the retail world, it's very easy. It's just the general consumer doesn't read, nor does the store owner."

Safina holds the same theory as many others I spoke with on why fraud is so pervasive in the artisanal trade. "The truffle business in Europe started off as an illegal operation, right?" he said. "You pick the truffles, you bring them to me, you negotiate a cash deal, there's no invoice. That's it. It always starts out as an illegal operation. Once it starts off as an illegal operation, and you are used to playing like that, you start to play other games too because I started this way and it worked fine. What's the big deal if I short-weight a can? What's the big deal if I color on the truffles? What's the big deal if the label, the ingredient statement's not real? One thing after another goes along with that mentality."

He met his current business partner, an Italian food scientist named Sandro Severi, at Urbani in the late 1980s. Both men left their respective roles with the company upset with its ethics and quality standards. "The old joke was, the only reason why Sandro was there was to make sure that no one got sick on the stuff that was made in the can. He says, 'My job was anti-botulism.' They did not care what was in the can as long as nobody got sick, and every year they spent more and more money on designing a more and more beautiful label." Sandro still lives close to the warehouse and encounters his old bosses at the local haunts; he is cordial to them. "He hates their guts," Safina said. "Proper Italian etiquette is to be cordial to people you know."

When they decided to work together again, part of the shared excitement was creating truffle products they could finally be proud of. Their fresh truffles come from small Umbrian parcels that have been certified as organic by the USDA, many of them near olive groves. To infuse the oil, Severi uses a process known as vacuum extraction, which can remove molecules from surfaces without soluble oil.

"You're having a dinner party," Safina said, "and you're serving USDA prime porterhouse and oven-roasted organic potatoes. Why would you want to buy a cheap bottle of something—I don't even call it truffles—and pour it on your friend's or guest's plate?"

For Safina, that would be like traveling back in time to certain moments of his life he wishes he could forget.

PART V

# THE PLATE · SEDUCTION

The truffle is not a positive aphrodisiac, but it can upon occasion make women tenderer and men more apt to love.

—Jean Anthelme Brillat-Savarin, in *The Physiology of Taste* (1825)

# CHAPTER ELEVEN

# Demanded, Delivered, Prepared

"THERE ARE SOME CHEFS WHO ARE REALLY PRIMA DONNAS," OLGA Urbani told me, wearing her gown and her expensive necklace, after making me wait far too long for our meeting. "They think they're the king of the world: 'You don't know who I am.' Yes, I know; yes, I know. But sometimes, you just don't have truffles. I mean, if I don't have, what can I do? I cannot produce in my factory."

Some chefs request perfectly round one-kilo white truffles for next-day delivery over the phone, as if large whites were not a rarity. "It depends on God," Olga said. "We pray if it comes out. If you don't have it, they start screaming at me. These people I hate—really hate—dealing with them. There are real problems in life. . . . People don't have enough money to eat, and you're screaming because you don't have one kilo of our truffles. We try to do it anyway." Her two sons will drive a thousand kilometers a day just to meet a hunter for a large set of white truffles, only to have the deal fall through when they can't agree on a price.

Even if truffles can be procured, there's the logistical challenge and price of constant international shipping, making profit margins slim for all larger truffle companies. A fresh white truffle loses almost its entire culinary appeal in five days, and a black truffle might only last ten, meaning the companies must move fresh product out almost as soon as it arrives on the company's premises.

The truffles travel to the United States on commercial airliners, stored in iceboxes in the cargo hold. The planes land at John F. Kennedy International Airport, and the truffles undergo a fifteen-minute inspection by USDA officials in the cargo receiving area. A few hours after being shuttled out of the airport by van and truck, the truffles are packed for delivery. Urbani pays couriers in Manhattan, Los Angeles, and San Francisco to hand deliver the goods to the back doors of kitchens.

Sabatino's Federico Balestra used the exact same language as Urbani to describe his strained relationships with some chefs over the years: prima donnas. His high-profile clients (Oprah, Celine Dion, Jimmy Kimmel, even the rich guy who flew all the way from Florida to New York because he wanted to see his truffles before he purchased them) are low maintenance compared with the chefs he used to encounter on his sales and delivery runs back when the company first entered the American market in the late 1990s. "They want to teach you everything," Balestra said. "How you can be an expert seeing half pound in a week? We see thousands of pounds a week. Obviously, they know less than us."

Ninety-nine percent of the comments he receives about the product, he said, are wrong. He recalled selling to one arrogant Manhattan chef who tried telling him that one of the white truffles with a red vein was "garbage." In fact, the vein appears when a truffle grows close to a pine tree. "When in Italy you find this truffle," he said, "red vein worth more money because the flavor's a lot more strong."

Before he was an owner at the company, Plantin's Christoph Poron sold and delivered truffles back door to back door in Manhattan for his father, Hervé. He quickly built a solid reputation among the city's chefs after moving there in 1998, at the age of twenty-one. His first customer was Daniel, the French gastronomic temple of the world-renowned chef Daniel Boulud. At that time, Alex Lee, a chef of equal talent to Boulud but with less name recognition, was the commander of the kitchen. Lee had a large party to please and requested 250 truffles, weighing twenty grams each, an order of around $4,500, or close to $7,000 in today's dollars. "Nice and round, but smaller," Poron said. That was the order that launched Plantin's business in the United States. Soon after, Scott Bryan, then the admired chef at Veritas, dubbed Poron "Truffle Boy." He registered the business as an American corporation, even though, at first, he was running the entire operation by himself out of his apartment.

Poron always packed heavy loads of fresh truffle underneath his arm when he left his apartment so the chefs he visited could select based on their particular predilections. He rode the bus and subway with them, where fusses would erupt about the unfamiliar scent. "Sometimes there was people like, 'Oh, it smells like dirty socks,'" Poron said. Once, after the World Trade Center towers fell, he heard someone say, "Oh my God, 'It smells like gas. Do you think he's got a bomb in his box?'" A parking attendant who had come to know him through all his deliveries warned him that a memo would circulate soon, directing people to report to the FBI any strange smells emanating from parked cars.

One winter's day, after driving directly from the airport to make deliveries in Manhattan, he headed back to his parking space to find that his car had disappeared. Confused, he wandered the icy sidewalks, then began to panic as he searched, thinking of the twenty-five kilos of black winter truffle inside it.

Two weeks later, a police detective called him. "We found your car," he said. "There's a lot of money in your car." The vehicle was a block away from where Poron had been looking, where he had parked it; it had never been stolen at all. "I was lucky enough that it snowed during those two weeks so the truffles kept okay," he said. His father called, demanding to know "what the hell" he was doing. His chefs, who had their scheduled deliveries delayed, didn't let him forget the episode.

Poron was never mugged during the course of his deliveries, but there were good reasons for his anxiety.

Back in France, someone had stolen truffles set to fly into New York for Poron from the Marseille airport's cargo area. "It was only thirty kilos," Poron said. "But it pissed me off because it was *my* thirty kilos. I didn't have enough to sell to my customers."

Whoever stole the product, likely a luggage attendant, later showed up offering the truffles to a restaurant somewhere to the east in the French department of Var, a stretch of Mediterranean coast known for absurdly high luxury. When he offered them to the restaurant's chef, the truffles were still in Plantin's marked boxes. "The guy was not very smart," Poron said. Word that Plantin had been robbed in Marseille traveled among regional truffle dealers and businesses. One of Plantin's competitors happened to be inside the kitchen at the same time as the thief. "Be careful," he told the chef. "They were mugged this week." One of the restaurant employees quietly called the gendarmerie, but the thief recognized something was amiss and fled.

American chefs couldn't always obtain truffles from enterprising young dealers at their back doors, or at all. The chef Ken Frank, who runs the Michelin-starred La Toque in Napa and has probably been cooking with truffles longer than any other American-trained chef, remembers a time when fresh truffles were merely tales whispered, by older French colleagues, in the steam and heat of the kitchen. He didn't encounter a truffle—of any kind—until doing grunt work in a fancy French restaurant in Pasadena, California. Even then, in 1974, in a place run by a somewhat renowned French chef, the truffles arrived in cans. "If you were in France, we would have fresh truffles," Frank's boss told him. "You can't believe how great they are." The American culinary scene was just beginning to take shape: Shallots and wild mushrooms were still considered exotic. With the exception of those who had lived or trained in France, few American chefs had handled them. The fresh truffle would soon become Frank's white whale.

In the mid-1970s, cooking was just beginning to become a respectable profession in the United States, and Frank decided to drop out of college to become a line cook. In Southern California, the only place an aspiring chef could hope to learn during this period was at a classical French restaurant, which always served the same dishes, in the same stuffy environment, and ran on the same set of kitchen rules. But it was better than the alternatives. "Italian restaurants were still serving spaghetti and meatballs," Frank said. During this time, some places he worked in simply used small circles of black olives as a substitute for truffles in the recipes that called for them. "They were black, so that was close enough," Frank told me. After a stint as a line cook in Newport Beach, Frank began dreaming of breaking French food of its haughty conventions.

In 1976, at the age of twenty-one, he landed the head chef's job at La Guillotine on the Sunset Strip. He remembers having to hunt for supplies, including shallots, leeks, and real Dijon mustard. Sun-dried tomatoes and sherry-wine vinegar were just starting to come into vogue. But still, he couldn't find a fresh truffle distributor. "Things that we take for granted now were just beginning," he said. He made fresh ingredients the very foundation of his culinary style, ensuring the placement of four perfectly cooked fresh vegetables on each entrée plate. Especially in the 1970s, this set him apart from competitors. The *Los Angeles Times* reviewer Lois Dwan called the restaurant one of L.A.'s best French establishments, many of which were run by actual Frenchmen. Eaters swarmed, and Frank's fame ballooned. He got a little cocky and began bad-mouthing crap ingredients other chefs in the region were using, especially frozen fish labeled as fresh. He soon earned a nickname for his candor: Enfant Terrible. When the owner at La Guillotine increased prices and packed in more tables, Frank left the restaurant for the head chef job at Club Elysee in Beverly Hills.

It was 1978, and by this time he was one of Los Angeles's most famous French chefs, but he still hadn't even glimpsed a fresh black truffle, one of French cuisine's most celebrated ingredients. French chefs he had worked with always spoke of fresh truffles in mythical terms. "If there was a truffle in this room, you could smell it thirty feet away," one of his bosses had said. Frank was intrigued and wanted badly to try one. Then he heard murmurs of a food supplier up in Sacramento named Darrell Corti who owned a legendary wine and food shop with his brother and was rumored to import fresh truffles directly from Italy. He immediately called him. Frank would soon be on the road to attend a cousin's wedding in Chico— could he pick up a pound of truffles en route? He flew to Sacramento, rented a car, and drove directly to the Corti Brothers' store. Corti, an Italian guy who loved truffles as much as he adored Barolo, also sold Frank on his very first bottles of Californian Cabernet Sauvignon, a few years before California's wine market exploded. (Corti has since been referred to as "the Indiana Jones of the culinary world.")

As soon as he arrived at his aunt Avis's house in Chico, Frank went about his first round of truffle prep. He had heard from other chefs that eggs would take on the flavor of the truffles if they were placed in the same tightly sealed container, so he did just that and placed it in the fridge overnight. The next morning, Frank woke up in anticipation of his first fresh truffle experience. He cooked truffle omelets, and his first forkful of eggs "blows my fucking mind," Frank recalled. His French colleagues weren't bullshitting. The magic was real.

He drove the rest of the truffles back to his kitchen in Los Angeles and began using them there on a few different menu items. He can't even remember what he put them on, because he realized almost instantly that the truffles were more important than their vehicle. Remembering the details would be like meeting the pope and reminiscing about his shoes. "I never stopped buying fresh black truffles in season ever since," he said. "They remain one of my favorite ingredients just because there's nothing like them."

In 1979, after a stop at another restaurant, Frank started his own place, the original La Toque in Los Angeles, funded by investments from Mel Brooks and Gene Wilder. In 1981, Frank had become so enamored of black truffles that he resolved to do a five-course truffle-tasting menu every January for the rest of his career. Early on, he realized that simply shaving them on plates worked well, but drawing out their true flavor took a bit more thought and experimentation. One of his earliest successes—a trick he still relies on today at La Toque in Napa—was pairing them with a triple-cream Brie-like cheese known as Brillat-Savarin. During his first truffle-tasting menu (in which each course was paired with a glass of a rare vintage of Château Mouton Rothschild), he used a fishing line to slice the Brillat into three layers, sprinkled finely chopped truffle between them, and then pressed the pieces back together for infusion. "It succeeded beyond anything that I imagined," he said. "That subtle, creamy cow's milk cheese, to this day, remains one of the best vehicles for absorbing a stupid amount of truffle flavor."

In the early years, Frank purchased his truffles directly from Corti's supplier, which happened to be Urbani. The American business had not yet been handed from Paul Urbani to Rosario Safina, but soon after Frank switched to a Los Angeles–based gourmet purveyor that he's been relying on for nearly thirty years. Later, he came to buy some of his truffles from a chef he knew during his Los Angeles days who moved back to Italy to help run his family's truffle business. "I find that getting truffles from people you know that you have a personal relationship with is very, very helpful. There's *a lot* of shady stuff in the truffle business. There's a lot of people in the truffle business that don't really understand the quality issues and how to really make sure that you're only using the very best. When you know someone who knows and you're a good customer and they hand select the best ones for you, you end up getting better stuff. It's very easy to launder truffles, as it were, from one place or another place, and there's a lot of incentive to cut corners. There are places that will sell you truffles that are two or three weeks old, and if you don't know any better, you settle for it." He prefers to rely on people whose homes he's been inside, whose families he knows, whose trust he can count on.

He's never had any issues with Urbani's fresh truffles, and from time to time he'll still order from them in a pinch. He's also ordered from Sabatino and Plantin, both of which he said have great truffles. But he can't stand the principles of any vendor that profits off truffle oil. "I've become a total Nazi on truffle oil," he said. "It just pisses me off because it's fake. I have zero tolerance for it. I have little patience for vendors that sell it. You can't tell me on the one hand you have integrity, and on the other hand you're still selling truffle oil. Come on, you know it's fake, but you can't resist the dough. It's five cents' worth of chemical in shitty olive oil. It's invariably way too strong. It stains the palate. You end up burping the damn chemical all day long. It makes it difficult to enjoy the more subtle but far more rewarding aroma of real fresh truffles. If your palate is conditioned to truffle oil popcorn, you're always going to think that I'm using shitty truffles. Even though I'm a hawk and will only use the best truffles that money can buy."

Even if the truffles come from Frank's two most trusted suppliers, when they arrive in the kitchen, Frank's La Toque staff subjects them to careful inspection. They study their surface and texture. They smell them. They slice them and taste. They regard truffles in the suspicious manner a prison guard regards new inmates.

But restaurants can commit culinary fraud too. There are plenty of chefs, Frank said, that serve Chinese truffles, dashed with a bit of truffle oil, and simply call them black truffles on the menu and charge equivalent prices. "You can't make anything delicious with them; they're just not that good," he said. The lower the price point, the higher the likelihood that there might be some funny truffle business going on. A low-cost entrée simply won't support the cost of real, fresh truffles.

——

In the years since his egg and cheese discoveries, Frank has developed many other truffle dishes, creating them with the focus and repetition of a guitarist searching for new jams. He makes slits in pieces of salmon, inserts slices of truffle, seals them in a seaweed bag with a touch of duck fat, and then cooks them at 125 degrees for twenty-five minutes. The inside of the salmon turns into a sort of pink truffle custard. He stuffs veal loin with strips of truffle and allows the flavor to seep through for two days before starting a roast.

The quality the truffle imparts to a dish is "nearly impossible" to describe, he said. A single truffle in a bigger batch can vary from an almost vanilla perfume to a darker, earthy scent. "There's something about them that is unmistakably compelling," Frank said. "There's something about them that is very primal. They get your attention at a very deep emotional level. There's something about the perfume that triggers something in the brain. We must react at some level in a similar way that pigs do." He feels he is only just beginning to unlock the ingredient's full potential. "It's only in recent years that I've understood how volatile the flavor compounds are," he said. "That heating them up too hot does more harm than good."

Frank has found he's happiest cooking with truffles in Napa, where winemakers and the quietly wealthy order truffles because they truly appreciate the experience rather than the glamour. In Los Angeles, he found that some celebrities came to his restaurant to be seen, often demanded adjustments to dishes that limited their enjoyment (no salt, no fat, no sugar), or ordered items, like Cristal champagne, simply because they were flashy or expensive. Their experiences of his food were about status, not taste.

No one besides the most fervent oenophiles would consider his customers in Napa famous. The ones with vast wine cellars and plenty of disposable income flock to the restaurant each year for the truffle menu because they've come to adore truffles the way Frank does. For one reason or another—usually an indelible experience during truffle season on vacation in some little French hamlet or Italian village—they've become obsessed. "For some people, truffle is bling," Frank said. "For my clientele, truffle is for flavor."

As the rise of Food Network popularized gourmet food and made people with extra cash more likely to blow it at a restaurant so they could brag about the trip to their friends, there were consumers who suddenly began to request truffle service because it was a little like owning a Porsche or getting a courtside seat at an NBA game. Truffles were cool. At least, that's what some cool chef on Food Network had said. And, well, there were their colleagues too, especially the ones who wouldn't shut up about Alba—all that Barolo and all that white truffle tagliatelle. All paid for by that crazy exit package from the hedge fund. If Oprah adored them, didn't they have to be good? They had to like them because truffles, like caviar or gold flakes, were expensive and therefore refined. These people wanted truffles because billionaires bought them at auctions for absurd sums, and, maybe, if they ordered truffles, it was a little like placing a bet on their future fortunes. And, hey, weren't they just worth it for the Insta and the glances when these smelly things rode in on a silver platter? This was the bling crowd. The walking-caricature crowd. The guys-who-might-actually-eat-one-of-Sandrino's-truffles-at-a-Trump-restaurant crowd.

At some point, the very early version of the bling crowd

supported the dreams of the aspirational crowd. These guys wanted to be the kind of someone who ordered truffles on a whim, but they didn't have the means to take that kind of an economic risk. Was there something cheaper that still contained the truffle's essence? At nicer restaurants without Michelin stars, chefs smelled this desire like blood in the water and began tapping it to increase revenue on lower-ticket menu items. They began tricking themselves into believing in the promise of truffle oil. It was greed for cash, preying upon greed for status. Satisfied with their approachable yet fancy fries and burgers, aspirational foodies started buying truffle oil at the grocery store, and truffle salt, and truffle popcorn. And then, one day, recognizing a critical mass, chains started getting in the truffle game. Suddenly some members of the aspirational crowd entered the bling crowd, and they ordered fresh truffle shavings as a celebration after the new job offer, and perhaps, like in Ken Frank's telling, they were sorely disappointed. Was this even real truffle? they thought. Yes, and it was the only real truffle they had ever tasted, spoiled by a once-desperate desire to become what they now were.

On the night of December 1, 2014, on an unremarkable stretch of Italian road in the suburban town of Cervere in Piedmont, inside a modest yellow brick and red-shutter facade of an old farmhouse, Gian Piero Vivalda closed an interior door to his restaurant and turned the lock. Like most days, he was the last person to walk out. But he was so committed to his craft that he lived upstairs, right above the kitchen.

The following morning, he would be one of the first people back there, ready to man the receiving door, where a procession of local truffle hunters would greet him and sell him some of the world's best white truffles, those found in Piedmont, in the sliver of land between the tiny villages of Barbaresco, San Rocco Seno d'Elvio, Neive, and Treiso. Vivalda had taken to using at least one kilogram of white truffles each day during the height of the season. He felt they were essential to a traditional Piedmontese dining experience, but he subjected the hunters to interrogation. One of Sandrino Romanelli's sub-middlemen, a guy named Fabio, might be one of them, arguing with him about the quality of what was on offer. Vivalda was far from arrogant, but he harbored passionate opinions about the necessary origins and characteristics of the white truffles he served to his customers.

Under Vivalda's leadership, Antica Corona Reale had earned two Michelin stars, the first in 2003 and the second in 2009. Michelin recognized Vivalda's nearly religious devotion to the quality of his regional ingredients, some of which were collected from the garden behind the building. Serving the finest Alba white truffles was part of honoring the tradition of Piedmontese cuisine, a distinct mixture of what hunters could catch and forage in the local foothills and mountains.

Vivalda's family had managed the restaurant for five generations, and it had run in some form for nearly two centuries. His great-grandfather and grandfather walked into the wilderness themselves to bring back ingredients. They hunted for white truffles, snails, leeks, mountain frogs, and river fish. In the early twentieth century, Italy's king, Vittorio Emanuele III, enlisted their services and made himself a regular, ordering pheasant with white truffle. But by the time Vivalda's father, Renzo, had taken over, the restaurant had lost a bit of its luster. In 1994, when the place had become little more than a café where old men played cards, Renzo considered closing. But Vivalda, who had left Cervere to train as a chef at a two-Michelin-star restaurant in Paris, wouldn't let it happen.

Vivalda operated with quiet ambition. He continued his family's legacy of quality, but he looked for new flourishes. He added delicacies to pair with regional staples: shrimp from the Ligurian Sea, Sicilian oils, Iranian caviar. He renovated the dining room. He turned glass into crystal, and steel into silver. He unfurled red Persian rugs and hung expensive fine paintings on the exposed-brick walls. He hired a host who wore a suit and tie.

Despite Antica's surroundings—run-down apartment buildings, a deserted pizzeria, and not much else—the Italian aristocracy began to flock there. At one point, the former head of Fiat, the late Giovanni Agnelli, and the former chairman of Ferrari, Luca Montezemolo, were both regulars. Robert De Niro, Hilary Swank, and the Rolling Stones drummer, Charlie Watts, found themselves making the fifty-minute detour from Turin to pass through its doors.

But Vivalda had not allowed any of the hype or his accolades to distract him from the business of producing perfect food. He knew he had to wake up at dawn and harvest his morsels from the garden. He knew he had to meet his suppliers and discuss the finer details of the ingredients they wanted to sell him. Like Frank, he believed in the quality of his ingredients above all else, which was why he always planned to return to the kitchen early in the morning.

After climbing the stairs to his residence, he wearily opened the door.

Four pale-skinned men hovered in his living room, waiting for his arrival. Before Vivalda could get his bearings, a fist slammed into his face. He pushed someone off, but the others grabbed him from behind and pulled him into a chair. The struggle continued as Vivalda squirmed, and the ruthless blows kept flying. Finally, someone began binding him to the chair with insulation tape.

They rifled through drawers. They grabbed his wristwatches. Then they descended the stairs and walked into the kitchen to search for what they'd really come for: his Piedmont white truffles. They were piled in the refrigerator, ready for service. They put all of them, all eight kilograms, into a bag. After collecting bottles of Barolo and Barbaresco as a bonus, the robbers walked into the night.

It had been an excellent season for white truffles, one of the best in recent memory. Vivalda came to suspect that was why he'd been selected for an ambush. He filed a police report and was hospitalized. Like most truffle thieves, the men were never captured.

❦

When I arrived at Antica Corona Reale the year after the attack, to meet one of the best white truffle chefs in the world, his assistant told me that he preferred to attend to his duties in the kitchen at least until I had finished lunch, courtesy of the chef. He had just finished buying truffles from the hunters out back.

Freshly baked bread arrived. A 2010 Barbera from Marina Coppi was poured; it had a silky and tart body, smelled of rose petals, and mostly defied the description of my untrained palate. I inhaled two small fresh garden vegetable and egg dollops and a salami crudo presented in a bright yellow cheese sauce. A cappelletti pasta, filled with the salted meat of a helmeted guinea fowl, was perfect—chewy on the knot and soft on the inside.

A former Italian soccer star for Juventus ambled in and sat down at a table not far from me. Then the gray- and frizzy-haired Vivalda, dressed in an all-white chef's uniform, came out of the kitchen to shake hands with everyone in the small dining room, as if he were campaigning for local public office. He did not have the nervous quality of someone who had been brutally beaten just a year before.

Finally, a cheese, egg, roe, and white truffle soup arrived on the table. After the waiter stirred it with a big spoon, the liquid turned from white to yellow, and shavings of white truffle bobbed below the surface. He came back to shave more truffle atop. The delicate gray-white flakes harmonized with the saltiness of the cheese, which browned at the edges of the bowl. By the time I finished, it felt as if I had spooned the very soul of a white truffle into my mouth.

"The truffle, in my kitchen, is always the undisputed main actor," Vivalda told me after I was done eating and we'd repaired to a table in the front room. He wholeheartedly disagrees with Sandrino Romanelli's assertion that a white truffle from Croatia can be as good as one from Piedmont. "Impossible," he said, when presented with the notion. "If you are lucky enough to taste a white truffle from Alba, there is nothing like it anywhere in the world. I use the truffles of Alba." But he goes even further, arguing that there are massive differences between different sections of the Piedmont region. "Those who tell you that all truffles in Piedmont are the same are perjurers," he said. The sliver of land near the village of Barbaresco is especially ideal. Vivalda believes the roots of the Barbaresco vineyards have made the soil perfect for the white truffle.

"What Romanelli told you is not positive for our economy," he said. "People who come here to eat, they come with a very precise idea: They want to drink Barbaresco and eat the truffle from our area, not the ones that come from Croatia, Umbria, or Tuscany. When they mix truffles from all these areas, they make an incredible damage to our region, and I say this with sadness in my heart. I understand that there are not enough truffles for everybody, so they come from everywhere. So tourists from Germany, China, U.S.A., et cetera are fooled, and that's not good at all."

Distributors and restaurants that advertise Alba truffles without actually checking on the truffle's origin infuriate him. "It's like buying a Louis Vuitton purse," he said. "What if a trader buys a lot of fake ones and then resells them as original? I don't mean to be a shark and say that today's market is bad, but some of us stay up every night to wait for the truffle hunters who you know go hunting in the proper areas; others do not even ask where the truffle they buy has been collected."

When Vivalda meets the hunters after their dawn hikes, he smells and weighs every piece he buys and checks the color. The white truffle should be a little fainter than the hue of a standard potato skin. Those from Alba tend to weigh more than truffles of the same size found in other areas because of the humidity. If he can't find hunters to do business with, the restaurant will simply go without truffles. "I certainly don't buy them from people I don't know," he said. "I don't let anyone else buy truffles for me. The restaurant is mine; it is my face I want the hunters to see when I buy truffles. I want and must know what I buy exactly."

When I finally asked him about the night that he was bloodied up and hospitalized, he seemed reluctant to say too much on the subject. "I tried to fight back, but it was useless," he said. The delivery was matter-of-fact, as if the whole event were as pedestrian as his preferences in cookware. Perhaps he thought recounting it, blow by blow, might give the thieves a false sense of triumph. Like most truffle handlers, he seemed to understand that the truffle gave pleasure and exacted pain, and not necessarily in equal measure. He had fully submitted to its twisted symbiosis.

# CHAPTER TWELVE

# Shaved

ON THE DAY OF MY VISIT TO URBANI, JUST BEFORE LUNCHTIME, OLGA led me up a flight of stairs in the modern, airy, glass-walled Accademia del Tartufo, or Truffle Academy, a building located right next to Urbani Tartufi's manufacturing facility in Sant'Anatolia di Narco, Umbria. Olga had slipped on her signature fur coat for the short walk over from the main building. I'd put on a worn peacoat with a dangling button. Everything inside the academy, including the furniture, was black, white, or silver, which made the colors of the green valley outside pop. Chefs from all over the world, Olga told me, travel here to cook with truffles; the academy is essentially a giant marketing tool.

Someone drew the upstairs curtains closed, and a projector was readied. When you're in the thrall of Olga's regal presence, things seem to appear out of the ether. A series of people who float at her periphery complete tasks, but it is sometimes difficult to track who exactly is doing them. "Three minutes, just to show you what is the tour of the truffle," Olga said. "With the tour of the truffle, you understand Urbani." On-screen, a flashy marketing video—of Hollywood-production quality—began. Set to a fast-paced classical composition, it followed the path an Urbani truffle takes, over a twenty-four-hour period, from Italian soil to a Manhattan plate. First, the truffle hunter walking with his dog, then a plane moving up through the air, an Urbani foot soldier hopping on a motorcycle to make restaurant deliveries in New York, and finally, a chef making final adjustments to the dish. Slick and effective, I thought. There was a beauty to the propulsion of the journey, even if parts of it were deliberately elided or obscured.

We walked downstairs and repaired to the open-air kitchen. Just as suddenly as the curtains had been drawn, we both had flutes full of sparkling Berlucchi wine from Franciacorta in our hands. Several plates of fresh bread and gourmet crackers piled with different Urbani truffle sauces had been placed atop the silver counter. "This has the taste of soil," Olga said, after picking up one of the black truffle spreads. Pans clanked as chefs behind the counter prepared to cook us lunch. She motioned to an hors d'oeuvre with white truffle. "This has the taste of gas, garlic," she said. There was a long pause as we took in the pleasure of the appetizers.

"It was really nice seeing the museum," I said, doing my best to make conversation rather than subject her to further interview questions. "I can't believe that is actually where—"

Olga interrupted me mid-sentence. "I'm thinking now, because if he wants to do something about the problems," she said, half speaking to her attaché and half addressing me, "I have a video to show you that was *never, never* seen. That he should see absolutely."

"Oh, really?" I asked breathlessly, barely containing my reportorial elation.

"I will never admit that I showed it to you, but I think it will help you very much. . . . I'm going to get it, but, please, someone will kill me if they know I showed it to you."

She rushed out of the room and back to her office to retrieve her laptop.

While she was gone, I sampled the traditional, runny Umbrian omelet. "This way, you can appreciate black truffles in there more," Sylvia said of the preparation. I also savored the creamy Camoscio d'Oro cheese with white truffles. In the center of the room, a group of Italian businessmen in suits—members of an entrepreneurial society—gathered to chat and laugh with one of Bruno's sons.

Olga darted back into the room, carrying her bulky PC. She found a spot, behind a few rows of champagne flutes, to set it down on the counter. She had put on a pair of red-framed glasses to search for the secret video. She fidgeted at the keyboard and mouse pad for long enough that I began to lose hope. But then, suddenly, her face twisted from confusion to excitement. She called me over from the truffle platters, and I sat down next to her at the counter. She pressed play.

It was a short Italian documentary, with English subtitles, that her "crazy friend" produced but had never sold to a broadcaster. It followed truffle hunters as they defied the law and trekked into the forest at night. "All on the dark side," Olga said. One of the police officers who told the interviewer that hunting was forbidden at night was a member of the nighttime poaching crew. "It's a crazy world," Olga said as we watched.

Olga seemed to think I'd be pleased to learn about the hunters and their dirty work, but I was more intrigued by her surprise cameo. Her friend, who seemed chiefly concerned with rule break-ing by truffle hunters, had used one of her off-the-cuff remarks, in passing, to establish why competition among hunters was so in-tense. White truffles were so scarce and global demand was so high that Olga herself was forced to buy all the white truffles she could from Slovenia and Hungary. This might have been a throwaway comment to her friend, but to me it was remarkable corroboration of ongoing deceit at the biggest truffle company in the world. And the fur-coated executive handed it to me herself—perhaps by mis-take or perhaps because of a feeling of utter invincibility. When I later checked the company's inventory online, I found that Urbani sells white truffles, or *Tuber magnatum pico*, at Italian prices ($3,200 for a pound), without any disclaimers about the possibility of their eastern European origin. Though it's not as daring a transgression as her father Paolo's selling of a counterfeit species, geographic grift of Olga's kind is still pursued by Italian law enforcement. When I reached out to inquire about whether the company had ever consid-ered making the eastern European provenance of its white truffles clear to consumers on its website, Olga evaded the question. "We are forced by the law to write the origin on the invoice," she wrote in an email. But invoices are issued after purchase, when informa-tion about origin is decidedly less useful, if it's noticed at all.

When the credits rolled, Olga suggested that her friend might have overplayed the criminal element of the industry. "I cannot tell you that that's really [the case], because I don't hear so many things like this around," she said. "You don't see everyday poison. I'm afraid that people make it bigger to make the story interesting." As the most powerful truffle executive in the world, she didn't seem particularly interested in claiming any accountability or responsi-bility for fixing the supply chain's more brutal problems.

We took our seats at the dining counter. Not long after I sat down, a hot plate of long *tagliolini* noodles, topped with a generous portion of shaved white truffle, arrived in a sauce of butter, Parmesan, and meat broth. Olga grabbed a wooden shaver on the counter, picked up a massive white truffle, and leaned over my plate to shave even more.

She describes herself as a white truffle obsessive. "For me, it's like a drug," she had told me earlier in the day, on the factory floor, as we stood next to a mound of them. "I am crazy for it." In the conference room, she had gone further: "I'm in love." She had fixed her eyes on an oddly shaped half-kilo specimen that her son had purchased and gushed, "Oh my God, that's so beautiful!" Afraid that she'd break it, the men on the floor didn't want her touching it, but she couldn't resist. "This is perfect," she said, as if she were caressing the statue of David's ankles.

She shaved and shaved and shaved, until the light yellow of the pasta was barely visible past several layers of thin light brown slivers. "You will remember that you were in Urbani," she said as she continued shaving. She then turned to her bowl of green pea soup and topped it with a heavy layer of white truffle as well.

The pasta was cooked to al dente perfection. The classical, simple Italian sauce burst with umami flavor, and the flaky shavings of white truffle—whether from Alba or Slovenia or Hungary—tasted as if they'd just been plucked, in that very form, from the earth. Each bite, with a perfect balance of texture and salt, produced unspeakable pleasure: the form that comes with measures of silence and involuntary purrs.

It was the kind of culinary pleasure that rips you away from concerns and anxieties. It made me forget where I was. It made me forget the violence, the personal betrayal, the fraud, the dog poisoning, and the theft that the truffle could have played an accomplice to on the way to my plate. It made me forget why I even cared. I could say I consciously looked the other way, but the truth is, the beauty of that moment, of that head space, was that I hadn't remembered to look at all.

After I finished eating, I was forced to leave for a meeting with a NAS detective in Rome. "I'm sorry," Olga said, "we have so many other things to eat." She told me that she would help in whichever way she could. "If you need hotels or something, feel free to call me. You never know. You're traveling in Italy, so consider us a family here for you."

We pecked cheeks and hugged, and I walked out into the rain. As I drove down the Urbani driveway and out onto the valley road, windshield wipers sloshing, I actually began to buy into the logic of her explanations for the past. I felt none of the repulsion I imagined I'd experience touring the facility or sharing a meal with such an infamous character. In fact, I wished I could have stayed there longer.

The seduction was primal. The flavor of the white truffle held me so tightly in its grasp that I reconsidered the very shape of Olga's character and the boundaries of moral behavior. The truffle drew me, momentarily, into an alternate universe, a place where flavor mattered more than truth and virtue.

With some horror, I came to realize that most diners would be defenseless against the truffle's power. In fact, we were the truffle underground's most useful accomplices. One exposure to the flavor was enough to unleash a barbaric id incapable of critical interrogation. We became criminals of pleasure, and we were exactly what the underground needed to thrive.

But why do the industry's victims remain? Despite the risks and crimes, they hover somewhere on its circuitous supply chain because, for many of them, it had become a part of who they were. The business doesn't make an honest person rich, but it gives people a connection to brotherhood and family and history and tradition. It gives them a brush with rarity. It gives them unsolvable riddles and opportunities to showcase their particular brand of genius. It gives them love, of their dogs, of the search and the adventure, of the silent stillness of the forest. It gives them relationships with foragers who work before dawn and after dusk, determined to find treasure. It gives them the thrill of one of the most esoteric forms of negotiation, and of evaluating a constant procession of shady colleagues. And, then, of course, it gives them the truffle itself: its otherworldly look, its indescribable scent, and its ineffable flavor. There is so much to savor that I finally understood why people might remain in this business even when its vices violently betrayed them.

But the most powerful gratification of all was left unspoken. They were members of a quiet cabal, bound by their persistence against the evils of the underground. And no matter what happened, each autumn and winter, they worked to pass this dark pleasure of the soil into the delicate light of a dining room, to a customer who knew nothing at all.

# ACKNOWLEDGMENTS

A HUGE TEAM OF PUBLISHING PROFESSIONALS, TRANSLATORS, FIXERS, colleagues, friends, family, and even a baby supported this book. It would never have existed without them.

My deepest and sincerest gratitude to my literary agent, Cassie Hanjian, of DeFiore and Company, who, from the very beginning, believed this was a story worth telling. Her friendship, feedback, support, and occasional therapy sessions made this book stronger and the process of writing it far more manageable. No matter the challenge or circumstances, she remained a steady, positive force and an incredible advocate who made me believe I could get the job done and done well. I will always be indebted to her for helping shape my vision of this book and for helping me execute it.

My sincerest thanks to Francis Lam, my editor at Clarkson Potter, for seeing the potential in this project and remaining enthusiastic about it throughout the entire editorial process. He forced me to see and do things I wouldn't have otherwise considered, things that brought the manuscript much closer to the vision of the book I wanted to write. His patience, understanding, and gentle craftsmanship were everything a writer could ask for in an editor. I am also thankful for the diligence, creativity, and support of Doris Cooper, Erica Gelbard, Amelia Zalcman, Lydia O'Brien, and countless others at Clarkson Potter, Crown Publishing, and Penguin Random House who helped get this book ready for market.

Huge props to my Italian fixers and translators, investigative journalists Lorenzo Bodrero and Cecilia Ferrara, who provided not only insights but also entertainment. And to my French translator Elodie Burgé, and French fixer, J.P. Gautier.

For a long while, I terrorized my friends and colleagues at *Pacific Standard* with uninvited thoughts about proposals, reporting, writing, revisions, and everything else that comes along with producing a book. All the beers to my good friend Nicholas Jackson, who encouraged me from the very beginning to the very end, and allowed me the time and space to complete the project while still remaining full-time at the magazine. Thanks also to colleagues Max Ufberg, Ted Scheinman, Kate Wheeling, Elena Gooray, and Jennifer Sahn, who all ably endured tedious book conversations.

Great gratitude to my former editors and colleagues at *The Atlantic*—Olga Khazan, Uri Friedman, John Gould, Paul Rosenfeld, and Sam Price-Waldman—who always entertained my strange ideas for stories about international crime and intrigue, including the one that eventually led to this book.

Speaking of tedious conversations, I would be remiss if I did not acknowledge my closest friends, who have made me a better person and a better writer: E.J. Schloss, Stephen Lanus, Creighton

Bledsoe, Michael Weiss, Max Heppermann, Justin Cohler, Alex Bergstrom, Dr. Thomas Clifford, Dr. Jack Dougherty, Lauren Caldwell, Sloane McNulty, and Raveen Reddy.

My family has an extremely high threshold for annoyance, and I took advantage of that many times over the years of working on this project. Biggest thanks to my dad, Patrick Jacobs, who always encouraged me to pursue writing and journalism and a career that didn't feel like a job. And to Kathye Citron, Kimi Murphy, Thomas Murphy, John Lee, Archimedes Lee, Dr. Sandra Fallico, Robert Miller, Abby Miller, Sophie Miller, Janet Fallico, and the Brewster family, for listening to truffle war stories and always believing that whatever I was up to was worth it.

Above all, I owe the greatest gratitude to my beautiful wife, Emily Miller. During the course of working on this book, we were engaged, married, and had our first child, Olive. She has supported this project in every way possible and managed to remain composed and calm while doing it, even when I had to work to finalize the initial manuscript from our Tahitian bungalow on our honeymoon. Even when we were forced to leave our home in Santa Barbara— through smoke and ash—when she was seven-months pregnant, during one of California's largest wildfires on record. Even when I had to trudge through late-night revisions during the first several months of our daughter's life (Olive, you won't remember this, but you helped make this book much, much better). She has endured enough truffle crime conversations to last her two lifetimes but has never wavered in her belief that this book was worth sweating over, even as some of the most important events of our lives happened alongside its production. I could not ask for a smarter, more patient, understanding, caring, and affectionate partner and family. You and Olive are everything.

# NOTES

THE SOURCES LISTED HERE SPECIFICALLY PERTAIN TO DETAILS AND other information that did not come directly from the substance of my own reporting efforts. However, many of the key phrases and assertions listed below were at least indirectly corroborated by interviews with living sources. To make the provenance of the facts in this book as clear as possible, I have also mentioned and quoted interview subjects throughout the text.

## Chapter 1: Black Diamond Bandits

11 **more than a hundred dollars per serving:** Ryan Sutton, "You'll Drop Mad Cash on Australian Truffles at Per Se," *Eater New York*, June 11, 2014, ny.eater.com.

11 **Puff Daddy once indelicately requested:** Josh Ozersky, "White Truffles: Why They're Worth $2,000 a Pound," *Time*, Oct. 20, 2010, content.time.com.

11 **Oprah refuses to travel:** Oprah Winfrey, "The Bucket-List Trip Oprah's Put Off for Years . . . Until Now," *Oprah*, January 13, 2015, oprah.com.

11 **In 2010, at an international auction:** "White truffles fetch $330,000 at auction," *The Guardian*, November 28, 2010, theguardian.com.

11 **a kilo routinely wholesales:** "Consumi, tartufo schizza 6000 euro al kg, massimo storico," Coldiretti, November 5, 2017, coldiretti.it.

11 **"the pungent memory of lost youth":** Ozersky, "White Truffles."

12 **At the beginning of each year's truffle season:** Wall text, Musee de la truffe et du vin, Richerenches, France.

12 **On the third Sunday in January:** Ibid.

15 **Somewhere outside the town of Bad Münstereifel:** David Crossland, "'Mushroom Mafia' Pillaging German Forests," *Spiegel Online*, October 8, 2013, spiegel.de.

17 **a focal point for a date on** *The Bachelor*: Rodger Sherman, "'The Bachelor' Recap: Finding Love Is Harder Than Finding Truffles, Apparently," *The Ringer*, February 12, 2018, theringer.com.

17 **McDonald's has experimented:** TasteTime, "McDonald's Truffle Mayo & Parmesan Loaded Fries," *YouTube*, August, 29, 2017, youtube.com.

## Chapter 2: Death in the Grove

26 **eleventh-century stone:** "Chateau de Grignan," Office de Tourisme: Couer de Drôme Provençale, tourisme-paysdegrignan.com.

26 **Roman tile:** "Grignan," *Provence Web*, provenceweb.fr.

29 **they hoped to ride the coattails:** Michael Reyne, "Auguste Rousseau (1808–1894), le père des truffes du Ventoux," Produits du Terroir, December 26, 2017, produits-du-terroir,over-blog.com.

31 **At six feet seven and 240 pounds:** Henry Samuel, "Death and intrigue in France's truffle wars," *The Telegraph*, May 30, 2015, telegraph.co.uk.

31 **the size of his feet:** Ibid.

31 **By day, he worked part-time:** Ibid.

33 **president of the department's young farmers' union:** Stèphane Blezy, "Procès du meurtre de la truffière de Grignan: suivez la 3e journée," *Le Dauphine*, May 28, 2015, ledauphine.com.

33 **member of the volunteer fire department:** "Drôme : 8 ans de prison pour le trufficulteur tueur," *Europe1*, May 29, 2015, europe1.fr.

34 **Rambaud encountered trespassers:** Blezy, "Procès du meurtre de la truffière de Grignan: suivez la 3e journée."

34 **On another occasion:** Ibid.

34 **At some point, the family discovered:** "Les truffes de la discorde," *Le Parisien*, May 30, 2015, leparisien.fr; Ibid.

34 **Rambaud's father asked him:** Stèphane Blezy, "Laurent Rambaud raconte la soiree du drame," May 29, 2015, ledauphine.com.

34 **He retrieved his 12-gauge:** "Drôme: Ernest Pardo tue pour des truffes," *Le Parisien*, May 26, 2015, leparisien.fr.

34 **He loaded the shells:** Blezy, "Laurent Rambaud raconte la soiree du drame."

34 **Startled, Rambaud bent down:** Ibid.

35 **the man staggered to his feet:** Ibid.

35 **his Citroën C15 van:** Blezy, "Procès du meurtre de la truffière de Grignan: suivez la 3e journée."

35 **With the assistance of his brother:** Ibid.

35 **Before the gendarmes arrived:** "Drôme: Ernest Pardo tue pour des truffes."

35 **He knew that Pardo had dabbled:** Blezy, "Procès du meurtre de la truffière de Grignan: suivez la 3e journée."

37 **Lately, farmers in and around Grignan:** Samuel, "Death and intrigue in France's truffle wars."

37 **about three hundred people:** "Drôme : 8 ans de prison pour le trufficulteur tueur."

37 **"did not deserve to be killed like a dog":** Ibid.

39 **On the day of his sentencing:** Blezy, "Procès du meurtre de la truffière de Grignan: suivez la 3e journée." All court testimony comes from this transcript.

39 **Of Rambaud's decision to pull:** Ibid.

39 **Another man, speaking on behalf of Pardo's parents:** Ibid.

41 **A farmer in Saint-Restitut told** *The Telegraph*: Samuel, "Death and intrigue in France's truffle wars."

## Chapter 3: The Peasant's Golden Secret

49 **The men believed they were being tailed:** Danièle Georget and Jean-Michel Verne, "Meurtrier pour une truffe," *Paris Match*, January 1, 2010, parismatch.com.

49 **watched as they moved:** Laurent Chabrun, "La guerre de la truffe," *L'Express*, January 17, 2011, lexpress.fr.

49 **They speculated that:** Ibid.

49 **"climate of psychosis":** Georget and Verne, "Meurtrier pour une truffe."

50 **a peasant named Joseph Talon:** *Garden: An Illustrated Weekly Journal of Gardening in All Its Branches* 9 (1876); Sabine Baring-Gould, *The Deserts of Southern France* (New York: Dodd, Mead, & Company, 1894); Jean-Marie Rocchia, *Truffles, the Black Diamond: And Other Kinds,* trans. Josephine Bacon (Avignon: Barthélemy, 1995); *Revue des Deux Mondes* vol. 8 (1875); C. de Ferry de la Bellone, *La truffe: Étude sur les truffes et les truffières* (Paris: Baillière, 1888). I was not there to witness Talon's discovery and its aftermath, but have reconstructed the events based on the available records from the nineteenth century (and others) listed here and

below, interviews with two local historians, a visit to Croagnes and the surrounding areas, and reasoned supposition based on all available facts.

50 **since ancient Amorite servants dug:** Elinoar Shavit, "Truffles Roasting in the Evening Fires," *Medicinal Mushrooms* vol. 1:3 Special Issue (2008), 18–22.

50 **a morsel of bread:** Baring-Gould, *Deserts of Southern France.*

51 **the Hôtel des Américains, the Hôtel de Provence:** Jean Anthelme Brillat-Savarin, *The Physiology of Taste* (New York: Dover Publications, Inc., 2011), First edition published December 1825.

51 **"The meal is almost unknown":** Brillat-Savarin, *The Physiology of Taste.*

51 **European royalty had long relished:** Ian R. Hall, Gordon Thomas Brown, Alessandra Zambonelli, *Taming the Truffle: The History, Lore, and Science of the Ultimate Mushroom* (Portland, Ore.: Timber Press, 2007); Zachary Nowak, *Truffle: A Global History* (London: Reaktion Books, 2015).

51 **Parisian dealers, noticing how truffles enhanced:** Brillat-Savarin, *The Physiology of Taste.*

52 **Some thought thunder:** Hall, *Taming the Truffle*; Elisabeth Luard, *Truffles* (London: Frances Lincoln, 2006).

52 **The naturalists and scientists:** Jacques de Valserres, *Culture lucrative de la truffe par le reboisement* (Paris: Librairie de la Société des Gens de Lettres, 1874).

53 **Talon's cousin, also named Joseph:** Baring-Gould, *Deserts of Southern France.*

54 **He plowed the space between:** Michel Wanneroy, "Truffe et Joseph Talon," *Archipal*, Issue 69 (2011).

54 **By 1820, he had sown:** Ibid.

55 **Word spread to Monsieur Vaison:** Adolphe Chatin, *La truffe: Botanique de la truffe et des plantes truffières, sol, climat, pays producteurs, composition chimique, culture, récolte, commerce, fraudes, qualités alimentaires, conserves, préparations culinaires* (Paris: J. B. Baillière, 1892).

55 **"A veritable school of trufficulture":** *Revue des Deux Mondes.*

55 **he possessed a rare:** Wanneroy, "Truffe et Joseph Talon."

55 **word of Talon's success reached Auguste Rousseau:** *Revue des Deux Mondes.*

55 **At this point, in 1847:** Valserres, *Culture lucrative de la truffe par le reboisement.*

55 **When Rousseau looked upon Puits-du-Plant:** *Revue des Deux Mondes.*

56 **In 1853, he recovered:** Ibid.

56 **The judges honored his product:** M. de Gasparin, "XI. — Fruits Secs Ou Frais," *Exposition universelle de 1855: Rapports du jury mixte international*, vol. 1. (1856).

56 **Parisian journalists swarmed:** Valserres, *Culture lucrative de la truffe par le reboisement.*

56 **"Here are the products I have gathered":** Ibid.

56 **Struck by the development, the Count of Gasparin:** M. de Gasparin, "XI.— Fruits Secs Ou Frais."

57 **Rousseau's pig ran wildly:** Ibid.

57 **When Gasparin returned home:** Ibid.

57 **The count reported his observations:** Valserres, *Culture lucrative de la truffe par le reboisement.*

57 **In November 1856:** Ibid.

57 **In a report, filed in 1869:** Henri Bonnet, *La truffe: Études sur les truffes comestibles* (Paris: A. Delahaye, 1869).

58 **"This is where I came into the world":** *Revue des Deux Mondes.*

58 **France's grapevines began to yellow:** Levi Gadye, "How The Great French Wine Blight Changed Grapes Forever," *io9*, March 17, 2015, io9.gizmodo.com.

58 **Knowing that a forest code:** Bellone, *La truffe: Étude sur les truffes et les truffières.*

58 **farmers in the southeast erected watchtowers:** "Rendons a Rousseau ce qui est a Rousseau," *Melano*, melano.free.fr.

58 **A book from the late nineteenth century:** Bellone, *La truffe: Étude sur les truffes et les truffières.*

59 **wealthy diners came to expect:** Baring-Gould, *Deserts of Southern France.*

59 **By 1895, Talon's method of cultivation:** Wanneroy, "Truffe et Joseph Talon."

60 **The world wars had a major impact:** S. Reyna-Domenech and S. Garcia-Barreda, "European Black Truffle: Its Potential Role in Agroforestry Development in the Marginal Lands of Mediterranean Calcareous Mountains," *Agroforestry in Europe: Current Status and Future Prospects*, (Springer, 2009).

60 **But in the 1970s, a group:** Ian R. Hall, Wang Yun, and Antonella Amicucci, "Cultivation of Edible Ectomycorrhizal Mushrooms," *Trends in Biotechnology* 21, no. 10 (Oct. 2003): 433-38.

65 **Hilarion Talon:** *Revue des Deux Mondes.*

## Chapter 4: A Scientific Mystery

79 **wore his long blond hair in a ponytail:** Joan Rigdon, "Californians Claim To Unearth Secret Of Raising Truffles," *The Wall Street Journal*, March 25, 1994, joanrigdon.com.

80 **Picart had attempted to corner:** Jeremy Iggers, "A new truffles crop grows at snail's pace," *Detroit Free Press*, August 11, 1982, newspapers.com.

80 **In 1978, he wrote a seventy-four-page:** François Picart, *Escargot from your garden to your table* (Self-published, 1978).

81 **who grew up watching pigs:** Wayne King, "Southwest Journal; A Passion in Truffles for Texas," *New York Times*, July 16, 1984, nytimes.com.

81 **licensed a black truffle inoculation technology:** Eugenia Bone, *Mycophilia: Revelations from the Weird World of Mushrooms* (New York: Rodale, 2011), 154–55.

81 **After some investigation, he had already settled:** Victoria Loe, "Oh, You Beautiful Fungus!," *Texas Monthly*, August 1982.

81 **his plans to retire:** Rigdon, "Californians Claim To Unearth Secret Of Raising Truffles."

82 **About four years later, in 1987:** Ibid.

82 **he applied rabbit manure:** Ibid.

83 **New Age crystals:** Ibid.

83 **more than three thousand truffle saplings:** King, "Southwest Journal; A Passion in Truffles for Texas."

83 **he dissolved his company:** California Secretary of State Statement Filing for Agri-Truffle Inc., businessfilings.sos.ca.gov.

83 **went on to expand his brother's:** Christophe Palierse, "Francois Picart l'autre Americain de la chaine de restauration," *Les Echos*, December 26, 2002, lesechos.fr.

83 **conspiring to poison the grove's production:** Alastair Bland, "Black Diamonds," *North Bay Bohemian*, December 3, 2008, metroactive.com.

84 **Griner and a new tenant, Don Reading:** Rigdon, "Californians Claim To Unearth Secret Of Raising Truffles."

84 **Griner was netting higher yields:** Ibid.

85 **In 2008, Griner died alone on the property:** Bland, "Black Diamonds"; Chris Smith, "The dog's coming along, the truffles, too," *Santa Rosa Press Democrat*, April 15, 2008, pressdemocrat.com.

## Chapter 5: Disappearance of the Dogs

99 **Icy gusts of Russian air had ripped:** Angelique Chrisafis, "Heaviest snowfall in decades wreaks havoc across Europe," *The Guardian*, February 5, 2012, theguardian.com.

99 **The uncharacteristic weather pattern:** Sarah Maslin Nir and Elisabetta Povoledo, "Hundreds of Deaths as Europe Struggles With Snow Amid an Intense Cold Snap," *New York Times*, February 5, 2012, nytimes.com.

## Chapter 6: Poison

123 **gas starts leaking:** Andrew P. Collins, "I Set Two Cars On Fire Last Night, Here's What I Learned," *Jalopnik*, March 11, 2014, jalopnik.com.

128 **In 2016, another nineteen dogs:** Michele di Franco, "Ateleta strage di cani da tartufo: 19 avvelenamenti," TeleAesse.it, November 24, 2016, teleaesse.it.

129 **at least 126 truffle dogs poisoned:** "Mappa dei bocconi avvelenati," *Andare a Tartufi*, December 16, 2015, andareatartufi.com.

## Chapter 7: Middlemen

143 **€300 million:** Judith Evenaar, "IWEMM8 in Cahors," The 8th International Workshop on Edible Mycorrhizal Mushrooms, 2016.

166 **Two truffles, each less than half this one's size, had sold:** "White truffles fetch $330,000 at auction."

166 **bids as high as $1 million:** "Can 'Big Boy' the truffle rake in a cool million?" *CBS News*, December 5, 2014, cbsnews.com.

166 **In an auction held at Sotheby's Manhattan offices:** "Auction Results: World's Largest White Truffle," Sotheby's, December 6, 2014, sothebys.com.

174 **In 2007, Pastrone was driving:** John Hooper, "Halt! Your truffles or your life!" *The Guardian*, November 5, 2007, theguardian.com.

## Chapter 8: Detectives and Fraudsters

186 **sold at least seven kilos:** "Venduti come tartufi del piemonte provenivano da croazia e molise," *La Stampa*, February 23, 2014, lastampa.it.

186 **honored as a special guest:** "New Yorkers Turn Out for Annual White Truffle Extravaganza at SD26," *Downtown Magazine NYC*, downtownmagazinenyc.com.

186 **In a court appearance in June 2014:** "Il bianco d'alba in realta era coratoanche. Il tartufo va a processo," *La Nuova Provincia*, June 11, 2014, lanuovaprovincia.it.

186 **But in March of 2016, the court acquitted:** "Frode in commercio trifulau assolti," *Ansa Piedmont*, March 18, 2016, ansa.it; Daniela Peira, "Processo tartufi: imputati assolti," *La Nuova Provincia*, March 22, 2016, lanuovaprovincia.it.

190 **the carabinieri seized 6,144 legs of ham:** Maria Teresa Improta, "Parmigiano contraffatto: l'ombra delle mafie nella Food Valley," *Parma Today*, December 26, 2012, parmatoday.it.

190 **criminal organizations, or the *agromafie*, make about $27 billion:** "IL BUSINESS DELLE AGROMAFIE AL SEMINARIO DELLA REGIONE VENETO CON INTERVENTO DEL PRESIDENTE DI COLDIRETTI VERONA CLAUDIO VALENTE," Coldiretti, February 27, 2018, verona.coldiretti.it.

194 **a type of desert truffle that thrives:** "Tuber oligospermum," Trufamania, trufamania.com.

198 **a €66 million tax fraud:** "Sora vendita tartufi scoperta maxi frode fiscal da 66 millioni," *TG24*, February 20, 2017, tg24.info.

198 **In 2018, an Italian citizen was arrested:** "Italian citizen fined by Turkey for smuggling truffle," *Hurriyet Daily News*, March 5, 2018, hurriyetdailynews.com; "Italian fined for trying to smuggle truffles out of Turkey," *The Local*, March 6, 2018, thelocal.it.

## Chapter 9: The King's Ascent

199 **Olga made a very public splash:** Lesley Stahl, "Truffles: The Most Expensive Food in the World," *60 Minutes*, June 4, 2012, cbsnews.com.

201 **to honor the memory of her father, Paolo:** "Museo del Tartufo Urbani," Tripadvisor, tripadvisor.com.

202 **Constantino Urbani:** "La famiglia Urbani," Urbani Tartufi, urbanitartufi.it.

203 **After visiting Carpentras to learn Rousseau's bottling technique:** Nowak, *Truffle: A Global History*.

203 **In 1946, the next leader of the company:** B.H. Fussell, "For the Gourmet, Trenton Truffles," *New York Times*, December 17, 1978, nytimes.com; M. D'Amato, "The Urbani Family From The Burg: Truffles," *Trenton Times*, August 27, 2001, mackstruckofwisdom.blogspot.com.

204 **already using those of French origin:** Ibid.

204 **He explained some of the basics:** June Owen, "News of Food: Truffles," *New York Times*, February 13, 1951, nytimes.com.

205 **By 1970, the Times had sent:** Craig Claiborne, "Those 'Black Diamonds' Called Truffles," *New York Times*, November 19, 1970, nytimes.com.

205 **Paul had made some significant inroads:** Fussell, "For the Gourmet, Trenton Truffles."

209 **She told one Italian publication:** "Urbani Tartufi," *Benvenuta Italia*, benvenuta italia.com.

## Chapter 10: The King's Betrayal

212 **market he had been trying to build up since 1946:** Lisa Wolff, "Urbani Truffles relinquishes name in U.S. legal settlement," *Gourmet News*, 2003, siliconinvestor .com.

220 **New York kitchens began to spot:** Florence Fabricant, "The Invasion of the Chinese Truffle," *New York Times*, February 15, 1995, nytimes.com.

221 **By this point, frozen and canned exports:** Nancy Harmon Jenkins, "White Truffle Fever Makes the Season Glow," *New York Times*, December 24, 1997, nytimes .com.

221 **truffle exports were undergoing an outlandish spike:** Nicola Galluzo, "Italian Tree Cultivation and Its Commercial Trend in the European Union Market," *International Journal of Agricultural Science and Research*, vol. 3 (June 2013): 47–58.

222 **forty-seven tons:** "OF THE TRUFFA DEL TRUFFA DEL TRUFFA: BUY AT 36MILA LIRE AND RESELLED TO 700MILA. A BUSINESS OF 33 BILLION THE MAYOR OF SGHEGGINO (PERUGIA) DENIED," *Avvertenze*, March 2, 1998, avvertenze.aduc.it.

229 **a report, by the Italian newspaper** *Corriere della Sera*: Haver Flavio, "Arrestati i fratelli Urbani, re del tartfuo," *Corriere della Sera*, March 26, 2001, archivio .corriere.it; Giano, "Right Company," *Ora d'Aria*, April 30, 2010, oradarialibera .blogspot.com.

231 **Urbani Tartufi filed civil lawsuits:** Wolff, "Urbani Truffles relinquishes name in U.S. legal settlement."

231 **"We didn't want to arrive":** Ibid.

231 **In a separate statement:** "Urbani Family Protects its Name in Suit With Former U.S. Distributor Rosario Epicureo Ltd.," *PRNewswire*, May 2003, prnewswire .com.

231 **the business was handed:** Wolff, "Urbani Truffles relinquishes name in U.S. legal settlement."

231 **The company settled:** Ibid.

232 **her interview with Lesley Stahl on CBS's** *60 Minutes*: Lesley Stahl, "Truffles: The Most Expensive Food in the World."

236 **they can move freely:** "One market without borders," European Union, europa.eu.

## Chapter 11: Demanded, Delivered, Prepared

244 **A fresh white truffle loses:** Rochelle Bilow, "So You've Got a Truffle? Cool. Here's How to Keep It Fresh," *Bon Appètit*, November 11, 2015, bonappetit.com.

248 **increased prices and packed in more tables:** Colman Andrews, "Views and Reviews of a Los Angeles Chef," *New York Times*, January 28, 1981, nytimes.com.

249 **"the Indiana Jones of the culinary world":** Rick Kushman, "The Tastemaker," *Sactown Magazine*, April 2012, sactownmag.com.

249 **In 1979, after a stop at another restaurant:** Colman Andrews, "Views and Reviews of a Los Angeles Chef."

256 **shrimp from the Ligurian Sea, Sicilian oils, Iranian caviar:** "Tempo, Spazio, Gusto," Antica Corona Reale, anticacoronareale.com.

256 **He turned glass into crystal:** Ibid.

256 **unfurled red Persian rugs and hung expensive fine paintings:** Ibid.

256 **pulled him into a chair:** "Fossano in manette autori di rapine furti e lesion," *IdeaWebTV*, March 17, 2015, ideawebtv.it.

257 **binding him to the chair with insulation tape:** Ibid.

Terrence Patrick

## ABOUT THE AUTHOR

RYAN JACOBS is an investigative reporter and has written for *The Atlantic*, *Mother Jones*, and *Pacific Standard*, where he serves as deputy editor and leads the magazine's investigations desk. Before joining *Pacific Standard*, he covered international crime for *The Atlantic*'s global channel, reporting on the largest diamond heist in French history, international carbon market scams, and the dark side of the truffle trade, among other subjects of intrigue. He graduated summa cum laude from Northwestern University's Medill School of Journalism. Find him online @ryanj899.